AIRCRAFT
OF
WORLD WAR
II

AIRCRAFT
OF
WORLD WAR
II

CHRIS CHANT

Grange
BOOKS

Copyright © 1999 Amber Books Ltd

This edition first published in 2000 for Grange Books
An imprint of Grange Books plc
The Grange
Kingsnorth Industrial Estate
Hoo, nr Rochester
Kent ME3 9ND
www.grangebooks.co.uk

Reprinted in 2001, 2002, 2003, 2004

ISBN: 1-84013-336-8

Editorial and design by Amber Books Ltd
Bradley's Close
74–77 White Lion Street
London N1 9PF

Design: Wilson Design Associates

Printed in Singapore

PICTURE CREDITS:
TRH Pictures

ARTWORK CREDITS:
All artworks Aerospace Publishing except the following:
Bob Garwood: 47, 93

CONTENTS

Introduction

World War II started in September 1939 with the German invasion of Poland and ended in August 1945 with the American atomic bombings of the Japanese cities of Hiroshima and Nagasaki. Air power had been increasingly important throughout this period at the tactical, operational and strategic levels, but with the annihilations of Hiroshima and Nagasaki it became clear that air power had attained a grand strategic capability, and as such had become an arbiter of the new world order that emerged from World War II.

Many clues about the nature of the warfare that was to characterise World War II became evident in the middle and late 1930s, especially during the Italian conquest of Abyssinia (1935-36), the Spanish Civil War (1936-39), in which the Republican government was supported by the USSR and the Nationalist insurgents by Germany and Italy, and the opening stages of the 2nd Sino-Japanese War (1937-45).

Above: During the early years of World War II, the Ju 87 'Stuka' enjoyed a reputation that struck terror into those, both civilian and military, on the ground beneath it.

Above: Contrary to popular opinion, it was the Hawker Hurricane (this is a Mk I version) that bore the brunt of the early battles with the Luftwaffe in 1940.

Over the same period there was a radical change in the technical nature of aircraft, already presaged during the late 1920s and early 1930s as fabric-covered biplanes of steel or light alloy construction were replaced in civil and then military service by monoplanes of light alloy construction covered increasingly with light alloy skinning. From about 1934, therefore, the tactical and operational nature of the air forces of the world's more advanced nations was advanced by the steady development, production and procurements of warplanes conforming to what may be termed the 'modern' monoplane configuration. These warplanes were typified by light alloy construction under a covering of stressed light alloy skinning, a cantilever low-wing monoplane layout, landing gear in which the main units were completely retractable, enclosed accommodation, trailing-edge flaps for enhanced take-off and landing performance, and propulsion by a high-powered engine (generally an air-cooled radial or liquid-cooled Vee unit) in a neat low-drag cowling, driving a variable-pitch propeller with three or more blades, cooled by a neat radiator installation, and boosted by a mechanically driven supercharger or, increasingly, an exhaust-driven turbocharger.

Also on the horizon, it should be noted, was the possibility of propulsion by reaction engines such as the rocket, which would offer an exceptionally high power/weight ratio but at the same time suffer from a prodigious specific fuel consumption of highly dangerous propellants. The turbojet offered a better power/weight ratio than the reciprocating engine and lower specific fuel consumption than the rocket, but suffered from major development problems in terms of its materials.

World War II started as a largely European matter starting with Germany's conquest of Poland in September 1939 and prompting British and French declarations of war. Between April and June 1940 the Germans turned north to overrun Denmark and Norway, and between May and June of the same year drive west to defeat the Netherlands, Belgium and France. This left only the UK in the war against Germany, which by now had been joined by Italy after the latter's declarations of war against France and the UK.

A NEW KIND OF WAR

So far as World War II in the air proper was concerned, the increasing effectiveness of bombing and of the close support for the ground forces by bombers and fighters were indicated by the campaigns in Abyssinia and Spain during the mid-1930s, a period of transition as modern monoplane warplanes were replacing older biplanes. The full potential of air warfare against ground targets were first clearly demonstrated, however, in the German 'Blitzkrieg' campaigns of 1939-41. But while the Germans revealed superb tactical efficiency in these campaigns, they had not grasped the full implications of air power as a new concept of warfare, as they employed their air forces essentially in support of their land forces. Although still searching for the right air doctrine, the British were nevertheless ahead of the Germans in their overall concept of air power, and it was this superiority of doctrine that combined with tactical and technical factors to give the British victory in the Battle of Britain.

Developed by the British and refined by the Americans, air doctrine had by the end of World War II reached an early definitive stage in which it comprised three closely related but still distinct major aspects: command of the air, long-range ('strategic') bombing of the enemy's war-making capabilities, and direct support of surface forces (both land and sea).

Command of the air, now better known as air superiority, was vital to effective offensive employment of air assets in the other two aspects and was also significant in two defensive roles. Command of the air, or at least the ability to mount an effective challenge to enemy control of the air, was important as a means of protecting one's own economic strength (otherwise war-making potential) against an enemy's long-range bombing, and also for the protection of one's own surface forces against an enemy's air attacks. Because the terrorising effect that an enemy's air attacks could exert on both civil and military personnel, moreover, command of the air was a vital factor in preserving the morale of one's own side.

Command of the air could be provided by means such as defensive air combat, attrition of enemy fighter strength through repeated long-range attacks (including escort of strategic bombing that lured the enemy's fighters into the air), attacks on air installations and, in the longer term, against the enemy's aircraft industry.

STRATEGIC BOMBING

Strategic bombing was the aspect that had for some time been seen by air power advocates as the decisive aspect of air power. The possession of long-range bombers for the first time made feasible direct offensive operations against an enemy's war-making capability rather than indirectly by blockade. The British, despite their overall inferiority of aircraft numbers and the need to concentrate on defensive fighter capability in the early days of the war, never lost sight of offensive air warfare as their primary air objective, and were undertaking long-range attacks on German industrial and commercial targets even during the Battle of Britain in 1940. The Germans quickly improved their fighter defence, however, and the British were then forced to switch to night attacks, in which the prevalence of poor visual conditions and indifferent nocturnal navigational accuracy dictated an alteration from precision attacks to area bombing against major industrial regions.

From a time late in 1942 US bombers, protected by armour and carrying numerous trainable guns, were able to bomb in daylight more effectively and, as a result of their use of a more effective sight, were able to strike at targets with greater accuracy. Moreover, such bombing raids drew the German fighters into the air to face attritional combat that led to a steady reduction of German fighter strength over occupied Europe and then over Germany itself. US losses to the Germans in these daylight raids grew to alarming proportions, however, and could be continued in 1944-45 only as a

Above: The Republic P-47 Thunderbolt, the total number of which exceeded 15,000. It was a fearsome aircraft, having devastating firepower and good range with drop tanks.

result of the introduction of longer-range fighters that could escort the bombers on their raids deep into Germany. Thus the UK's RAF Bomber Command and the USA's 8th and 15th Army Air Forces respectively struck at area targets by night and point targets by day, and this so-called combined bomber offensive was a major force in speeding Germany's industrial and military collapse, especially after the focus for the attacks had become communications and energy producing installations.

Although it differed in detail, the US strategic bombing of Japan followed a course basically similar to that employed against Germany. The distances were greater, of course, which lessened the overall efficiency of the bomber offensive. However, with the capture of Iwo Jima in March 1945 US bombers and long-range fighters were able to take off from the island's two landing fields to strike at the Japanese homeland, and effectively destroy the enemy's industrial infrastructure.

At the tactical level, the doctrine for close air support of ground forces reached its definitive form in World War II largely as a cooperative effort by two British formations – the Desert Air Force and the 8th Army – in North

Africa during 1942. The key feature of this concept was its command arrangement, in which full control of all air units was retained by the air commander rather than ground force commanders. This provided a flexibility in fulfilling ground force requirements and in dealing with unexpected threats that was wholly beyond systems such as that employed by the Germans, whose air units were generally assigned to ground force command. It must be admitted, however, that the British system effectively prevented full integration of air support units into the land warfare team.

THE TRIUMPH OF THE FIGHTER-BOMBER

One vital aspect of the air support doctrine was the availability of the genuine fighter-bomber. Fast and agile, this type of warplane was ideally suited to the task of delivering precise low-level bombing and strafing attacks against ground targets, but was also the only effective weapon against comparable enemy types. Thus the first task of such fighter-bombers, assisted by light and medium bombers attacking the enemy's air installations, was to operate in the fighter role for the gaining of local air superiority, without which no other types of aircraft could undertake their tasks without heavy and possibly prohibitive losses to enemy fighters.

Above: The Boeing B-17 Fortress was a giant among the combat aircraft of World War II. A total of 12,731 were built, the majority serving in the skies over Europe.

The role of aircraft in support of surface forces at sea was similar in concept but differed in important details. The most important revelation about the nature of maritime air power became evident right at the beginning of the war, when it became clear that the capability of bomber and torpedo aircraft against surface ships was so great that air superiority translated into surface superiority even in situations in which the enemy had a considerable superiority in surface strength. The validity of this concept was definitely proved in the Battle of Midway in June 1942, when the air power of a numerically inferior US force provided almost total victory over a superior Japanese force. Though the Americans lost 150 aircraft in the battle, their air arm sank four Japanese carriers, an event which marked the turning point of the sea war in the Pacific.

THE PRIMACY OF AIR POWER

The conclusion was that carrierborne aircraft were no longer mere supports for the surface forces but rather the primary attack element. Even the heaviest-armed and armoured battleship was vulnerable to air attack, as the sinking of the giant battleship *Yamato* by US aircraft in April 1945 illustrated (though it took seven bombs and 11 torpedoes to send her to the bottom). As a result, it was quickly realised that the aircraft carrier had replaced the battleship as the capital vessel of modern warfare, and that the aircraft carrier was vital in its smaller forms as an escort or light carrier in the defeat, in collaboration with long-range aircraft operating from land bases, of the submarine that was the other major threat to surface vessels, both naval and mercantile, and in the provision of tactical air support for amphibious forces landed on enemy shores.

As World War II ended, opinion about the capabilities and limitations of air power was widely divided among professional leaders, who otherwise agreed that air power had become an indispensable element of what was now a 'triphibious' combat team.

The aircraft featured in this book include all the major fighters, bombers and ground attack aircraft deployed by the combatant nations during World War II. As well as the famous aircraft that graced the skies between 1939 and 1945, the more unusual and less well known flying machines are featured, such as those built by Poland, France and Sweden. Variants of the most important and influential aircraft that flew with either the Allied or Axis nations are also featured.

Aeronca L-3 Grasshopper

After using converted biplane attack aircraft as its observation types for many years, the US Army Air Corps decided to adopt larger and more capable purpose-designed aircraft but then came to the conclusion in the early 1940s that minimum-change adaptations of two-seat civil lightplane types offered considerably greater advantages. Such aircraft were cheap to buy and operate, could fly in the liaison as well as observation roles, and as a result of their low observability and high agility were less vulnerable to ground defences. Short-field performance was particularly impressive, making the aircraft a useful asset to ground commanders. The USAAC and its successor, the US Army Air Forces, therefore procured large numbers of these aircraft in several types, all characterised by an enclosed cabin, high-set braced wing and fixed tailwheel landing gear. The Aeronca Model 65 was typical of the breed, 1740 being procured in L-3 to L-3J variants.

Country of origin:	USA
Type:	(L-3) two-seat light liaison and observation aeroplane
Powerplant:	one 65hp (48.5kW) Continental O-170-3 flat-four engine
Performance:	maximum speed 140km/h (87mph); initial climb rate 123m (405ft) per minute; service ceiling 2360m (7750ft); range 351km (218 miles)
Weights:	empty 379kg (835lb); maximum take-off 590kg (1300lb)
Dimensions:	span 10.67m (35ft 0in); length 6.40m (21ft 0in); height 2.34m (7ft 8in)
Armament:	none

Aichi B7A Ryusei 'Grace'

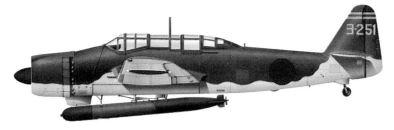

In 1941 the Imperial Japanese navy air force issued an exacting requirement for a carrierborne attack bomber to replace the Nakajima B6N torpedo bomber and Yokosuka D4Y dive-bomber. Aichi's response was the AM-23 design, and the first of nine B7A1 prototypes flew in May 1942. The development programme was constantly delayed by engine teething problems, and it was April 1944 before the type entered production as the B7A2, which offered very good handling and excellent performance. Although production in three factories was planned, only two in fact came on stream and production totalled a mere 105 aircraft (80 from Aichi and 25 from the 21st Naval Air Arsenal). These had to operate from land bases as the Japanese navy had no operational aircraft carriers by this time. The aircraft pictured is a B7A2 of the Yokosuka Kokutai and is carrying a 'Long Lance' torpedo, one of the most effective weapons of its type.

Country of origin:	Japan
Type:	(B7A2) two-seat carrierborne and land-based torpedo bomber and dive-bomber
Powerplant:	one 2000hp (1491kW) Nakajima NK9C Homare 12 18-cylinder two-row radial engine
Performance	maximum speed 566.5km/h (352mph); climb to 4000m (13,125ft) in 6 minutes 55 seconds; service ceiling 11,250m (36,910ft); range 3038km (1888 miles)
Weights:	empty 3810kg (8400lb); maximum take-off 6500kg (14,330lb)
Dimensions:	span 14.40m (47ft 3in); length 11.49m (37ft 8.33in); height 4.07m (13ft 4.5in)
Armament:	two 20mm fixed forward-firing cannon in wing l.e, and one 13mm trainable rearward-firing machine gun in the rear cockpit, plus an internal bomb and torpedo load of 800kg (1764lb)

Aichi D3A 'Val'

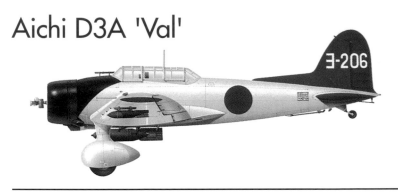

Best remembered as one of the two main attack types involved in the Japanese attack on Pearl Harbor in December 1941, the D3A resulted from a 1936 requirement for a D1A successor and was a trim low-wing monoplane with enclosed accommodation but fixed and nicely faired landing gear. The first of eight prototype and service trials aircraft flew in January 1938, and there followed production of 470 D3A1 aircraft with the 1000hp (746kW) Mitsubishi Kinsei 43 or 1070hp (898kW) Kinsei 44 engine. It was this type that was the Japanese navy's mainstay early in World War II. The improved D3A2 (1016 aircraft) entered service in the autumn of 1942. By this time the type was obsolescent, however, and from 1943 most of the surviving aircraft were adapted as D3A2-K trainers. Many were later used for *kamikaze* attacks on Allied shipping. The aircraft pictured is a D3A1 of the Yokosuka Kokota, in 1940 colours.

Country of origin:	Japan
Type	(D3A2) two-seat carrierborne and land-based dive-bomber
Powerplant:	one 1300hp (969kW) Mitsubishi Kinsei 54 14-cylinder two-row radial engine
Performance	maximum speed 430km/h (267mph); climb to 3000m (9845ft) in 5 minutes 48 seconds; service ceiling 10,500m (34,450ft); range 1352km (840 miles)
Weights	empty 2570kg (5666lb); maximum take-off 4122kg (9100lb)
Dimensions:	span 14.37m (47ft 2in); length 10.20m (33ft 5.4in); height 3.8m (12ft 7.5in)
Armament:	two 7.7mm fixed forward-firing machine guns in the upper part of the forward fuselage, and one 7.7mm trainable rearward-firing machine gun in the rear cockpit, plus an external bomb load of 370kg (816lb)

Aichi D1A 'Susie'

In response to a 1932 requirement for an advanced carrierborne dive-bomber for the Japanese Navy, Nakajima adapted the Heinkel He 66, of which a single example had been imported from Germany, with a Japanese engine to create the Aichi Special Bomber prototype. Late in 1934 the Imperial Japanese navy air force ordered Aichi to proceed with the finalisation of its AB-9 design for production as the D1A1 with the 580hp (432.5kW) Nakajima Kotobuki 2 Kai 1 or Kotobuki 3 radial engine. Deliveries of this initial model totalled 162 aircraft. The company then built 428 of the improved D1A2 model with spatted wheels and an uprated engine. The D1A saw widespread service during the Sino-Japanese war, but by the time of Japan's entry into World War II in 1941, all surviving D1A1 and most D1A2 aircraft had been relegated to training units, with a mere 68 D1A2 machines operating in second-line roles until 1942.

Country of origin:	Japan
Type:	(D1A2) two-seat carrierborne and land-based dive-bomber
Powerplant:	one 730hp (544kW) Nakajima Hikari 1 nine-cylinder single-row radial engine
Performance:	maximum speed 309km/h (192mph); climb to 3000m (9845ft) in 7 minutes 51 seconds; service ceiling 6980m (22,900ft); range 927km (576 miles)
Weights:	empty 1516kg (3342lb); maximum take-off 2610kg (5754lb)
Dimensions:	span 11.40m (37ft 4.75in); length 9.30m (30ft 6.125in); height 3.41m (11ft 2.25in)
Armament:	two 7.7mm fixed forward-firing machine guns in the upper part of the forward fuselage, and one 7.7mm trainable rearward-firing machine gun in the rear cockpit, plus an external bomb load of 310kg (683lb)

Aichi E13A 'Jake'

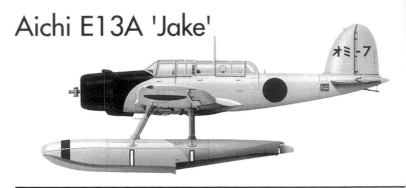

The E13A resulted from a 1937 requirement for a long-range reconnaissance floatplane and first flew in prototype form during 1940. This paved the way for the E13A1 initial production model that entered service late in 1941. Production by three manufacturers totalled 1418 including an unknown number of prototypes, and these machines were delivered in variants such as the E13A1 baseline model, E13A1-K dual-control trainer, E13A1a with detail improvements as well as exhaust flame-dampers in a nocturnal subvariant, and E13A1b with air-to-surface radar. Numbers of E13A1a and E13A1b floatplanes were later adapted to the light anti-ship role with a 20mm cannon in a trainable downward-firing installation. The aircraft in Imperial Japanese Navy service regularly undertook patrol sorties lasting up to 15 hours, but many came to a rather ignominious end during the latter stages of the war on *kamikaze* operations.

Country of origin:	Japan
Type:	(E13A1a) three-seat reconnaissance floatplane
Powerplant:	one 1080hp (805kW) Mitsubishi Kinsei 43 14-cylinder two-row radial engine
Performance:	maximum speed 377km/h (234mph); climb to 3000m (9845ft) in 6 minutes 5 seconds; service ceiling 8730m (28,640ft); range 2089 km (1298 miles)
Weights:	empty 2642kg (5825lb); maximum take-off 4000kg (8818lb)
Dimensions:	span 14.50m (47ft 7in); length 11.30m (37ft 1in); height 4.70m (15ft 5in)
Armament:	one 20mm trainable downward-firing cannon in the ventral position (field modification on late-production floatplanes), and one 7.7mm trainable rearward-firing machine gun in the rear of the cockpit, plus an external bomb load of 250kg (551lb)

Amiot 143

First flown in April 1931, the Amiot 140 was designed to meet a 1928 requirement for a day and night bomber, long-range reconnaissance, and bomber escort type. Ordered into production in November 1934 with Lorraine W-type engines, the type became the Amiot 143 with the powerplant changed to Gnome-Rhône engines. The Amiot 143M.4 entered service in 1935, and production totalled 138 aircraft, the later examples with 7.5mm MAC 1934 machine guns in place of the original Lewis guns, a longer nose, and fixed rather than jettisonable auxiliary fuel tanks. This obsolete type still equipped six *groupes de bombardement* at the start of World War II but suffered heavy losses when switched from night to day operations. The surviving aircraft were operated as transports to Vichy French forces in North Africa until 1944. The aircraft pictured is a 143M, the 78th production aircraft, of the 3rd Escadrille of GB II/35, based at Pontarlier in September 1939.

Country of origin:	France
Type:	(Amiot 143M.4) four/six-seat night bomber and reconnaissance warplane
Powerplant:	two 870hp (640kW) Gnome-Rhône 14Kirs/Kjrs Mistral-Major 14-cylinder two-row radial engines
Performance:	maximum speed 310km/h (193mph); climb to 4000m (13,125ft) in 14 minutes 20 seconds; service ceiling 7900m (25,920ft); range 2000km (1243 miles)
Weights:	empty 6100kg (13,448lb); maximum take-off 9700kg (21,385lb)
Dimensions:	span 24.53m (80ft 5.75in); length 18.26m (59ft 11in); height 5.68m (18ft 7.75in)
Armament:	up to six 7.5mm machine guns, plus an internal and external bomb load of 1600kg (3527lb)

Amiot 354

Having produced the extraordinarily ungraceful Amiot 143 during the late 1920s, in the early 1930s the Amiot design team then acquired a flair for graceful design and evolved the beautiful Amiot 341 long-range mailplane. This aircraft paved the way for the Amiot 340 bomber prototype that developed by a number of steps into the Amiot 354B.4 production bomber. The 354B.4 was one of the best aircraft of its type to enter production before World War II. Some 900 of this type were ordered and offered good performance and potent defensive firepower. However, development and production delays meant that only about 45 had been completed before the fall of France in June 1940. The survivors were used mainly as high-speed transports, four being taken over by the Luftwaffe for clandestine operations. The aircraft pictured was the 39th delivered to the Armée de l'Air. After the war the sole surviving aircraft was operated by the French Air Ministry.

Country of origin:	France
Type:	(Amiot 354B.4) four-seat medium bomber
Powerplant:	two 1060hp (790kW) Gnome-Rhòne 14N-48/49 14-cylinder two-row radial engines
Performance:	maximum speed 480km/h (298mph); climb to 4000m (13,125ft) in 8 minutes 42 seconds; service ceiling 10,000 m (32,810ft); range 3500km (2175 miles) with an 800kg (1764lb) bomb load
Weights:	empty 4725kg (10,417lb); maximum take-off 11,300kg (24,912lb)
Dimensions:	span 22.83m (74ft 10.75in); length 14.50m (47ft 6.75in); height 4.08m (13ft 4.5in)
Armament:	one 20mm trainable rearward-firing cannon in the dorsal position, one 7.5mm trainable forward-firing machine gun in the nose, and one 7.5mm trainable rearward-firing machine gun in a ventral mounting, plus an internal bomb load of 1200kg (2646lb)

Arado Ar 68

The Ar 68 was Germany's last biplane fighter, and entered service in the summer of 1936 as successor to the Heinkel He 51. The Ar 68 was typical of late-generation biplane fighters in its clean design, comparatively high-powered engine and cantilever main landing gear units, but survived in first-line service only to 1938, by which time it had been superseded by the Messerschmitt Bf 109. The two main models, in order of their entry into service, were the Ar 68F-1 with the 750hp (559kW) BMW VI Vee engine, and the Ar 68E-1 that was the main production variant with the revised powerplant of one Junkers engine. By the start of World War II the Ar 68 was serving as an interim night-fighter, but by the spring of 1940 was used only for the advanced flying and fighter lead-in training roles. Pictured is an Arado Ar 68F night fighter of 10 (Nacht) JG 53 based at Oedheim/Heilbron during September 1939.

Country of origin:	Germany
Type:	(Ar 68E-1) single-seat fighter
Powerplant:	one 690hp (515kW) Junkers Jumo 210Ea 12-cylinder Vee engine
Performance:	maximum speed 335km/h (208mph); climb to 6000m (19,685ft) in 10 minutes 0 seconds; service ceiling 8100m (26,575ft); range 415km (258 miles)
Weights:	empty 1840kg (4057lb); maximum take-off 2475kg (5457lb)
Dimensions:	span 11.00m (36ft 1in); length 9.50m (31ft 2in); height 3.28m (10ft 9in)
Armament:	two 7.92mm fixed forward-firing machine guns in the upper side of the forward fuselage, plus an external bomb load of 60kg (132lb)

Arado Ar 232

The Ar 232 was designed as a general-purpose transport with multi-wheel landing gear for operation into front-line airfields. The aircraft first flew in prototype during the summer of 1941 with a powerplant of two 1600hp (1193kW) BMW 801MA radial engines. The design incorporated innovative features with provision for easy loading into and unloading from the pod-like main section of the fuselage. BMW 801 engines were required more urgently for combat aircraft, such as the Focke Wulf 190, and the third prototype introduced the powerplant of four BMW Bramo 323 radial engines on the leading edges of a centre section of increased span. This basic configuration was retained for the 19 or so Ar 232B production aircraft that were completed (one of them fitted with captured French Gnome-Rhòne engines) for intensive service between 1942 and 1945. Most of these aircraft served with KG 200, the Luftwaffe's special operations unit.

Country of origin:	Germany
Type:	(Ar 232B-0) Four-seat medium transport
Powerplant:	four 1200hp (895kW) BMW Bramo 323R-2 Fafnir nine-cylinder single-row radial engines
Performance	maximum speed 340km/h (211mph); climb to 4000m (13,125ft) in 15 minutes 48 seconds; service ceiling 6900m (22,640ft); range 1335km (830 miles)
Weights:	empty 12,800kg (28,219lb); maximum take-off 21,160kg (46,649lb)
Dimensions:	span 33.50m (109ft 10.75in); length 23.52m (77ft 2in); height 5.70m (18ft 8.25in)
Armament:	one 20mm trainable cannon in the dorsal turret, one 13mm trainable forward-firing machine gun in the nose position, and one or two 13mm trainable rearward/downward-firing machine guns in the rear of the fuselage pod

Armstrong Whitworth Whitley

Obsolescent at the beginning of World War II, the Whitley was nonetheless one of Bomber Command's mainstays in 1939 and enjoyed an important role in the early days of the war as a night bomber before passing to Coastal Command as a patrol and anti-submarine type and ending its days as a glider-towing and paratroop training machine. The Whitley Mk I (34 aircraft) entered service in March 1937 with Armstrong Siddeley Tiger radial engines, which were retained in the 126 improved Mk II and Mk III aircraft, while the 33 Whitley Mk IV bombers switched to Rolls-Royce Merlin engines and introduced a powered tail turret. The main variant was the Mk V with a longer rear fuselage, revised tail unit and greater fuel capacity, and these 1,466 aircraft were followed by the 146 Mk VII aircraft for Coastal Command with air-to-surface search radar. The aircraft pictured wears pre-war insignia and was operated by No 10 Squadron, RAF, from Dishworth in 1937.

Country of origin:	United Kingdom
Type:	(Whitley Mk V) five-man long-range night bomber
Powerplant:	two 1145hp (854kW) Rolls-Royce Merlin X 12-cylinder Vee engines
Performance:	maximum speed 370km/h (230mph); climb to 4570m (15,000ft) in 16 minutes 0 seconds; service ceiling 7925m (26,000ft); range 2655km (1650 miles) with standard fuel and a 1361kg (3000lb) bomb load
Weights:	empty 8777kg (19,350lb); maximum take-off 15,195kg (33,500lb)
Dimensions:	span 25.60m (84ft 0in); length 21.49m (70ft 6in); height 4.57m (15ft 0in)
Armament:	one 0.303in trainable forward-firing machine gun in the nose turret, and four 0.303in trainable rearward-firing machine guns in the tail turret, plus an internal bomb load of 7000lb (3175kg)

Armstrong Whitworth Albemarle

The Albemarle medium bomber was designed by Bristol during 1939, but production was transferred to Armstrong Whitworth when it became clear that the latter had spare design and production capacity. Subsequently the Albemarle was redesigned as a reconnaissance bomber with an airframe of steel and wood (thereby reducing demand on strategic light alloys) that could be produced largely by subcontractors for assembly on a single line. The first of two prototypes flew in March 1940, and was a poor performer as a result of its great structural weight. Production of 600 aircraft was then undertaken in the revised airborne forces support role for service from January 1943 as the first British operational aeroplane with tricycle landing gear. The Mks I, II and VI differed only in details and were completed as paratroop transports and glider tugs, while the Mk V was only a glider tug.

Country of origin:	United Kingdom
Type:	(Albemarle Mk II) three-seat paratroop transport and glider tug
Powerplant:	two 1590hp (1186kW) Bristol Hercules XI 14-cylinder two-row radial engine
Performance:	maximum speed 426km/h (265mph); initial climb rate 279m (980ft) per minute; service ceiling 5485m (18,000ft); range 2092km (1300 miles)
Weights:	empty 11,497kg (25,347lb); maximum take-off 16,556kg (36,500lb)
Dimensions:	span 23.47m (77ft); length 18.26m (59ft 11in); height 4.75m
	(15ft 7in); wing area 74.65 sq m (803.5 sq ft)
Armament:	two 0.303in trainable machine guns in the dorsal position

Arado Ar 196

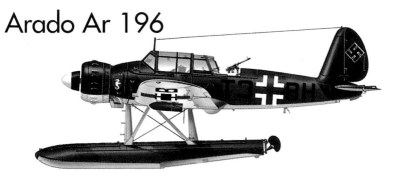

The Ar 196 was designed from late 1936 as a successor to the Heinkel He 50—the catapult-launched spotter and reconnaissance floatplane carried by German warships. The Ar 196 was initially built to the extent of five prototypes (three and two with single- and twin-float alighting gear respectively), of which the first flew in the summer of 1938. The twin-float arrangement was selected for the Ar 196A production model (536 aircraft) that entered service in the autumn of 1939 in variants such as the Ar 196A-0 pre-production model, Ar 196A-1 baseline model with two fixed forward-firing machine guns, Ar 196A-2 improved model with two 20mm fixed forward-firing cannon added, Ar 196A-3 structurally strengthened major production model, Ar 196A-4 with extra radio equipment, Ar 195A-5 with revised armament. There were also five Ar 196B-0 pre-production aircraft with single-float alighting gear.

Country of origin:	Germany
Type:	(Ar 196A-3) two-seat reconnaissance and light attack floatplane
Powerplant:	one 970hp (723kW) BMW 132K nine-cylinder single-row radial engine
Performance:	maximum speed 320km/h (199mph); initial climb rate 415m (1362ft) per minute; service ceiling 7000m (22,960ft); range 1070 km (665 miles)
Weights:	empty 2572kg (5670lb); maximum take-off 3730kg (8223lb)
Dimensions:	span 12.40m (50ft 9.5in); length 11.00m (36ft 0.5in); height 4.45m (14ft 7.25in)
Armament:	two 20mm fixed forward-firing cannon in wing, i.e one 7.92mm fixed forward-firing machine gun in starboard side of forward fuselage, and one 7.92mm trainable rearward-firing machine gun in rear of cockpit, plus an external bomb load of 220lb (100kg)

Arado Ar 234 Blitz

T he Blitz (lightning) was the only turbojet-powered bomber to achieve
operational status in World War II, and as such was an important milestone in
the development of military aviation. The origins of the type can be traced to a 1940
requirement issued by the German air ministry for a turbojet-powered fast
reconnaissance aeroplane. An intensive programme of design and development
resulted in no fewer than 18 prototypes with a powerplant of two Junkers 004 or
four BMW 003 turbojets, provision for rocket-assisted take-off units, a cabin with or
without pressurisation and a pilot's ejection seat, and a clumsy combination of a
drop-away trolley for take-off and extendable skids for landing. Four B-1s were
operated by Sonderkommando Götz based at Rheine from July 1944 for the
reconnaissance role, and form early October reconnaissance missions were being
flown over Allied-occupied Europe and the British Isles.

Country of origin:	Germany
Type:	(Ar 232 V3) single-seat reconnaissance aeroplane
Powerplant:	two 1852lb (8.24kN) Junkers Jumo 109-004A-0 turbojet engines
Performance:	(estimated) maximum speed 780km/h (485mph); service ceiling 16,370m (36,090ft); range 2000km (1243 miles)
Weights:	empty 4800kg (10,580lb); maximum take-off 8000kg (17,637lb)
Dimensions:	span 14.40m (47ft 3.25in); length 12.65m (41ft 5.5in)
Armament:	none

Arado Ar 234B Blitz

The wheeled trolley/skid used in the Ar 234 prototypes for take-off and landing was clearly impractical for an operational aeroplane, so plans for the Ar 234A production derivative of the Ar 234 V3 were dropped in favour of the Ar 234B. This utilised tricycle landing gear in which all three units retracted into the fuselage, an arrangement pioneered in the Ar 234 V9. The Ar 234B was intended for the reconnaissance bomber role with hardpoints under the fuselage and two engine nacelles for bombs up to 1102lb (500kg) weight. Some 20 Ar 234B-0 pre-production aircraft were followed by 210 Ar 234B-1 reconnaissance aircraft with drop tanks in place of bombs, and Ar 234B-2 reconnaissance bombers. The type entered service in September 1944, and the Ar 234B was complemented by just 14 examples of the Ar 234C with the revised powerplant of four 1764lb st (7.85kN) BMW 109-003A-1 turbojets.

Country of origin:	Germany
Type:	(Ar 234B-2) single-seat reconnaissance bomber
Powerplant:	two 1984lb (8.825kN) Junkers Jumo 109-004B-1/2/3 Orkan turbojet engines and provision for two 1102lb (4.90kN) Walter HWK 109-500 (R I-202b) RATO units
Performance:	maximum speed 742km/h (461mph); climb to 6000m (19,685ft) in 12 minutes 48 seconds with a 500kg (1102lb) bomb load; service ceiling 10,000m (32,810ft); range 1630km (1013 miles)
Dimensions:	span 14.11m (46ft 3.5in); length 12.64m (41ft 5.5in); height 4.30m (14ft 1.25in)
Weights:	Empty 5200kg (11,464lb); maximum take-off 9850kg (21,715lb)
Armament:	two 20mm fixed rearward-firing cannon in the underside of the rear fuselage, and an external bomb load of 1500kg (3307lb)

Avia B-534

Avia developed the last Czechoslovak fighter biplane to enter service, the B-534, from the earlier B-34. The B-534 first flew in 1933; for it's time it was one of the best fighters in the world. The type was developed through five main variants, namely the B-534-I (47 with pairs of 7.7mm machine guns in the fuselage and lower wing), B-534-II (99 with four 7.7mm machine guns in the fuselage), B-534-III (46 including Greek and Yugoslav orders with spatted wheels and enlarged supercharger inlet), B-534-IV (272 with an enclosed cockpit) and Bk-534 (35 with one 7.7mm machine gun firing through the propeller shaft and provision for this weapon to be replaced by a 20mm cannon). After Germany's seizure of Czechoslovakia in 1939 some of the aircraft were allocated to the puppet Slovak regime and they continued in this service until 1944, but the majority were used by Germany as advanced trainers.

Country of origin:	Czechoslovakia
Type:	(B-534-IV) single-seat fighter
Powerplant:	one 830hp (619kW) Avia (Hispano-Suiza) 12Ydrs 12-cylinder Vee engine
Performance:	maximum speed 415km/h (251.5mph); climb to 5000m (16,405ft) in 4 minutes 28 seconds; service ceiling 10,600m (34,775ft); range 580km (360 miles)
Weights:	empty 1460kg (3219lb); normal take-off 1980kg (4365lb); maximum take-off 2120kg (4674lb)
Dimensions:	span 9.40m (30ft 10in); length 8.20m (26ft 10.8in); height 3.10m (10ft 2in)
Armament:	four 7.7mm or 7.92mm fixed forward-firing machine guns, plus an external bomb load of 120kg (265lb)

Avro Anson Mk I

Enjoying a production run that lasted from 1934 to 1952, the Anson was built in larger numbers than any other British aeroplane except the Hawker Hurricane and Supermarine Spitfire. The type was initially schemed as a light transport but then adapted as a coastal reconnaissance type to meet a May 1934 requirement. The prototype first flew in March 1935, and the type was ordered into production as the Anson Mk I (later Anson GR.Mk I) with a revised tail unit, a larger cabin window area, Cheetah IX radial engines, and full military equipment. The first of these aircraft flew in December 1935, and the type entered service in March of the following year at the start of a programme that saw the delivery of 6915 aircraft, the later aircraft completed to a five-seat trainer standard with dual controls and different equipment. Pictured is an Anson Mk 1 of No 220 Squadron, RAF Coastal Command. The aircraft has a typical pre-war silver finish.

Country of origin:	United Kingdom
Type:	(Anson Mk I) three/five-seat coastal reconnaissance aeroplane or multi-role trainer
Powerplant:	two 335hp (250kW) Armstrong Siddeley Cheetah IX or, in later aircraft, 395hp (295kW) Cheetah XIX seven-cylinder single-row radial engines
Performance:	maximum speed 302.5km/h (188mph); initial climb rate 293m (960ft) per minute; service ceiling 5790m (19,000ft); range 1271 km (790km)
Weights:	empty 2438kg (5375lb); maximum take-off 4218kg (9300lb)
Dimensions:	span 17.22m (56ft 6in); length 12.88m (42ft 3in); height 3.99m (13ft 1in)
Armament:	up to four 0.303in machine guns on cabin mountings (or in dorsal turret for the trainer model), plus a 227kg (500lb) internal bomb load

Avro Anson Mk II to C.Mk 19

Realisation that the Anson Mk I was too small for as a practical utility or coastal patrol aircraft led to the delivery of later aircraft as multi-role trainers. Production types included the Canadian-built Anson Mk II (1050 aircraft) with 330hp (246kW) Jacobs L-6MB radial engines, British-built Anson Mk III (559 aircraft completed in Canada with L-6MB engines, British-built Anson Mk IV (223 aircraft) completed in Canada with 300hp (224kW) Wright R-760-E1/E3 Whirlwind engines, Canadian-built Anson Mk V (1070 aircraft) with a fuselage of moulded plywood and 450hp (335.5kW) Pratt & Whitney R-985-AN-12B/14B Wasp Junior engines, Anson Mk X transport (103 aircraft) with a strengthened floor, Anson Mk XI transport (90 aircraft), and Anson Mk XII transport (276 aircraft) with 420hp (313kW) Cheetah XV engines. Illustrated is an Anson C.Mk 19 Series 2 in post-war colours and dayglo trim, serving in the communications role with Fighter Command.

Country of origin:	United Kingdom
Type:	(Anson Mk XI) two-crew utility transport aeroplane
Powerplant:	two 395hp (295kW) Armstrong-Siddeley Cheetah XIX seven-cylinder single-row radial engines
Performance:	maximum speed 306km (190mph); initial climb rate 223m (730ft) per minute; service ceiling 4570m (15,000ft); range 982km (610 miles)
Weights:	empty 3365kg (7419lb); maximum take-off 2957kg (9700lb)
Dimensions:	span 17.22m (56ft 6in); length 12.88m (42ft 3in); height 4.22m (13ft 10in)
Armament:	none

Avro Manchester

By the mid-1930s the steady improvement in aeronautical design allowed the Air Ministry to plan a new generation of advanced medium bombers, and in 1936 issued a requirement that elicited responses from both Avro and Handley Page. Both companies received prototype orders although the Handley Page did not progress beyond the drawing board. The Avro type was the Manchester medium bomber that first flew in July 1939 after an initial order for 200 aircraft had been built. The Manchester Mk I became operational in November 1940, and these 20 aircraft were followed by 180 examples of the Manchester Mk IA with larger endplate vertical surfaces on the tail, allowing the removal of the Mk I's centreline surface. The Manchester had an ideal airframe, but was rendered a failure by its wholly unreliable Vulture engines and finally retired in June 1942. Pictured is a Mk I of No 207 Squadron, RAF Bomber Command in early 1941.

Country of origin:	United Kingdom
Type:	(Manchester Mk I) seven-seat medium bomber
Powerplant:	two 1760hp (1312kW) Rolls-Royce Vulture I 24-cylinder X-type engines
Performance:	maximum speed 426km/h (265mph); service ceiling 5850m (19,200ft); range 2623km (1630 miles) with 3674kg (8100lb) of bombs
Weights:	empty 13,350kg (29,432lb); maximum take-off 25,402kg (56,000lb)
Dimensions:	span 27.46m (90ft 1in); length 21.14m (69ft 4.25in); height 5.94m (19ft 6in)
Armament:	two 0.303in trainable forward-firing machine guns in the nose turret, two 0.303in trainable machine guns in a ventral turret later replaced by a dorsal turret, and four 0.303in trainable rearward-firing machine guns in the tail turret, plus an internal bomb load of 10,350lb (4695kg)

Avro Lancaster Mk I

The most successful and celebrated heavy night bomber used by the Royal Air Force in World War II, the Lancaster was a development of the Manchester with the revised powerplant of four Rolls-Royce Merlin Vee engines. The Lancaster first flew on January 9, 1941, and entered service from the beginning of 1942. The original Lancaster Mk I soon developed an enviable reputation as a sturdy aeroplane that handled well in the air, possessed moderately good performance and had good defensive and offensive firepower. The fact that the type was essentially 'right' from its beginning is indicated that few changes were made other than minor engine and equipment details in the course of a long production run that saw the delivery of 7,378 aircraft including 3,294 examples of the Lancaster Mk I (later Lancaster B.Mk I and finally B.Mk X). Pictured is a Lancaster Mk 1 of No 463 Squadron, RAF, based at Waddington in spring 1945.

Country of origin:	United Kingdom
Type:	(Lancaster Mk I) seven-seat heavy night bomber
Powerplant:	four 1640hp (1223kW) Rolls-Royce Merlin XX, 22 or 24 12-cylinder Vee engines
Performance:	maximum speed 462km/h (287mph); initial climb rate 76m (250ft) per minute; service ceiling 5790m(19,000ft); range 2784km (1730 miles) with a 5443kg (12,000lb) bomb load
Weights:	empty 16,783kg (37,000lb); maximum take-off 29,484kg (65,000lb)
Dimensions:	span 31.09m (102ft); length 21.18m (69ft 6in); height 6.25m (20ft 6in)
Armament:	two 0.303in trainable machine guns in the nose turret, two 0.303in trainable machine guns in the dorsal turret, four 0.303in trainable machine guns in the tail turret, and provision for one 0.303in trainable machine gun in a ventral turret, plus an internal bomb load of 8165kg (18,000lb)

Avro Lancaster Mk I (Special)

In 1943 the British decided that a major blow could be struck at Germany's war-making industries by the destruction of the dams controlling the flow of river water through the Ruhr industrial region. This decision led to one of the most celebrated bombing raids of the war, using 'bouncing' bombs that were spun backward and then released at a precise height, speed and distance from the target dam to skip over the water, hit the rear face of the dam and then sink down the face before exploding with devastating force. No.617 Squadron was created for the task, and on 17 May 1943 this unit flew 19 converted Lancaster B.Mk Is to attack five of the dams, of which three were breached for the loss of eight aircraft. The raid was an enormous morale-booster to the British, but did not achieve the strategic results anticipated. Note the serial ED912/G on the aircraft pictured, which indicates a special aircraft that must be kept under armed guard when on the ground.

Country of origin:	United Kingdom
Type:	(Lancaster Mk I Special) six-seat special mission bomber
Powerplant:	four 1640hp (1223kW) Rolls-Royce Merlin 24 12-cylinder Vee engines
Performance:	maximum speed 462km/h (287mph); initial climb rate 76m (250ft) per minute; service ceiling 5790m (19,000ft); range 2784km (1730 miles) with a 5443kg (12,000lb) bomb load
Weights:	empty 16,783kg (37,000lb); maximum take-off 29,484kg (65,000lb)
Dimensions:	span 31.09m (102ft); length 21.18m (69ft 6in); height 6.25m (20ft 6in)
Armament:	two 0.303in trainable machine guns in the nose turret, four 0.303in trainable machine guns in the tail turret and one 0.303in trainable machine gun in the ventral position, plus a 3900kg (8599lb) 'bouncing bomb' semi-recessed under the fuselage

Avro Lancaster Mk III and Mk X

When it became clear that production by Rolls-Royce of its great Merlin engine would not be able to keep pace with the manufacture of the airframes designed to use it, the decision was made to use the American licence-built version, namely the Packard V-1650 in its Merlin 28, 38 or 224 forms. When this engine was installed in the Lancaster Mk I, the aeroplane was known as the Lancaster Mk III (later B.Mk III and finally B.Mk 3), and deliveries of this model totalled 3,020 aircraft. The Lancaster Mk III was also selected for production in Canada by Victory Aircraft Ltd. of Toronto, which delivered 430 examples of the Lancaster Mk X (later B.Mk X and finally B.Mk 10) that were identical in all important respects to the Mk III machines. KB861 was one of a batch of 300 aircraft built as Lancaster Mk Xs by Victory Aircraft, with Packard engines and the Martin 250-CE23 electrically driven mid-upper turret with 0.5in guns.

Country of origin:	United Kingdom
Type:	(Lancaster Mk III) seven-seat heavy night bomber
Powerplant:	four 1640hp (1223kW) Packard (Rolls-Royce) Merlin 28, 38 or 224 12-cylinder Vee engines
Performance:	maximum speed 462km/h(287mph); initial climb rate 76m (250ft) per minute; service ceiling 5790m (19,000ft); range 2784km (1730 miles) with a 5443kg (12,000lb) bomb load
Weights:	empty 16,783kg (37,000lb); maximum take-off 29,484kg (65,000lb)
Dimensions:	span 31.09m (102ft 0in); length 21.18m (69ft 6in); height 6.25m (20ft 6in)
Armament:	two 0.303in trainable machine guns in the nose, turret, two 0.303-in trainable machine guns in the dorsal turret and four 0.303in trainable machine guns in the tail turret, plus an internal bomb load of 8165kg (18,000lb)

Avro Lancaster B.Mk I (Special)

After it had gained experience with the accurate delivery of single Deep Penetration-type bombs with the 12,000lb (5443kg) 'Tallboy' (of which 854 were dropped in anger) the Royal Air Force agreed to undertake missions with the heaviest weapon of this class, the 22,000lb (9979kg) 'Grand Slam'. This was designed to penetrate deep into the earth before detonating, thus creating an earthquake effect. The bomber designed to carry this weapon from March 1945 was the Lancaster B.Mk I (Special), of which 33 were built by converting Lancaster B.Mk I aircraft with a lengthened and doorless bomb bay and, to save weight, no nose or dorsal turrets. The aircraft were operated by No.617 Squadron, which dropped 41 such bombs, with considerable success, on U-boat pens and transportation chokepoints. This unusual colour scheme was worn by one of the aircraft of the squadron's C Flight. Note the retaining chain under the bomb.

Country of origin:	United Kingdom
Type:	(Lancaster B.Mk I [Special]) five-seat special mission bomber
Powerplant:	four 1640hp (1223kW) Rolls-Royce Merlin 24 12-cylinder Vee engines
Performance:	maximum speed 462km/h (287mph); initial climb rate 76m (250ft) per minute; service ceiling 5790m (19,000ft); range 2494km (1550 miles) with a 9979kg (22,000lb) bomb load
Weights:	empty 16,083kg (35,457lb); maximum take-off 32,659kg (72,000lb)
Dimensions:	span 31.09m (102ft 0in); length 21.18m (69ft 6in); height 6.25m (20ft 6in)
Armament:	four 0.303in trainable machine guns in the tail turret, plus a semi-internal bomb load of one 22,000lb (9979kg) 'Grand Slam' bomb

Avro Lancaster Mk VI

To perform the role of electronic countermeasures and electronic counter-countermeasures for the Pathfinder Force, a total of nine Lancaster bombers were converted from Mk 1 and Mk III aircraft, (two and nine respectively). These were re-engined with the two-stage supercharged Merlin 85/87 in circular cowlings (with curved ventral radiator) that were later used on Lincolns and Shackletons. With four-bladed paddle propellors the Mk VI had tremendous performance, especially as all armament except the tail turret was removed. One was logged at 555km/h (345 mph). The Mk VI also benefited from an improved version of the H2S bombing radar; the main antenna for this unit was protected by a ventral fairing. This example served with No 635 Squadron, a dedicated Pathfinder unit. To identify aircraft operating in the Pathfinder role the fins were painted with high-visibility stripes, as can be seen above.

Country of origin:	United Kingdom
Type:	(Lancaster B.Mk VI) five-seat special mission bomber
Powerplant:	four 1640hp (1223kW) Packard Merlin 85/87 12-cylinder Vee engines
Performance:	maximum speed 555km/h (345mph); initial climb rate 76m (250ft) per minute; service ceiling 6500m (21,418ft); range 2494km (1550 miles) with a 9979kg (22,000lb) bomb load
Weights:	empty 16,083kg (35,457lb); maximum take-off 32,659kg (72,000lb)
Dimensions:	span 31.09m (102ft 0in); length 21.18m (69ft 6in); height 6.25m (20ft 6in)
Armament:	four 0.303in trainable machine guns in the tail turret.

Bell P-39 Airacobra

The P-39 was a bold attempt to create an advanced fighter by locating the engine in the fuselage behind the cockpit, from where it drove the tractor propeller by means of a long extension shaft. This was intended to leave the nose free for a concentrated forward-firing battery of guns, improve agility by locating the engine nearer the centre of gravity than was common, and facilitate the use of tricycle landing gear. The XP-39 prototype first flew in April 1938, and a number of prototype and pre-production standards appeared before the P-39D entered service as the first operational model. Despite the fact that it served with 13 groups, the US Army never deemed the P-39 genuinely successful, and 4924 of the 9590 aircraft were shipped to the USSR for use mainly in the ground-attack role. The other main variants were the P-39F, J, K, L, M, N and Q. This Airacobra Mk 101 wears the colours on No 601 Squadron, the only operational RAF unit to fly the type.

Country of origin:	USA
Type:	(P-39N) single-seat fighter and fighter-bomber
Powerplant:	one 1125hp (839kW) Allison V-1710-85 12-cylinder Vee engine
Performance:	maximum speed 605km/h (376mph); climb to 4570m (15,000ft) in 6 minutes 6 seconds; service ceiling 11,665m (38,270ft); range 1569km (975 miles)
Weights:	empty 2903kg (6400lb); maximum take-off 3992kg (8800lb)
Dimensions:	span 10.36m (34ft); length 9.2m (30ft 2in); height 3.79m (12ft 5in)
Armament:	one 37mm fixed forward-firing cannon and two 0.5in fixed forward-firing machine guns in the nose, and four 0.3in fixed forward-firing machine guns in the leading edges of the wing, plus an external bomb load of 227kg (500lb)

Bell P-59 Airacomet

The Airacomet was the first American-designed aeroplane to fly with a turbojet-engine and was also the first Allied warplane of World War II to take to the air after being designed from the outset for turbine power. The first of three XP-59A prototypes made its maiden flight in October 1942 with General Electric I-A turbojets derived from a British engine, the Whittle W.2. There followed 13 YP-59A service test aircraft with uprated I-16 (J31) engines and armament, but flight trials highlighted indifferent performance and handling and persuaded the US Army that the production variant could be used only as a fighter trainer. The two production models were the P-59A and P-59B: the 20 P-59A aircraft delivered from the autumn of 1944 had J31-GE-5 engines and a lengthened fuselage. Illustrated is the third and last prototype, in USAAF markings whilst undergoing evaluation at Muroc Dry Lake in summer 1943.

Country of origin:	USA
Type:	(P-59A) single-seat fighter and fighter-bomber
Powerplant:	two General Electric J31-GE-3 turbojets
Performance:	maximum speed 664.5km/h (413mph); climb to 6095m (20,000ft) in 7 minutes 24 seconds; service ceiling 14,080m (46,200ft); range 837km (520 miles)
Weights:	empty 3704kg (8165lb); normal take-off 5008kg (11,040lb); maximum take-off 6214kg (13,700lb)
Dimensions:	span 13.87m (45ft 6in); length 11.62m (38ft 1.5in); height 3.66m (12ft)
Armament:	one 37mm fixed forward-firing cannon and three 0.5in fixed forward-firing machine guns in the nose, plus an external; bomb and rocket load of 907kg (2,000lb)

Bell P-59B Airacomet

The service P-59A (20 built) and P-59B (30 built) Airacomets had a shorter fin than the prototypes. The P-59B also incorporated a raised canopy first seen on the YP-59 aircraft and had additional fuel tankage. Pilots reported the aircraft was a delight to fly, but nonetheless it was only ever used for secondary duties. Performance was similar to the early Gloster Meteors: it had inadequate performance and proved to be an indifferent gun platform. The Airacomet was flown for test and evaluation purposes by the USAAF's 412th Fighter Group, a specially formed unit. The aircraft pictured served with the USAF on drone control operations, fitted with nose armament and drop tanks, and having an open cockpit in the nose to seat a drone operator. Note the position of the fairy high tailplane position, designed so that it would be clear of the efflux from the two General Electric turbojets.

Country of origin:	USA
Type:	(P-59B) single-seat fighter and fighter-bomber
Powerplant:	two 2000lb st (8.90kN) General Electric J31-GE-5 turbojets
Performance:	maximum speed 664.5km/h (413mph); climb to 6095m (20,000ft) in 7 minutes 24 seconds; service ceiling 14,080m (46,200ft); range 837km (520 miles)
Weights:	empty 3704kg (8165lb); normal take-off 5008kg (11,040lb); maximum take-off 6214kg (13,700lb)
Dimensions:	span 13.87m (45ft 6in); length 11.62m (38ft 1.5in); height 3.66m (12ft)
Armament:	one 37mm fixed forward-firing cannon and three 0.5in fixed forward-firing machine guns in the nose, plus an external; bomb and rocket load of 907kg (2000lb)

Besson MB.411

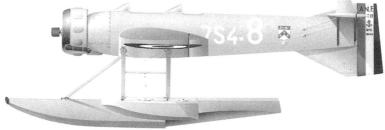

This small floatplane was specifically designed for disassembled carriage (in the watertight cylindrical hangar abaft the conning tower of the submarine cruiser *Surcouf*) before rapid assembly and launch as a reconnaissance type or as a spotter for the submarine's pair of 8in guns. Early trials had involved the MB.35 and MB.410 floatplanes, the latter paving the way for the MB.410 that first flew in June 1935 as a low-wing monoplane with single-float alighting gear. Only one other MB.411 was built, and the concept of their operation proved practical if not actually very effective as a result of the time it took to assemble and then disassemble the type before and after any mission. Neither of the two floatplanes was on board the submarine when it was lost in February 1942, after being rammed in darkness by an American freighter. Plans to operate the MB.411 from a British merchant ship never came to fruition.

Country of origin:	France
Type:	(MB.411) two-seat submarine-borne reconnaissance and observation floatplane
Powerplant:	one 175hp (130kW) Salmson 9Nd nine-cylinder single-row radial engine
Performance:	maximum speed 190km/h (118mph); initial climb rate not available; service ceiling 5000m (16,405ft); range 650 km (404 miles)
Weights:	empty 760kg (1676lb); maximum take-off 1140kg (2513lb)
Dimensions:	span 12.00m (39ft 4.5in); length 8.25m (27ft 0.75in); height 2.85m (9ft 4.25in)
Armament:	none

Beriev KOR-2 (Be-4)

The KOR-1 was designed in 1934-35 by Beriev as successor to the Heinkel HD 55 floatplane carried by catapult-equipped Soviet warships. The aircraft first flew in prototype form in around April 1936. The type entered service in the following year, and despite the fact that its utility was hampered by seaworthiness problems as well as a lack of structural rigidity on the water and during catapult launches, the type remained in production (about 300 aircraft) up to 1940. As Beriev sought to rectify the KOR-1's structural problems, most of the early aircraft were restricted to shore-based operations. It was only in 1939, when it had received the updated designation KOR-2, that the type was granted full release for naval use, and then only without armament and with a restriction to water take-off rather than catapult launch. Only a small number of the aircraft had been completed before the Beriev factory at Taganrog was overrun by German troops in the autumn of 1941.

Country of origin:	USSR
Type:	(KOR-1) two-seat reconnaissance floatplane
Powerplant:	one 900hp (671kW) M-25A nine-cylinder single-row radial engine
Performance:	maximum speed 360km/h (223mph); climb to 1000m (3280ft) in 3 minutes 12 seconds; service ceiling 8100m (26,575ft); range 950km (590 miles)
Weights:	empty 2055kg (4530lb); normal take-off 2486kg (5480lb); maximum take-off 2760kg (6085lb)
Dimensions:	span 12.00m (39ft 4.5in); length 10.5m (34ft 5.25in); height 4.05m (13ft 3in)
Armament:	one 7.62mm trainable machine gun in aft cockpit, plus an external bomb load of 300kg (661lb)

Beriev MBR-2

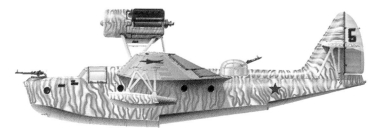

The MBR-2 was intended to provide the Soviet naval air arm with a coastal flying boat for the reconnaissance bomber role, and first flew in prototype form during October 1932. Trials revealed structural strength, good performance, and problem-free handling on the water and in the air, and the type was therefore ordered into production. The first of an initial 100 or so MBR-2/M-17 boats was delivered in the spring of 1934 with the M-17 Vee engine rated at 500hp (373kW). Beriev then developed the type into the MBR-2/M-34 with the uprated M-34NB engine, structural strengthening for greater weights and higher speeds, a revised tail unit with curved rather than angular outlines, a deepened hull, a revised cockpit of the enclosed type, and improved defensive armament. Production of some 1200 boats lasted to 1942. This MBR-2 has sea green streaking camouflage. The type served for nearly a decade after World War II on fishery patrol duties.

Country of origin:	USSR
Type:	(MBR-2/M-34) four-seat coastal reconnaissance and bomber flying boat
Powerplant:	one 860hp (641kW) Mikulin M-34NB 12-cylinder Vee engine
Performance:	maximum speed 238km/h (148mph); initial climb rate not available; service ceiling 7900m (25,920ft); range 800km (497 miles)
Weights:	empty 2718kg (5992lb); normal take-off 4100kg (9039lb); maximum take-off 4000kg (9921lb)
Dimensions:	span 19.00m (62ft 4in); length 13.50m (44ft 3.75in); height not available
Armament:	one 7.62mm trainable forward-firing machine gun in the bow position, and one 7.62mm trainable machine gun in the dorsal turret, plus an external bomb load of 500kg (1102lb)

Blackburn Baffin

After the Finnish Air Force had replaced the Napier Lion W-type engine with a radial engine in most of its licence-built Blackburn Ripon torpedo bombers, Blackburn followed a similar course to create the two T.5J (Ripon Mk V) private-venture prototypes. These aircraft were then redesigned as the B-4 and B-5 with 650hp (485kW) Armstrong Siddeley Tiger I and 545hp (406kW) Bristol Pegasus IMS radial engines respectively. The prototypes flew in 1932, and there followed two Pegasus IM3-powered T.8 pre-production aircraft. These paved the way for the Baffin Mk I, of which 97 were delivered up to June 1935 in the form of 38 and 30 Ripon Mk IIA and Mk IIC conversions as well as 29 new-build aircraft. The Baffin was declared obsolete in September 1937, and this allowed New Zealand to buy 19 aircraft for coastal patrol service up to 1942. Pictured is one of the B-5 aircraft operated by the Finnish Air Force

Country of origin:	United Kingdom
Type:	(Baffin Mk I) two-seat carrierborne and land-based torpedo and level bomber
Powerplant:	one 565hp (421kW) Bristol Pegasus IM3 nine-cylinder single-row radial engine
Performance:	maximum speed 219km/h (136mph); initial climb rate 146m (480ft) per minute; service ceiling 4570m (15,000ft); range 869km (450 miles)
Weights:	empty 1452kg (3200lb); maximum take-off 3452kg (7610lb)
Dimensions:	span 13.88m (45ft 6.5in); length 11.68m (38ft 3.75in); height 3.91m (12ft 10in)
Armament:	one 0.303in fixed forward-firing machine gun in the upper port side of the forward fuselage, and one 0.303in trainable rearward-firing machine gun in the rear cockpit, plus an external torpedo and bomb load of 907kg (2000lb)

Blackburn Botha

Designed to meet a 1935 requirement for a twin-engined reconnaissance bomber with a bomb bay large enough to accommodate an 18in (457mm) torpedo, the Botha first flew in prototype form during December 1938. Trials revealed that the type had a number of handling problems and was also seriously underpowered, but the handling problems were cured and the type was placed in production (580 aircraft) with the option of marginally uprated engines. The first aircraft to be delivered to the RAF was the third aircraft off the Dumbarton production line, which arrived at No 12 Maintenance Unit, Kemble, in December 1939. Entering service in May 1940, the Botha proved so inadequate for coastal reconnaissance and attack purposes that only two operational squadrons converted to the type, which was soon relegated to second-line duties. The Botha survived as a navigation and gunnery trainer into 1944, and was unsuccessful even in this secondary role.

Country of origin:	United Kingdom
Type:	(Botha Mk I) four-seat reconnaissance and torpedo bomber used mainly for training and communications
Powerplant:	two 930hp (694kW) Bristol Perseus XA nine-cylinder single-row radial engine
Performance:	maximum speed 401km/h (249mph); initial climb rate 300m (985ft) per minute; service ceiling 5610m (18,400ft); range 2044km (1270 miles)
Weights:	empty 5366kg (11,830lb); maximum take-off 8369kg (18,450lb)
Dimensions:	span 17.98m (59ft 0in); length 15.56m (51ft 0.5in); height 4.46m (14ft 7.5in)
Armament:	one 0.303in fixed forward-firing machine gun in the nose, and two 0.303in trainable machine guns in the dorsal turret, plus an internal bomb and torpedo load of 907kg (2000lb)

Blackburn Firebrand

In March 1939 the Admiralty issued a requirement for a two-seat fleet-defence
fighter with an armament of four 20mm wing-mounted cannon, later revised to
cover a single-seat type. The Blackburn design was deemed more promising than
Hawker's navalised Typhoon concept, and the first of three Firebrand prototypes
made its maiden flight in February 1942. By this time the Supermarine Seafire had
been accepted for service, and plans were then made for the Firebrand to be used
as torpedo fighter. The first nine aircraft were too advanced in construction for
adaptation, however, and were completed as Firebrand F.Mk I fighters before the
advent of the Firebrand TF.Mk II with external carriage of one torpedo. Only 12
aircraft were completed before the type was revised for post-war production with
the Bristol Centaurus radial engine. Illustrated is a Firebrand TF.5 of No 813
Squadron, with torpedo carrying MAT Mk IV directional stablising fins.

Country of origin:	United Kingdom
Type:	(Firebrand Mk II) single-seat carrierborne and land-based torpedo fighter
Powerplant:	one 2305hp (1719kW) Napier Sabre III 24-cylinder h-type engine
Performance:	maximum speed 571km/h (355mph); initial climb rate 701m (2300ft) per minute; service ceiling not available; range 1239km (770 miles)
Weights:	empty 5368kg (11,835lb); maximum take-off 6826kg (15,049lb)
Dimensions:	span 15.63m (51ft 3.5in); length 11.63m (38ft 2in); height 4.06m (13ft 4in)
Armament:	four 20mm fixed forward-firing cannon in the leading edges of the wing, and an external torpedo or bomb load of 839kg (1850lb)

Blériot-SPAD S.510

T he S.510 was the last biplane fighter to serve with the French Air Force. Its origins lay in the S.91 designed by Blériot-SPAD to meet a 1926 requirement for a lightweight (or 'Jockey') fighter. The S.510 was clearly a linear descendant of the S.91, but had a number of more modern features including nicely faired and spatted main units of the divided type for the fixed tailskid landing gear. The S.510 had a tortuous design history and proved inferior to the rival Dewoitine D.510 monoplane, but the French air ministry was persuaded to order 60 examples of the obsolescent S.510 in parallel with the D.510. The S.510C.1 entered service early in 1936, and was still in limited service on the outbreak of World War II, seeing limited operational use in France before being relegated to second-line service in North Africa. The aircraft pictured was operated by ERC 4/561 of the Armée de l'Air, based at Havre-Octeville in October 1939.

Country of origin:	France
Type:	(S.510C.1) single-seat fighter
Powerplant:	one 690hp (515kW) Hispano-Suiza 12Xbrs 12-cylinder Vee engine
Performance::	maximum speed 372km/h (231mph); climb to 4000m (13,125ft) in 4 minutes 31 seconds; service ceiling 10,500m (34,450ft); range 875km (544 miles)
Weights:	empty 1250kg (2756lb); maximum take-off 1830kg (4034lb)
Dimensions:	span 8.84m (29ft); length 7.46m (24ft 5.75in); height 3.72m (12ft 2.5in)
Armament:	two 7.5mm fixed forward-firing machine guns in the upper part of the forward fuselage and two 7.5mm fixed forward-firing machine guns in gondola fairings below the lower wing, or four 7.5mm fixed forward-firing machine guns in gondola fairings under the lower wing

Bloch MB.151 and MB.152

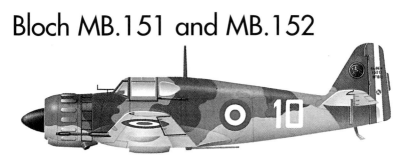

As first completed in MB.150.01 prototype form, this fighter refused even to take-off, but after revision to MB.151.01 standard with a larger wing finally flew in August 1938. The type was ordered into production as the MB.151C.1; the first 25 of the 140 aircraft had the 920hp (686kW) Gnome-Rhône 14N-11 engine, later production aircraft had the improved 14N-25 engine. Performance and handling were indifferent, and the type was generally used as a fighter lead-in trainer. In parallel there emerged 481 production examples of the MB.152C.1 with an uprated engine and a different armament fit. The type saw limited service in the defence of France in May and June 1940, and remained in service with the Vichy regime after France's defeat. Germany took over a number of the aircraft as trainers, and later passed 20 MB.151 and MB.152 fighters to Romania. Pictured is an MB. 152 of the 1st Escadrille, Groupe de Chasse I/1, based at Chantilly-les-Aigles in May 1940.

Country of origin:	France
Type:	(MB.152C.1) single-seat fighter
Powerplant:	one 1080hp (805kW) Gnome-Rhône 14N-25 or 1060hp (790kW) Gnome-Rhône 14N-49 14-cylinder two-row radial engine
Performance:	maximum speed 509km/h (316mph); climb to 4000m (13,125ft) in 6 minutes 55 seconds; service ceiling 10,000m (32,810ft); range 540km (335 miles)
Weights:	empty 4758lb (2158kg); maximum take-off 6173lb (2800kg)
Dimensions:	span 10.54m (34ft 7in); length 9.10m (29ft 10.5in); height 3.03m (9ft 11.25in)
Armament:	four 7.5mm fixed forward-firing machine guns, or two 20mm fixed forward-firing cannon and two 7.5mm fixed forward-firing machine guns, in each case in the leading edges of the wing

Bloch MB.155

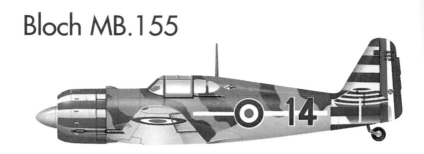

With the MB.155.01 prototype conversion from MB.152C.1 standard, the MB.150 series finally began to come of age as a genuinely effective fighter. The main change in the MB.155 was the installation of the engine inherited from the MB.152. The prototype first flew in 1940, and there followed for the Vichy French Air Force a total of 33 production aircraft with the designation MB.155C.1. These differed from the prototype is having their cockpit repositioned farther to the rear, which permitted the introduction of a new fuel tank for an enlarged overall capacity and the addition of more armour protection. After the German occupation of Vichy France in November 1942, several of the aircraft were seized for subsequent German use as fighter trainers. The colourful, even lurid paint scheme applied to this aircraft indicates that it was the personal mount of Groupe de Chasse II/8. This Vichy French Air Force unit was based at Marignane in July 1940.

Country of origin:	France
Type:	(MB.155C.1) single-seat fighter
Powerplant:	one 1060 hp (790kW) Gnome-Rhône 14N-49 14-cylinder two-row radial engine
Performance:	maximum speed 520km/h (323mph); climb to 4000m (13,125ft) in 6 minutes; service ceiling 10,000m (32,810ft); range 1050km (652 miles)
Weights:	empty 2158kg (4757lb); normal take-off 2748kg (6058lb); maximum take-off 2850kg (6283lb)
Dimensions:	span 10.54m (34ft 7in); length 9.05m (29ft 8.33in); height 3.03m (9ft 11.25in)
Armament:	two 20mm fixed forward-firing cannon and two or four 7.5mm fixed forward-firing machine guns, or six 7.5mm fixed forward-firing machine guns in the leading edges of the wing

Bloch MB.174

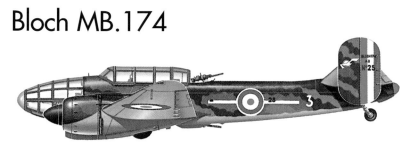

The origins of the Bloch MB.174 can be traced to a time late in 1936, when Bloch began to plan the MB.170 multi-role warplane that could be operated in the A.3 three-seat army co-operation or AB.2 two-seat attack bomber roles. The MB.170 first flew in February 1938, and the type was eventually ordered as the MB.174, primarily for reconnaissance and target-marking operations but with light bombing as a secondary role. The MB.174A.3 retained the flying surfaces, landing gear and powerplant of the MB.170B.3 in combination with a redesigned fuselage. The cockpit was moved farther to the rear and the nose received a fair measure of glazing. Only 56 of this model were completed and played a modest part in the defensive campaign that preceded France's capitulation in June 1940. Pictured is one of the aircraft operated by Groupe de Reconnaissance II/33 during the Battle of France. Some were later used by the Vichy Air Force.

Country of origin:	France
Type:	(MB.174A.3) three-seat light reconnaissance bomber
Powerplant:	two 1140hp (850kW) Gnome-Rhône 14N-48/49 14-cylinder two-row radial engines
Performance:	maximum speed 530km/h (329mph); climb to 8000 m (26,250ft) in 11 minutes 0 seconds; service ceiling 11,000m (36,090ft); range 1285km (798 miles) with an 400kg (882lb) bomb load
Weights:	empty 5600kg (12,346lb); maximum take-off 7160kg (15,784lb)
Dimensions:	span 17.90m (58ft 8.75in); length 12.25m (40ft 2.25in); height 3.55m (11ft 7.75in)
Armament:	two 7.5mm fixed forward-firing machine guns in the leading edges of the wing, two 7.5mm trainable rearward-firing machine guns in the dorsal position and three 7.5mm rearward-firing machine guns in the ventral position, plus an internal bomb load of 400kg (882lb)

Bloch MB. 200

Designed to replace the obsolete Liorè-et-Olivier LeO 20 in the night bomber role, the Bloch MB.200 was typical of the highly angular French warplanes of the late 1920s and early 1930s and first flew in MB.200.01 prototype form in June 1933. An initial 30 MB.200B.4 bombers were ordered in December of the same year, and the type entered service in 1934. Eventual French production by six companies – Bloch, Breguet, Hanriot, Loire, Potez and SNCASO – was 208 aircraft, and another 124 aircraft were built under licence in Czechoslovakia by the Aero and Avia companies. The type was obsolete by 1939, and most French aircraft were soon relegated to the training role. Many continued in service after France's defeat. A number of the aircraft were expropriated by the Germans for their own use and transfer to allies. Pictured is one of the aircraft operated by Section de Remorquage d'Orange in May 1940.

Country of origin:	France
Type:	(MB.200B.4) four-seat medium bomber
Powerplant:	two 870hp (649kW) Gnome-Rhône 14Kirs/Kjrs Mistral-Major 14-cylinder two-row radial engines
Performance:	maximum speed 283km/h (176mph); climb to 4000m (13,125ft) in 13 minutes; service ceiling 8000m (26,245ft); range 1000km (621 miles)
Weights:	empty 4300kg (9840lb); maximum take-off 7480kg (16,490lb)
Dimensions:	span 22.45m (73ft 7.88in); length 15.80m (51ft 10in); height 3.92m (12ft 10in)
Armament:	one 7.5mm trainable forward-firing machine gun in the nose turret, one 7.5mm trainable machine gun in the dorsal turret and one 7.5mm trainable rearward-firing machine gun in the ventral gondola, plus an external bomb load of 1200kg (2646lb)

Blohm und Voss Bv 138

The Bv 138 was projected and built in prototype form as the Ha 138, with three Junkers Jumo 205D Diesel engines, before undergoing a virtually total redesign in 1938, the year in which the Hamburger Flugzeugbau was absorbed fully into Blohm und Voss. The first of six Bv 138A-0 pre-production flying boats made its maiden flight in February 1939. These machines were followed by 25 Bv 138A-1 production 'boats with three 600hp (447kW) Jumo 205C-4 engines, and the type saw its first operational service in April 1940. Six and 14 Bv 138B-0 and B-1 machines introduced a strengthened structure and greater power respectively, while the definitive Bv 138C-1 (about 227 'boats) had more strengthening and better defensive armament. The designation Bv 138MS was used for minesweeper conversions. Pictured here is a BV 138C-1 of 2/KüF/Gr. 406, based in northern Norway in March 1942.

Country of origin:	Germany
Type:	(Bv 138C-1) five-seat maritime reconnaissance flying boat
Powerplant:	three 1000hp (746kW) Junkers Jumo 205D 12-cylinder vertically opposed Diesel engines
Performance:	maximum speed 285km/h (177mph); climb to 3000m (9845ft) in 22 minutes 48 seconds; ceiling 5000m (16,405ft); range 4300km (2672 miles)
Weights:	empty 11,770kg (25,948lb); maximum take-off 17,650kg (38,912lb)
Dimensions:	span 26.94m (88ft 4.75in); length 19.85m (65ft 1.5in); height 5.90m (19ft 4.25in)
Armament:	one 20mm trainable forward-firing cannon in the bow turret, one 20mm trainable rearward-firing cannon in the rear-hull turret, one 13mm trainable rearward-firing machine gun behind the central engine nacelle, and one 7.92mm trainable lateral-firing machine gun in starboard hull position, plus a bomb load of 300kg (661lb)

Blohm und Voss Bv 141

Designed as a tactical reconnaissance aeroplane to the same requirement as the Focke-Wulf Fw 189, the Bv 141 had a highly unusual asymmetric layout with the fully glazed crew nacelle offset to starboard of the centreline and a boom (carrying the engine at its front and a tail unit at its rear) offset to port. The first of three prototypes flew in February 1938, and there followed five Bv 141A-0 pre-production aircraft. The type had poor performance as a result of its use of the 865hp (645kW) BMW 132N engine, so the next five aircraft were redesigned Bv 141B-0 machines with an uprated powerplant as well as a strengthened structure and a revised tail unit. These aircraft were used for operational trials over the UK and the USSR from the autumn of 1941, but there were development delays and the programme was ended in 1943. Depicted is one of the pre-production aircraft (BV 141A-04), as evaluated by the Luftwaffe at the Erprobungstelle factory in late 1939.

Country of origin:	Germany
Type:	(Bv 141B-0) three-seat tactical reconnaissance and observation aeroplane with limited close support capability
Powerplant:	one 1560hp (1163kW) BMW 801A 14-cylinder two-row radial engine
Performance:	maximum speed 438km/h (272mph); initial climb rate not available; service ceiling 10,000m (32,810ft); range 1900km (1181 miles)
Weights:	empty 4700kg (10,362lb); maximum take-off 6100kg (13,448lb)
Dimentions:	span 17.46m (57ft 3.5in); length 13.95m (45ft 9.25in); height 3.60m (11ft 9.75in)
Armament:	two 7.92mm fixed forward-firing machine guns in the front of the crew nacelle, one 7.92mm trainable rearward-firing machine gun in the dorsal position, and one 7.92mm trainable rearward-firing machine gun in the rotating tailcone position, plus an external bomb load of 200kg (441lb)

Blohm und Voss Bv 222 Wiking

The Wiking (Viking) started life as a 1937 project for a 24-passenger flying boat airliner to operate between Berlin and New York. The type was then revised as a long-range maritime reconnaissance type and was the largest flying boat to enter operational service in World War II. There were eight prototypes, the first of them flying in September 1940, the Bv 222B was the unrealised civil model, and the military version was planned as the Bv 222C, of which only four Bv 222C-0 pre-production examples were completed. The prototypes entered transport service in mid-1941, mainly in the Mediterranean, and from 1943 were revised for the reconnaissance role and supplemented by the four pre-production 'boats. The 'boats then served over the Atlantic, Baltic and Arctic regions. Only four 'boats survived to the end of the war. One of these was flown to RAF Calshot for evaluation, and later equipped No 201 Squadron.

Country of origin:	Germany
Type:	(Bv 222C) transport and maritime reconnaissance flying boat
Powerplant:	six 1000hp (746kW) Junkers Jumo 207C 12-cylinder vertically opposed Diesel engines
Performance:	maximum speed 390km/h (242mph); initial climb rate 144m (473ft) per minute; ceiling 7300m (23,950ft); range 6100 km (3790 miles)
Weights:	empty 30,650kg (67,572lb); maximum take-off 49,000kg (108,025lb)
Dimensions:	span 46m (150ft 11in); length 37m (121ft 4.75in); height 10.90m (35ft 9in)
Armament:	one 20mm trainable cannon in the dorsal turret, one 20mm trainable cannon in each of the two power-operated wing turrets, one 13mm trainable forward-firing machine gun in the bow position, and one 13mm trainable lateral-firing machine gun in each of the four lateral hull positions

Boeing B-17C Flying Fortress

The Model 299 was designed to meet a 1934 requirement for a multi-engined medium bomber and envisaged primarily for the coast-defence role. The aircraft first flew as a private-venture prototype with provision for a 4800lb (2177kg) bomb load and was later evaluated as the XB-17. Orders were then placed for 14 YB-17 and YB-17A service test aircraft that were later accepted as B-17 and B-17A aircraft, and paved the way for the 39 B-17B aircraft with a modified nose, 38 B-17B aircraft with greater power and defensive armament, and 42 B-17D aircraft with an additional crew member. Some 20 B-17Cs were transferred to the UK as Fortress Mk I machines; most of the B-17D bombers were stationed in the Far East, where about half were destroyed by Japan's pre-emptive attacks of December 7, 1941. Note the ventral bathtub and flush waist positions on the B-17C illustrated here. The B-17C was the fastest of all versions, with a maximum speed of 515km/h (320 mph).

Country of origin:	USA
Type:	(B-17C) nine-seat medium bomber
Powerplant:	four 1200hp (895kW) Wright R-1820-65 nine-cylinder single-row radial engines
Performance:	maximum speed 515km/h (320 mph); climb to 3050m (10,000ft) in 7 minutes 30 seconds; service ceiling 11,280m (37,000ft); range 5471km (3400 miles)
Weights:	empty 13,880kg (30,600lb); maximum take-off 22,521kg (49,650lb)
Dimensions:	span 31.62m (103ft 9in); length 20.70m (67ft 11in); height 4.70m (15ft 5in)
Armament:	two 0.3in forward-firing machine guns in cheek positions, three 0.5in machine guns in dorsal positions, two 0.5in machine guns in the ventral position, and one 0.5in machine gun in each of the two waist positions, plus an internal bomb load of 4761kg (10,496lb)

Boeing B-17F Flying Fortress

The B-17D paved the way for the first large-scale production model of the Flying Fortress, the B-17E. Some 512 were delivered and featured a wholly redesigned and enlarged tail unit for improved stability at high altitude, and a completely revised defensive scheme including a twin-gun tail position and power-operated twin-gun dorsal and ventral turrets. The B-17E entered service in 1942, and was soon supplemented by the B-17F. This was the definitive model, as indicated by a production total of 3,405 aircraft from three manufacturers. The B-17F introduced a frameless Plexiglas nose transparency, structural strengthening for higher-weight operations, and further refinement of the defensive armament. Small numbers of B-17E and B-17F bombers were operated by the British with the designations Fortress Mk IIA and Fortress Mk II respectively. A number were captured intact by the Germans and evaluated in Luftwaffe markings.

Country of origin:	USA
Type:	(B-17F) 10-seat medium bomber
Powerplant:	four 1200hp (895kW) Wright R-1820-97 nine-cylinder single-row radial engines
Performance:	maximum speed 523km/h (325mph); climb to 6095m (20,000ft) in 25 minutes 42 seconds;ceiling 11,430m (37,500ft);range 7113km (4420 miles)
Weights:	empty 16,206kg (35,728lb); maximum take-off 32,6591kg (72,000lb)
Dimensions:	span 31.63m (103ft 9.38in); length 22.78m (74ft 9in); height 5.85m (19ft 2.5in)
Armament:	two 0.3in trainable forward-firing machine guns in cheek positions, three 0.5in trainable machine guns in dorsal positions, two 0.5in trainable machine guns in the ventral position, and one 0.5in trainable lateral-firing machine gun in each of the two waist positions, plus an internal bomb load of 4761kg (10,496lb)

Boeing B-17G Flying Fortress

The B-17G Flying Fortress resulted directly from the experience of the US bomber crews in 1943, which revealed that the B-17F lacked adequate defence against head-on fighter attack. The primary change in the B-17G was therefore the introduction of a power-operated chin turret armed with two 0.5in machine guns and controlled remotely from the glazed nose position. This proved to be a more practical unit as it lost the one or two manually operated 0.5in machine guns that had been fitted in the B-17F. Deliveries began in September 1943. A number of other operational improvements were steadily incorporated during the production of 8680 aircraft from three manufacturers in the period up to April 1945. The B-17G was the cornerstone of the US Army Air Forces' bomber effort in Europe during 1944 and 1945. The aircraft pictured is the famed B-17G *A Bit o'Lace* of the 711th BS, 447th BG, based at Rattlesden.

Country of origin:	USA
Type:	(B-17G) 10-seat heavy bomber
Powerplant:	four 1200hp (895kW) Wright R-1820-97 nine-cylinder radial engines
Performance:	maximum speed 486km/h (302mph); climb to 6095m (20,000ft) in 37 minutes; service ceiling 10,850m (35,600ft); range 2897km (1800 miles)
Weights:	empty 20,212kg (44,560lb); maximum take-off 32,659kg (72,000lb)
Dimensions:	span 31.63m (103ft 9.4in); length 22.78m (74ft 9 in); height 5.82m (19ft 1in)
Armament:	two 0.5in machine guns in chin turret, one 0.5in machine gun in each cheek position, two 0.5in trainable machine guns in dorsal turret, one 0.5in machine gun in roof position, two 0.5in machine guns in ventral turret, one 0.5in machine gun in each waist position, two 0.5in machine guns in tail, plus a bomb load of 7983kg (17,600lb)

Boeing B-29 Superfortress

The B-29 is generally remembered as the warplane which, on 6 and 9 August 1945, dropped atomic weapons that destroyed the cities of Hiroshima and Nagasaki, persuading the Japanese to surrender. Yet by this time the B-29 had been at the forefront of a campaign to neutralise the war-making potential of Japan by burning her cities, destroying her communications network and crippling her industries. First entering service from the summer of 1944, the Superfortress was an extremely clean bomber with turbocharged engines. The baseline B-29, of which 2458 were completed, was complemented by the B-29A of which 1119 were manufactured with greater span and a four- rather than two-gun forward dorsal barbette, and the B-29B of which 310 were delivered with reduced defensive armament but a greater bomb load and higher speed. The aircraft pictured was allocated to the 500th Bomb Group of the 73rd Bomb Wing.

Country of origin:	USA
Type:	(B-29) nine-seat long-range heavy bomber
Powerplant:	four 2200hp (1640kW) Wright R-3350-23 18-cylinder two-row radial engines
Performance:	maximum speed 576km/h (358mph); climb to 6095m (20,000ft) in 38 minutes; service ceiling 9710m (31,850ft); range 9382km (5830 miles)
Weights:	empty 31,816kg (70,140lb); normal take-off 47,628kg (105,000lb); maximum take-off 56,246kg (124,000lb)
Dimensions:	span 43.05m (141ft 2.75in); length 30.18m (99ft); height 9.02m (29ft 7in)
Armament:	one 20mm trainable rearward-firing cannon and two 0.5in trainable rearward-firing machine guns in the tail position, and two 0.5in trainable machine guns in each of two dorsal and two ventral barbettes, plus an internal bomb load of 9072kg (20,000lb)

Boeing B-29

The Boeing B-29 made a highly significant contribution to the Allied war effort, quite out of proportion with its length of service. Although most aircraft were completed as heavy bombers, many were later modified for different tasks such as air/sea rescue, turbojet research or air refuelling. In 1942 Boeing began development of a transport version of the Boeing B-29 with a large upper lobe to create a 'double bubble' fuselage. This was designated Model 367 and first flew in November 1944. Together with Consolidated C-87s and modified B-24s, the B-29 was pressed into service as a tanker to bring to Chinese airfields the fuel needed for missions over Japan. Many were permanently modified as tankers, an example being B-29-1-BW- 42-6242 *Esso Express*, one of the first production block, which served with the 486th BG. This aircraft is painted in early olive-drab camouflage; later aircraft were unpainted to reduce drag.

Country of origin:	USA
Type:	(B-29) nine-seat long-range heavy bomber
Powerplant:	four 2200hp (1640kW) Wright R-3350-23 18-cylinder two-row radial engines
Performance:	maximum speed 576km/h (358mph); climb to 6095m (20,000ft) in 38 minutes; service ceiling 9710m (31,850ft); range 9382km (5830 miles)
Weights:	empty 31,816kg (70,140lb); normal take-off 47,628kg (105,000lb); maximum take-off 56,246kg (124,000lb)
Dimensions:	span 43.05m (141ft 2.75in); length 30.18m (99ft); height 9.02m (29ft 7in)
Armament:	one 20mm trainable rearward-firing cannon and two 0.5in trainable rearward-firing machine guns in the tail position, plus an internal bomb load of 9072kg (20,000lb)

Boulton Paul Defiant

In the 1930s there developed an enthusiasm for the turret fighter in which fixed forward-firing armament was replaced by a multi-gun turret. The two main attractions of such a fighter were a reduction in pilot workload and the turreted armament's significantly greater field of fire. The British response to this idea was the Defiant, which entered service in December 1939. On entering combat in May 1940 the type was initially successful as a result of its novelty, but German pilots soon learned to use the greater agility of their lighter fighters to engage the Defiant head-on or from below, where the guns could not be trained. The Defiant was subsequently utilised as a night-fighter and finally for target-towing duties. Production was 723 Mk I and NF.Mk I machines, 210 Mk II and NF.Mk II aircraft with the 1260hp (939.5kW) Merlin XX engine, and 140 TT.Mk I machines ordered as Mk II fighters.

Country of origin:	United Kingdom
Type:	(Defiant Mk I) two-seat fighter
Powerplant:	one 1030hp (768kW) Rolls-Royce Merlin III 12-cylinder Vee engine
Performance:	maximum speed 489km/h (304mph); climb to 4800m (15,750ft) in 8 minutes 30 seconds; service ceiling 9250m (30,350ft); range 748km (465 miles)
Weights:	empty 2757kg (6078lb); maximum take-off 3788kg (8350lb)
Dimensions:	span 11.99m (39ft 4in); length 10.77m (35ft 4in); height 4.39m (14ft 5in)
Armament:	four 0.303in trainable machine guns in the dorsal turret

Breda Ba 88 Lince

First flown in October 1936, the Lince (lynx) proved fiercer in name than deed. Great things were expected of the type, which set a number of records during development. However, the addition of military equipment added weight and drag resulting in wholly inadequate performance and degraded handling, despite the adoption of an uprated powerplant and two rather than one vertical tail surfaces. The first 88 aircraft were completed between May and October 1939. In the first phase of the North African campaign the aircraft proved tactically useless, and the survivors were soon being used as decoys for attacking British warplanes. By this time 155 aircraft had been made, but most of the new aircraft were scrapped. The designation Ba 88M was used for three aircraft converted in 1943 as dive-bombers with a lengthened wing, downrated powerplant and revised armament. Pictured is a Ba 88 of the 7th Gruppo, 5th Stormo da Combattimento, based in Libya in 1940.

Country of origin:	Italy
Type:	two-seat ground-attack warplane
Powerplant:	two 1000hp (746kW) Piaggio P.XI RC.40 14-cylinder two-row radial piston engines
Performance:	maximum speed 490km/h (304mph); climb to 3000m (9845ft) in 7 minutes 30 seconds; service ceiling 8000m (26,245ft); range 1640km (1020 miles)
Weights:	empty 4650kg (10,252lb); maximum take-off 6750kg (14,881lb)
Dimensions:	span 15.60m (51ft 2in); length 10.79m (35ft 5in); height 3.10m (10ft 2.75in)
Armament:	three 12.7mm fixed forward-firing machine guns and one 7.7mm trainable rearward-firing machine gun, plus an internal bomb load of 1000kg (2205lb)

Breguet Bre.521 Bizerte

After buying a single example of the Short S.8 Calcutta flying boat from the UK and building four more under licence with the designation S.8/2, Breguet developed its own version as the Bre.521 Bizerte. This first flew in prototype form during September 1933, and was followed by three pre-production 'boats and then 27 'boats to the full production standard with an uprated powerplant and other improvements. The Bre.521Hy.8 entered service late in 1935, and at the start of World War II the French had 20 'boats in service with four squadrons of the French naval air service. After the defeat of France the surviving 'boats were entrusted to two Vichy French units, and when in November 1942 the Germans occupied Vichy France they seized eight Bizertes for continued use in the air/sea rescue role. One is seen here in the colours of 1.Seentostaffel of the Luftwaffe, based at Brest-Hourtin in north west France in winter of 1943-44.

Country of origin:	France
Type:	(Bre.521Hy.8) eight-seat maritime reconnaissance and bomber flying boat
Powerplant:	three 900hp (671kW) Gnome-Rhône 14Kirs-1 Mistral-Major 14-cylinder two-row radial engines
Performance:	maximum speed 243km/h (151mph); climb to 2000m (6560ft) in 8 minutes 46 seconds; service ceiling 6000m (19,685ft); range 3000 km (1864 miles)
Weights:	empty 9470kg (20,878lb); maximum take-off 16,600kg (36,597lb)
Dimensions:	span 35.15m (115ft 4in); length 20.48m (67ft 2.25in); height 7.48m (24ft 6.5in)
Armament:	five 7.5mm trainable machine guns mounted singly in the tail position, two port and starboard forward positions, and two port and starboard waist positions, plus external bomb load of 300kg (661lb)

Breguet Bre.693

The Bre.690 resulted from a 1934 requirement for a three-seat heavy fighter, but after the selection of the Potez 630 was revised as the Bre.691 two-seat attack warplane, and was ordered only in 1937, first flying in this form in March 1938 and paving the way for 78 Bre.691AB.2 production aircraft with two Hispano-Suiza 14 radial engines. Although thought was given to the creation of a Bre.692 with Gnome-Rhône 14N radial engines, the next model was the Bre.693 evolution of the Bre.691 with Gnome-Rhône 14M radial piston engines and, in later aircraft, one obliquely downward- and rearward-firing 7.5mm machine gun in the rear of each engine nacelle. The first Bre.693AB.2 flew in March 1940, and 254 such aircraft were delivered, later aircraft serving with the Vichy French air force after the fall of France in June 1940. In November 1942 the aircraft were confiscated by the Germans and transferred to the Regia Aeronautica for use as trainers.

Country of origin:	France
Type:	two-seat light attack bomber
Powerplant:	two 700hp (522kW) Gnome-Rhône 14M-6/7 Mars 14-cylinder two-row radial engines
Performance:	maximum speed 475km/h (295mph); climb to 4000m (13,125ft) in 7 minutes 12 seconds; ceiling 8500m (27,885ft); range 1350km (839 miles)
Weights:	empty 3010kg (6636lb); maximum take-off 5500kg (12,125lb)
Dimensions:	span 15.36m (50ft 5in); length 9.67m (31ft 8.75in); height 3.19m (10ft 5.75in)
Armament:	one 20mm fixed forward-firing cannon and two 7.5mm fixed forward-firing machine guns, one 7.5mm fixed obliquely rearward-firing machine gun, two 7.5mm fixed obliquely downward/rearward-firing machine guns and one 7.5mm trainable rearward-firing machine gun, plus an internal bomb load of 400kg (882lb)

Breguet Bre.695

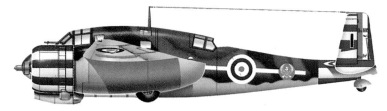

Worried about the strategic danger to the country as a result of its limited aero engine manufacturing capability, France decided in 1939 to adopt a policy of ensuring that every major warplane type in French service would be capable of accepting an imported American or British engine. This led to the Bre.695.01 that was the Bre.690.01 prototype revised with two Pratt & Whitney R-1830-SB4G Twin Wasp radial engines, which were of lighter weight and greater power than the French engines they replaced but also of larger diameter. The Bre.695.01 first flew in March 1940, and while flight trials confirmed the overall viability of the revised powerplant, they also revealed a number of problems. Even so, large-scale orders for the Bre.695AB.2 were planned, but only 50 had been completed before France's defeat in June 1940. Pictured is a Breguet 695 AB.2 of the 1e Escadrille, GBA I/151 of the Armée de l'Air de l'Armistice, based at Lézignan-Corbières in June 1942.

Country of origin:	France
Type:	two-seat light attack bomber
Powerplant:	two 825hp (640.5kW) Pratt & Whitney R-1830-SB4G Twin Wasp 14-cylinder two-row radial engines
Performance:	maximum speed 560km/h (348mph); service ceiling 9000m (29,530ft); range 1500km (932 miles)
Weights:	maximum take-off 5400kg (11,905lb)
Dimensions:	span 15.36m (50ft 5in); length 9.67m (31ft 8.75in); height 3.19m (10ft 5.75in)
Armament:	one 20mm fixed forward-firing cannon and two 7.5mm fixed forward-firing machine guns, one 7.5mm fixed obliquely rearward-firing machine gun, two 7.5mm fixed obliquely downward/rearward-firing machine guns and one 7.5mm trainable rearward-firing machine gun, plus an internal bomb load of 400kg (882lb)

Breguet Bre.19

Almost certainly built in larger numbers (perhaps 1500 aircraft including 400 licence-built machines) than any other warplane type in the period between the world wars, the Bre.19 was designed to succeed the Bre.14 that had performed so magnificently in World War I. The prototype made its maiden flight in November 1921, and production versions included the Bre.19A.2 observation and reconnaissance model with engines in the power range between 400 and 860hp (298 and 693kW), the Bre.19B.2 light bomber with provision for an external bomb load, and the Bre.19GR reconnaissance model. Many were sold to foreign clients for evaluation or operational service. Variants built in smaller numbers included the Bre.19bis, ter, T, Tbis, 19.1, 19.2, 19.7, 19.8 and 19.9. The type was still in first-line service with Greece when it was invaded by Italy during October 1940. Pictured is one of the 50 Bre.19.7s ordered by Turkey in 1933.

Country of origin:	France
Type:	(Bre.19A.2) two-seat army cooperation and reconnaissance aircraft
Powerplant:	one 513hp (382.5kW) Renault 12Kb 12-cylinder Vee engine
Performance:	maximum speed 235km/h (146mph); climb to 5000m (16,405ft) in 29 minutes 50 seconds; service ceiling 6900m (22,640ft); range 1200km (746 miles)
Weights:	empty 1722kg (3796lb); maximum take-off 3110kg (6856lb)
Dimensions:	span 14.83m (48ft 7.75in); length 9.51m (31ft 2.5in); height 3.69m (12ft 1.25in)
Armament:	one 7.7mm or 7.5mm fixed forward-firing machine gun in the starboard side of the forward fuselage, one or two 7.7mm or 7.5mm rearward-firing machine guns in the rear cockpit, and provision for one 7.7mm or 7.5mm trainable machine gun in the ventral position, plus a bomb load of 1764lb (800kg)

Brewster F2A and Buffalo

Ordered as the US Navy's first monoplane fighter, the F2A first flew in XF2A-1 prototype form in January 1938 and paved the way for 11 F2A-1 production aircraft that entered service in July 1939 with the 940hp (701kW) R-1820-34 engine, then 43 and 108 examples of the F2A-2 and F2A-3, the former with an uprated engine and the latter with more armour and a longer nose. The F2A was generally unsuccessful in American service, the type was also ordered in B-239 (44 for Finland, which was the sole country to operate the type with major success), B-339B (40 for Belgium of which 38 were delivered to the UK as Buffalo Mk Is), B-339D (72 for the Netherlands East Indies), B-339E (170 for the UK as Buffalo Mk Is), and B-439 (20 for the Netherlands East Indies but all impressed by the US Army that later delivered 17 to Australia) form. Pictured here is a Brewster F2A-2 of VF-2 'The Flying Chiefs', US Navy, aboard USS *Lexington* in March 1941.

Country of origin:	USA
Type:	(F2A-3) single-seat carrierborne and land-based fighter/fighter-bomber
Powerplant:	one 1200hp (895kW) Wright R-1820-40 Cyclone nine-cylinder single-row radial engine
Performance:	maximum speed 517km/h (321mph); initial climb rate 698m (2290ft) per minute; service ceiling 10,120m (33,200ft); range 2704km (1680 miles)
Weights:	empty 2146kg (4732lb); normal take-off 2867kg (6321lb); maximum take-off 3247kg (7159lb)
Dimensions:	span 10.67m (35ft); length 8.03m (26ft 4in); height 3.68m (12ft 1in)
Armament:	two 0.5in fixed forward-firing machine guns in upper part of the forward fuselage; two 0.5in fixed forward-firing machine guns in the leading edges of the wing, plus an bomb load of 105kg (232lb)

Bristol Beaufighter Mks X and XI

The Beaufighter TF.Mk X was an improved version of the Beaufighter Mk VIC with Hercules XVII engines optimised for the low- rather than medium-altitude as required for anti-shipping operations. An AI.Mk VIII radar was fitted in a 'thimble' nose for use in tracking surface vessels, a dorsal gun provided defensive fire, and provision was made for underwing bomb and rocket loads as alternatives to the underfuselage torpedo. The combination of a large dorsal fin and enlarged elevators improved control at high weights. Production of the Beaufighter TF.Mk X, which was the most important British anti-ship attack weapon from 1944 in Europe and the Far East, totalled 2205 aircraft, and another 163 machines were completed to the Beaufighter Mk XIC standard that differed from the Beaufighter TF.Mk X only in possessing no torpedo capability. The aircraft pictured is a TF. Mk X of No 455 Squadron, RAF.

Country of origin:	United Kingdom
Type:	(Beaufighter TF.Mk X) two/three-seat anti-ship attack fighter
Powerplant:	two 1770hp (1320kW) Bristol Hercules XVII 14-cylinder two-row radial engines
Performance:	maximum speed 512km/h (318mph); climb to 1525m (5000ft) in 3 minutes 30 seconds; service ceiling 4570m (15,000ft); range 2913km (1810 miles)
Weights:	empty 7076kg (15,600lb); maximum take-off 11,431kg (25,200lb)
Dimensions:	span 17.63m (57ft 10in); length 12.70m (41ft 8in); height 4.83m (15ft 10in)
Armament:	four 20mm fixed forward-firing cannon in the underside of the forward fuselage, and one 0.303in trainable rearward-firing machine gun in the dorsal position, plus an external torpedo, bomb and rocket load of 1111kg (2450lb)

Bristol Beaufighter Mk VI

The Beaufighter was a derivative of the Beaufort torpedo bomber and was first flown in July 1939 as a heavy fighter with a smaller fuselage and an uprated powerplant. of two 1400hp (1044kW) Bristol Hercules III or 1500hp (1118kW) Hercules XI radial engines. Some 553 Mk IF radar-equipped night-fighters and 397 Mk IC coastal fighters were fitted with Hercules engines and were later complemented by 597 Mk IIF night-fighters with 1280hp (954kW) Rolls-Royce Merlin XX Vee engines. The type came into its own during 1942 in its Mk VI form. There were three subvariants, namely the Beaufighter Mk VIC torpedo fighter (693 aircraft), the Beaufighter Mk VIF night-fighter (879 aircraft) and the Beaufighter Mk VI Interim Torpedo Fighter (60 aircraft) with underwing provision for eight 60lb (27kg) rockets, providing a heavier punch against ships and surfaced submarines. This aircraft is a Mk VIF, serving with the 416th Night Fighter Squadron, USAAF.

Country of origin:	United Kingdom
Type:	(Beaufighter Mk VIF) two-seat night-fighter
Powerplant:	two 1635hp (1219kW) Bristol Hercules VI 14-cylinder two-row radial engines
Performance:	maximum speed 536km/h (333mph); initial climb rate not available; service ceiling not available; range 2478km (1540 miles)
Weights:	empty 6622kg (14,600lb);maximum take-off 9798kg (21,600lb)
Dimensions:	span 17.63m (57ft 10in); length 12.70m (41ft 8in); height 4.82m (15ft 10in)
Armament:	four 20mm fixed forward-firing cannon in the underside of the forward fuselage, and six 0.303in fixed forward-firing machine guns in the leading edges of the wing (two to port and four to starboard)

Bristol Beaufighter Mk 21

The Royal Australian Air Force evinced an interest in the Beaufighter from an early stage. Reliable twin-engined powerplant, heavy firepower and good overall performance (especially in range) were attractive to a force facing the possibility of Japanese attack on the north coast of Australia, a region that was both inhospitable and lacking in a network of closely spaced airfields. As a result the Department of Aircraft Production commenced building the Beaufighter TF.Mk X as the Beaufighter TF.Mk 21 with two Hercules XVIII engines rated for optimum performance at medium altitude. Other changes included removal of the torpedo shackles, the radar and the dorsal fin fillet, modification of the wing for four 0.5in machine guns, and addition of a bulge in the nose for a Sperry autopilot that was in fact seldom fitted. The first of 364 such aircraft flew in May 1944. The aircraft pictured wears the colours of No 22 Squadron, RAAF.

Country of origin:	Australia (from a British design)
Type:	(Beaufighter Mk 21) two/three-seat multi-role heavy fighter
Powerplant:	two 1770hp (1320kW) Bristol Hercules XVIII 14-cylinder two-row radial engines
Performance:	maximum speed 512km/h (318mph); climb to 1525m (5000ft) in 3 minutes 30 seconds; service ceiling 4570m (15,000ft); range 2913km (1810 miles)
Weights:	empty 7076kg (15,600lb); maximum take-off 11,431kg (25,200lb)
Dimensions:	Span 17.63m (57ft 10in); length 12.70m (41ft 8in); height 4.83m (15ft 10in)
Armament:	four 20mm fixed forward-firing cannon in forward fuselage, four 0.5in fixed forward-firing machine guns in the leading edges of the wing, and one 0.303in rearward-firing machine gun in the dorsal position, plus an external bomb and rocket load of 2450lb (1111kg)

Bristol Bombay

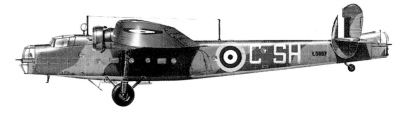

As first flown in June 1935, the Bombay was a comparatively simple high-wing monoplane with fixed tailwheel landing gear, and resulted from a 1931 requirement for dual-role transport and bomber optimised for service in Africa, the Middle East and India. Thus the new type had to be able to carry 24 troops or an equivalent weight of freight (including items as large as an aero engine), be fitted with defensive armament, and possess the capability for service as a bomber with an externally carried bomb load. Orders were placed for 50 production aircraft, and these entered service in March 1939, by which time they were technically obsolete. Even so, the aircraft performed valuable service in the North African and Mediterranean theatres as transports and were also used at times as bombers. The survivors were retired mid-way through World War II. Shown here in the colours of No 216 Squadron, RAF, based in Egypt in 1940-1, is a Bombay Mk 1.

Country of origin:	United Kingdom
Type:	(Bombay Mk I) three/six-seat transport and bomber
Powerplant:	two 1010hp (753kW) Bristol Pegasus XXII nine-cylinder radial engines
Performance:	maximum speed 309km/h (192mph); climb to 4570m (15,000ft) in 20 minutes; service ceiling 7620m (25,000ft); range 2230 miles (3589km)
Weights:	empty 6260kg (13,800lb); maximum take-off 9072kg (20,000lb)
Dimensions:	span 29.18m (95ft 9in); length 21.11m (69ft 3in); height 5.94m (19ft 6in)
Armament:	one 0.303in trainable forward-firing machine gun in nose turret and one 0.303in trainable rearward-firing machine gun in tail turret; option of one 0.303in trainable machine gun in each of two beam positions, plus a bomb load of 907kg (2000lb)

Bristol Blenheim Mk I

Developed as a militarised version of the Type 142 high-speed light transport, the Type 142M prototype paved the way for the Blenheim Mk I light bomber that entered service in 1939. The Royal Air Force hoped this aircraft would provide a measure of operational capability as well as helping to create a pool of skilled aircrews pending the development of high-performance types. The Blenheim saw extensive service but never was truly effective; the first variant was the Blenheim Mk I of which 1365 were produced by three British manufacturers, 45 and 16 generally similar aircraft being built in Finland and Yugoslavia respectively. In addition a small number were presented to Romania as a diplomatic bribe in 1939, with the result that the Blenheim fought both for and against the Allies during World War II. A number of British aircraft were converted to Blenheim Mk IF night-fighter standard with a ventral pack of four 0.303in machine guns and radar.

Country of origin:	United Kingdom
Type:	(Blenheim Mk I) three-seat light bomber
Powerplant:	two 840hp (627kW) Bristol Mercury VIII nine-cylinder single-row radial engines
Performance:	maximum speed 459km/h (285mph); climb to 4570m (15,000ft) in 9 minutes 58 seconds; service ceiling 8315m (27,280ft); range 1810km (1125 miles)
Weight:	empty 4013kg (8839lb); maximum take-off 5947kg (13,100lb)
Dimensions:	span 17.17m (56ft 4in); length 12.12m (39ft 9in); height 3.00m (9ft 10in)
Armament:	one 0.303in fixed forward-firing machine gun in the leading edge of the port wing, and one 0.303in trainable machine gun in the dorsal turret, plus an internal bomb load of 454kg (1000lb)

Bristol Blenheim Mk IV

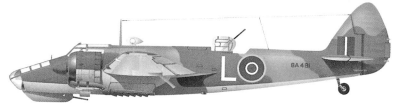

The Blenheim Mk IV was designed to overcome the operational deficiencies of the Blenheim Mk I, and differed in its uprated powerplant and significantly increased fuel capacity. Another revsion was the forward fuselage, which was lengthened by some 0.91 m (3ft) to include a navigator's station under a glazed upper surface with a downward-scalloped port side. The Blenheim Mk IV entered production early in 1939, and by the outbreak of war the RAF had 13 squadrons of Mk IVs. British production by three companies (Bristol, Avro and Rootes) totalled 3285. Finland also produced 10 aircraft for its own use, and 676 aircraft were produced in Canada with the name Bolingbroke. The Blenheim Mk IV bomber equipped 25, 19 and one squadrons in the UK, Middle East and Far East respectively, and numbers of the aircraft were later converted to Blenheim Mk IVF night-fighter standard with a ventral gun pack and radar.

Country of origin:	United Kingdom
Type:	(Blenheim Mk IV) three-seat light bomber
Powerplant:	two 995hp (742kW) Bristol Mercury XV nine-cylinder single-row radial engines
Performance:	maximum speed 428km/h (266mph); initial climb rate 457m (1500ft) per minute; service ceiling 6705m (22,000ft); range 2350km (1460 miles) with a 454kg (1000lb) bomb load
Weights:	empty 4456kg (9823lb); maximum take-off 6804kg (15,000lb)
Dimensions:	span 17.17m (56ft 4in); length 12.98m (42ft 7in); height 3.90m (12ft 9.5in)
Armament:	One 0.303in fixed forward-firing machine gun in the leading edge of the port wing, two 0.303in trainable machine guns in the dorsal turret, and two 0.303in trainable rearward-firing machine guns in undernose blister position, plus internal bomb load of 454kg (1000lb)

Bristol Blenheim Mk V

The Blenheim Mk V (originally Bisley Mk I) was a final attempt to wring improved performance out of the Bristol Type 142 airframe. It was schemed in 1940 as a low-level bomber with the possibility of development into a low-level fighter and dual-control trainer. The two-seat Blenheim Mk V was basically the Blenheim Mk IV with a revised forward fuselage (including a fixed forward-firing armament of four 0.303in machine guns in its port side), an improved windscreen, some 272kg (600lb) of external armour protection, a dorsal turret with a gyro sight, and engines optimised for medium-altitude operations. Production eventually totalled 942 aircraft to the Mk V bomber, Mk VA ground-attack, Mk VB operational trainer, and Mk VD tropicalised Mk VA standards. The type entered service in North Africa during November 1942, but served mainly with Far East squadrons. Their poor performance prompted their withdrawal after only nine months of service.

Country of origin:	United Kingdom
Type:	(Blenheim Mk VA) three/two-seat light bomber
Powerplant:	two 950 hp (708kW) Bristol Mercury XXX nine-cylinder single-row radial engines
Performance:	maximum speed 418km/h (260mph); service ceiling 9450m (31,000ft); range 2575km (1600 miles)
Weights:	empty 4990kg (11,000lb); maximum take-off 7711kg (17,000lb)
Dimensions:	span 17.17m (56ft 4in); length 13.39m (43ft 11in); height 3.90m (12ft 9.5in)
Armament:	two 0.303in trainable machine guns in the dorsal turret and two 0.303in trainable rearward-firing machine guns in the undernose blister position, plus an internal bomb load of 454kg (1000lb)

CAMS 55

A development of the CAMS 53 transport flying boat with features of the unsuccessful CAMS 51 and CAMS 54GR reconnaissance types, the CAMS 55 first flew in prototype form in 1928. Successful trials of the five prototypes paved the way for service from 1930 of an eventual 107 production 'boats. The survivors were still in limited service at the start of World War II but were scrapped after France's June 1940 defeat. The main variants were the baseline CAMS 55.1 with two 600hp (522kW) Hispano-Suiza 12Lbr Vee engines; these 43 'boats were followed by 29 examples of the CAMS 55.2 with 480hp (358kW) Gnome-Rhône 9Akx Jupiter radial engines, 28 examples of the CAMS 55.10 upgraded version of the CAMS 55.2, and four examples of the long-range CAMS 55.10 Col. for colonial service. Pictured is a CAMS 55/2 of Escadrille 4S1, Aéronavale (French Naval Air Force), based in North Africa during the 1930s.

Country of origin:	France
Type:	(CAMS 55.10Hy.5) five-seat maritime reconnaissance flying boat
Powerplant:	two 530hp (395kW) Gnome-Rhône 9Kbr Mistral nine-cylinder single-row radial engines
Performance:	maximum speed 215km/h (134mph); climb to 2500m (8200ft) in 28 minutes; service ceiling 3400m (11,155ft); range 1300 km (808 miles)
Weights:	empty 4640kg (10,231lb); maximum take-off 6530kg (14,396lb)
Dimensions:	span 20.39m (66ft 11in); length 15m (49ft 2.5in); height 5.41m (17ft 9in)
Armament:	two 7.7mm trainable forward-firing machine guns in the bow position, and two 7.7mm trainable rearward-firing machine guns in the dorsal position, plus an external bomb load of 150kg (330lb)

CANT Z.501 Gabbiano

The first Gabbiano (Seagull) made its maiden flight in 1934, and gave notice of its capabilities by establishing a world seaplane distance record of 3080 miles (4955 km) between Trieste and Berbera in British Somaliland. Production for the Italian air force started in 1936, and some 202 'boats of this type were in service when Italy entered World War II in June 1940. Operational experience in the maritime reconnaissance role soon revealed that the Z.501 lacked the performance and defensive firepower for successful operation against fighter opposition, resulting in the type's relegation to the air/sea rescue and coastal patrol tasks. Even so production continued to the middle of 1943 and resulted in the overall delivery of 444 'boats including small numbers delivered to Romania and Nationalist Spain. Pictured is one of the aircraft operated by 2 Escuadrilla, Grupo 62, Agrupacion Espanola (Spanish nationalist air force) based in Majorca in 1939.

Country of origin:	Italy
Type:	(Z.501) five-seat maritime reconnaissance and bomber flying boat
Powerplant:	one 900hp (671kW) Isotta-Fraschini Asso XI R2C.15 12-cylinder Vee engine
Performance:	maximum speed 275km/h (171mph); climb to 4000m (13,125ft) in 16 minutes; service ceiling 7000m (22,965ft); range 2400km (1491miles)
Weights:	empty 3840kg (8466lb); maximum take-off 7050kg (15,542lb)
Dimensions:	span 22.50m (73ft 9.75in); length 14.30m (46ft 11in); height 4.40m (14ft 6in)
Armament:	one 7.7mm trainable forward-firing machine gun in the bow position, one 7.7mm trainable machine gun in the nacelle turret, and one 7.7mm trainable rearward-firing machine gun in the dorsal turret, plus an external bomb load of 640kg (1411lb)

CANT Z.506 Airone

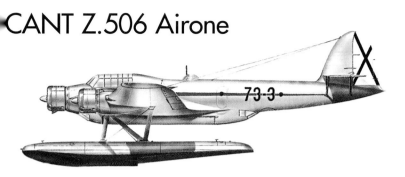

The Z.506 was derived from the Z.505 prototype that was planned as a mailplane to connect Italy with its East Africa colonies, which lacked major airfields. The aircraft was subsequently placed in production as a 15-passenger civil transport (20 aircraft) before production switched to the Z.506B Airone (heron) military derivative that entered service in 1938. Production of the Z.506B totalled some 324 aircraft, of which 95 were in service at the time of Italy's entry into World War II. The type was initially operated in the bomber role, but then revised with stronger defensive armament and reassigned to the maritime reconnaissance, convoy escort, and anti-submarine roles. A number of aircraft were also converted to the Z.506S standard for the air/sea rescue task, and a number of the aircraft were retained in service up to 1959. Illustrated here is a Z.506B wearing the colours of Grupo 73, Agrupacion Espanola, based at Majorca in 1939

Country of origin:	Italy
Type:	(Z.506B) five-seat maritime reconnaissance and bomber floatplane
Powerplant:	three 750hp (559kW) Alfa Romeo 126 RC.34 nine-cylinder single-row radial engines
Performance:	maximum speed 350km/h (217mph); climb to 4000m (13,125ft) in 20 minutes; service ceiling 8000m (26,245ft); range 1705 miles (2745 km)
Weights:	empty 8300kg (18,298lb); maximum take-off 12,705kg (28,008lb)
Dimensions:	span 26.50m (86ft 11.33in); length 19.24mn (63ft 1.7in); height 7.45m (24ft 5.5in)
Armament:	one 12.7mm trainable machine gun in the dorsal turret, one 7.7mm trainable rearward-firing machine gun in the rear of the ventral gondola, and one 7.7mm trainable lateral-firing machine gun in each of the two lateral positions, plus an internal bomb load of 1200kg (2646lb)

CANT Z.1007 Alcione

First flown in prototype form during March 1937, the Z.1007 Alcione (kingfisher) entered service late in 1938 and became one of Italy's most important medium bombers. Production of the Z.1007 totalled only about 35 aircraft with 840hp (626kW) Piaggio Asso XI radial engines and a defensive armament of four 7.7mm machine guns. This initial variant was followed by 526 examples of the Z.1007bis and Z.1007ter. The former introduced a larger airframe, an uprated powerplant with engines in revised nacelles, and different armament as well as two types of tail unit (single vertical surface in first three batches and twin surfaces in the last six batches). The latter had the uprated powerplant of three 1175hp (876kW) Piaggio P.XIX radial engines but a reduced 1000kg (2205lb) bomb load. This aircraft has the markings of the Aviazione Nazionale Republicana, the air force formed from the remnants of the Regia Aeronautica in late 1943.

Country of origin:	Italy
Type:	(Z.1007bis) five-seat medium bomber
Powerplant:	three 1000hp (746kW) Piaggio P.XI R2C.40 14-cylinder two-row radial engines
Performance:	maximum speed 466km/h (290mph); climb to 4000m (13,125ft) in 10 minutes 30 seconds; service ceiling 8200m (26,900ft); range 1750km (1087 miles) with a 1200kg (2646lb) bomb load
Weights:	empty 9396kg (20,715lb); maximum take-off 13,621kg (30,029lb)
Dimensions:	span 24.80m (81ft 4.33in); length 18.35mn (60ft 2.5in); height 5.22m (17ft 5in)
Armament:	one 12.7mm trainable machine gun in the dorsal turret, one 12.7mm trainable rearward-firing machine gun in the ventral step position, and one 7.7mm lateral-firing machine gun in each of the two beam positions, plus an internal bomb load of 1200kg (2646lb)

Caproni Ca 101

In 1927 Caproni introduced the Ca 101 transport as an enlarged tri-motor development of the Ca 97 transport that was produced with one, two and three engines. The type was soon ordered by the Italian air force as a bomber with three 370hp (276kW) Piaggio P.VII radial engines. The Ca 101 did not remain in Italian metropolitan service for long, and after their relegation from this primary role the aircraft were revised for dual-role bomber and transport service in Italy's East African colony of Eritrea with less powerful but more reliable and economical Alfa Romeo Dux or D.2 radial engines. Some 20 aircraft were sold to Hungary, which operated them on the Eastern Front against the USSR, phasing the aircraft out of service only at the start of 1943. Pictured is a Ca 101 of the C./III Bombázó Osztály, Magyar Királyi Légierö (Royal Hungarian air force), based at Papa in Hungary, early in 1941.

Country of origin:	Italy
Type:	(Ca.101) three-seat light reconnaissance bomber
Powerplant:	three 240hp (179kW) Alfa Romeo D.2 nine-cylinder single-row radial engines
Performance:	maximum speed 165km/h (103mph); climb to 5000m (16,405ft) in 40 minutes 30 seconds; ceiling 6100m (20,015ft); range 2000km (1243 miles)
Weights:	empty 3275kg (7221lb); maximum take-off 4975kg (10,968lb)
Dimensions:	span 19.68m (64ft 6.75in); length 14.37m(47ft 1.75in); height (3.89m) 12ft 9.25in
Armament:	one 7.7mm trainable machine gun in the dorsal position, one or two 7.7mm trainable rearward-firing machine guns in the ventral position, and on some aircraft one 7.7mm trainable lateral-firing machine guns in each of the one or two beam positions, plus an internal and external bomb load 500kg (1102lb)

Caproni Bergamasca Ca 310 Libeccio

A close relative of the Ca 308 Borea civil transport and Ca 309 Ghibli multi-role colonial warplane (with fixed undercarriage), the Ca 310 Libeccio (south-west wind) was the first of a major series of attack, bomber, reconnaissance, torpedo and trainer aircraft with retractable landing gear. The Ca 310 first flew in prototype form during April 1937 and entered limited Italian service in 1938, when 16 aircraft were sent to Spain for operational trials. Caproni was more successful in the export market, soon capturing orders from Hungary, Norway, Peru and Yugoslavia. Not all the aircraft were delivered after the customers found that performance was well below that promised, and 33 aircraft returned by Hungary were taken onto Italian Air Force strength as temporary replacements for the unsatisfactory Breda Ba 65. Pictured is a Ca 103M of the 8a Escuadrilla, Grupo num 18, Agrupacion Espanola in Spain during late 1938.

Country of origin:	Italy
Type:	(Ca 310) three-seat light reconnaissance bomber
Powerplant:	two 470hp (350.5kW) Piaggio P.VII C.35 seven-cylinder single-row radial engines
Performance:	maximum speed 365km/h (227mph); climb to 4000m (13,125ft) in 12 minutes 23 seconds; service ceiling 7000m (22,965ft); range 1200km (746 miles)
Weights:	empty 3040kg (6702lb); maximum take-off 4650kg (10,251lb)
Dimensions:	span 16.20m (53ft 1.75in); length 12.20m (40ft 0.33in); height 3.52m (11ft 6.5in)
Armament:	two 7.7mm fixed forward-firing machine guns in the leading edges of the wing and one 7.7mm trainable machine gun in the dorsal turret, plus an internal bomb load of 400kg (882lb)

Caproni Bergamaschi Ca 135

Intended as a fast medium bomber of modern concept, the Ca 135 proved a major disappointment to the Italians. The prototype first flew in April 1935, and the Italian Air Force ordered 14 Ca 135 tipo Spagna aircraft for operational evaluation in the Spanish Civil War. In the event deliveries were made too late for this to happen. Some 32 generally similar Ca 135 tipo Peru bombers were delivered to the Peruvian Air Force. After evaluation of two Ca 135 tipo Spagna aircraft revised with two 1000hp (746kW) Fiat A.80 RC.41 radial engines, which proved unreliable, the main production model was the Ca 135/P.XI with Piaggio radial engines. About 100 of these aircraft were completed for delivery to the Hungarian Air Force, which relegated the survivors from the operational to the training role in the second half of 1942. One of these aircraft is depicted here, wearing recognition markings indicative of service in southern Russia.

Country of origin:	Italy
Type:	(Ca 135/P.XI) four-seat medium bomber
Powerplant:	two 1000hp (746kW) Piaggio P.XI RC.40 14-cylinder two-row radial engines
Performance:	maximum speed 440km/h (273mph); climb to 5000m (16,405ft) in 17 minutes 24 seconds; service ceiling 6500m (21,325ft); range 1200km (746 miles) with a 1600kg (3527lb) bomb load
Weights:	empty 6050kg (13,340lb); maximum take-off 9550kg (21,050lb)
Dimensions:	span 18.80m (61ft 8in); length 14.40m (47ft 2.75in); height 3.40m (11ft 1.75in)
Armament:	one 12.7mm trainable forward-firing machine gun in the nose turret, one 12.7mm trainable machine gun in the dorsal turret, and one 12.7mm trainable machine gun in the ventral turret, plus an internal bomb load of 1600kg (3527lb)

Caproni Ca 133

An improved version of the Ca 101 dual-role bomber and transport, the Ca 133 introduced a number of drag-lowering features, namely neat long-chord cowlings (housing three uprated engines), together with faired legs and spatted wheels for the main landing gear units, an improved tail unit and split flaps on the wing trailing edges. The Italian Air Force soon realised that despite its improvements the type was suitable only for colonial use in North and East Africa. Ca 133 production totalled 419 aircraft, and conversions included 21 Ca 133S air ambulances and 329 Ca 133T pure transports with reduced defensive armament. The Ca 133 during heavy losses at the hands of British fighters after Italy's entry into World War II in June 1940. A small batch of Ca 133 aircraft was also exported to Austria in the mid-1930s. Pictured is one of the aircraft operated by Bomberstaffel 1B, Fliegerregiment Nr 2 of the Austrian air force, based at Zeltwig in 1937.

Country of origin:	Italy
Type:	(Ca 133) three-seat bomber and transport
Powerplant:	three 460hp (343kW) Piaggio Stella P.VII C.16 seven-cylinder single-row radial engines
Performance:	maximum speed 265km/h (165mph); service ceiling 5500m (18,045ft); range 1350km (838 miles)
Weights:	empty 4190kg (9237lb); maximum take-off 6700kg (14,771lb)
Dimensions:	span 21.24m (68ft 8in); length 15.36m (50ft 4.75in); height 4.00m (13ft 1in)
Armament:	one 7.7mm trainable machine gun in the dorsal position, two 7.7mm trainable rearward-firing machine guns in the ventral position, and one 7.7mm trainable lateral-firing machine gun in the door on the port side of the fuselage, plus an external bomb load of 1200kg (2646lb)

Caproni Ca 148

The Ca 148 was the last development of the Ca 101, and appeared in 1938 as an 18-passenger transport with a powerplant of three 460hp (343kW) Piaggio Stella P.VII RC radial engines each driving a three-blade metal propeller of the variable-pitch type. The cockpit was moved forward by 0.60 m (1ft 11.6in) from its original location under the wing leading edge, the fuselage door was relocated from its original position under the port wing root trailing edge to a position farther to the rear, and the landing gear strengthened to cater for an increased maximum take-off weight. Production totalled 106 aircraft intended mainly for civil and military operation in East Africa, but a number of the aircraft were operated as military transports by the Germans as well as the Italians in the European theatre. Some Ca 148s aircraft remained in Italian service until the late 1940s. Ca 148 I-ETIO of the Italian airline Ala Littoria saw service duirng the Abyssinian campaign.

Country of origin:	Italy
Type:	(Ca 148) two-seat transport with accommodation for 18 troops
Powerplant:	three 460hp (343kW) Piaggio Stella P.VII C.16 seven-cylinder single-row radial engines
Performance:	maximum speed 265km/h (165mph); service ceiling 5500m (18,045ft); range 1350km (838 miles)
Weights:	empty 4190kg (9237lb); normal take-off 4970kg (10,596lb)
Dimensions:	span 21.24m (68ft 8in); length 15.36m (50ft 4.75in); height 4.00m (13ft 1in)
Armament:	none

Caudron C.445 Goéland

Designed as an advanced monoplane to capture a slice of the emerging feederliner and executive transport market, the Goéland (seagull) first flew in 1934 as the C.440 and entered production with two 220hp (164kW) Renault Bengali-Six engines. These were replaced in the C.441 with identically rated Renault 6Q-01 engines. The C.441 also introduced a modified wing that was retained in the C.444 (with Renault 6Q-00/01 engines) and then the C.445 with increased outer wing dihedral. The C.445 entered civil and military service. The French Air Force ordered the C.445M for the light transport, communications and crew training roles, and in a slightly revised form with a glazed nose for the bombardier training role. Production of the C.445M accounted for 404 of the eventual 1,702 aircraft of the Goéland series. A number of aircraft were flown to the UK in June 1940, and operated wearing the Lorraine Cross of the Free French forces.

Country of origin:	France
Type:	(C.445M) two-seat light transport with accommodation for six passengers
Powerplant:	two 220hp (164kW) Renault 6Q-00/01 or -08/09 six-cylinder inverted inline engines
Performance:	maximum speed 300km/h (186mph); climb to 2000 m (6560ft) in 10 minutes 15 seconds; service ceiling 5600m (16,570ft); range 1000km (621 miles)
Weights:	empty 2300kg (5071lb); maximum take-off 3500kg (7716lb)
Dimensions:	span 17.60m (57ft 9in); length 13.80m (45ft 3.75in); height 3.50m (11ft 6in)
Armament:	none

Caudron C.714 Cyclone

An interesting but ultimately unsuccessful attempt to create a cheap and quickly built light interceptor out of a highly successful series of wooden racing aircraft, the C.714 began military life as the C.710.01 prototype that first flew in July 1936 with the 450hp (335.5kW) Renault 12R-01 engine and an armament of two 20mm cannon. This was turned into the C.713.01 prototype by the introduction of retractable main landing gear units and the revision of the vertical tail surface. The C.713 was in turn developed into the C.714.01 prototype with a strengthened structure and a revised wing, and this was followed by the C.714C.1 production model, of which 92 (including six for Finland) were completed for limited service from early in 1940. After France's fall nine of the aircraft were used as fighter trainers by Vichy France and by Germany respectively. Pictured is a C.714 of the Groupe de Chasse Polonaise, based at Lyon-Bron in May 1940.

Country of origin:	France
Type:	(C.714C.1) single-seat lightweight interceptor fighter
Powerplant:	one 500hp (373kW) Renault 12R-03 12-cylinder inverted-Vee engine
Performance:	maximum speed 460km/h (286mph); climb to 4000m (13,125ft) in 9 minutes 40 seconds; service ceiling 9100m (29,855ft); range 900km (559 miles)
Weights:	empty 1395kg (3076lb); maximum take-off 1880kg (4045lb)
Dimensions:	span 8.97m (29ft 5.13in); length 8.63m (28ft 3.88in); height 2.87m (9ft 5in)
Armament:	four 7.5mm fixed forward-firing machine guns in two flush-fitting trays under the wing

Chance Vought V-166 Corsair

The Corsair was undoubtedly one of the finest aircraft of the war, and was virtually unmatched in the Pacific theatre after its service entry in February 1943. Development of the V-166B began in 1938, with the aim of tailoring the smallest possible airframe to fit the powerful Pratt & Whitney XR-2800 Double Wasp engine. The highly cranked wing was designed to allow clearance for the large diameter propeller, without the need for overlong main gear units. The XF4U-1 prototype first flew in May 1940, but it was not until the following February that the US Navy placed and order for 585 F4U-1 production aircraft. Carrier evaluation proved disappointing, leading to changes in the landing gear and cockpit height to improve forward view. Most aircraft were modified on the production line and were designated F4U-1A. Initial operational service was with the USMC (February 1943), but the aircraft later distinguished itself with both the US Navy and Fleet Air Arm.

Country of origin:	USA
Type:	(F4U-1A) single-seat shipborne and land-based fighter
Powerplant:	one 2,000hp (1491kW) Pratt & Whitney R-2800-8 Double Wasp radial engine
Performance:	maximum speed 671km/h (417mph); climb to 951m (3,120ft) in 1 minute; service ceiling 11,245m (36,900ft); range 1633km (1015 miles)
Weights:	empty 4074kg (8982lb); maximum take-off 6350kg (14,000lb)
Dimensions:	span 12.5m (41ft); length 10.16m (33ft 4in); height 4.9m (16ft 1in)
Armament:	six 0.5in fixed forward-firing machine guns in the leading edge of the wing

Commonwealth Wirraway

In 1936 the Australian government decided to embark on a programme to create a national aircraft industry that could eventually make Australia independent of imported aircraft, and created the Commonwealth Aircraft Corporation. CAC's first product was the CA-1 Wirraway, which was the Australian version of the North American NA-33, an improved version of the NA-26 advanced trainer produced for the US Army Air Corps as the BC-1. Of the two CA-1 prototypes, the first flew in March 1939 and paved the way for the Wirraway Mk I, of which 755 were built in seven blocks during World War II. The type entered service in June 1939, and as a result of its good performance and armament was pressed into limited operational service during 1942. Pictured is a CA-5 Wirraway, one of 30 completed for the Royal Australian Air Force, and operated by No 4 Squadron in New Guinea during December 1942. The pilot of this aircraft clearly has a kill of some sort to his credit.

Country of origin:	Australia
Type:	(Wirraway Mk I) two-seat advanced flying and armament trainer
Powerplant:	one 600hp (447kW) CAC-built Pratt & Whitney R-1340-S1H1-G Wasp nine-cylinder single-row radial engine
Performance:	maximum speed 354km/h (220mph); initial climb rate 594m (1950ft) per minute; service ceiling 7010m (23,000ft); range 1159km (720 miles)
Weights:	empty 1811kg (3992lb); maximum take-off 2991kg (6595lb)
Dimensions:	span 13.11m (43ft); length 8.48m (27ft 10in); height 2.66m (8ft 8.75in)
Armament:	two 0.303in fixed forward-firing machine guns in the upper side of the forward fuselage, and provision for one 0.303in trainable rearward-firing machine gun in the rear of the cockpit, plus an external bomb load of 1000lb (454 kg)

Commonwealth Boomerang

Given the very real possibility that it may become isolated from sources of major equipment items, Australia decided in 1941 to develop an indigenous weapons design and manufacturing capability. The Boomerang was ordered as an emergency fighter that was based on many assemblies and components already in production for the Wirraway trainer, itself a development of the North American NA-33, and a powerful Australian-built US engine. The resulting Boomerang fighter-bomber prototype first flew in May 1942, only 14 weeks after the design had been approved. Production of the basically similar Boomerang Mk I totalled 105 aircraft delivered by June 1943, and there followed 95 Boomerang Mk II warplanes that differed only in minor details. The Boomerang combined adequate performance with good armament, low-level agility and strength. Pictured is a Boomerang Mk 1 of No 2 Operational Training Unit, RAAF, based at Port Pirie in South Australia in late 1942.

Country of origin:	Australia
Type:	(Boomerang Mk II) single-seat fighter and fighter-bomber
Powerplant:	one 1200hp (895kW) Pratt & Whitney R-1830-S3C4G Twin Wasp 14-cylinder two-row radial engine
Performance:	maximum speed 491km/h (305mph); climb to 6095m (20,000ft) in 9 minutes 12 seconds; service ceiling 10,365m (34,000ft); range 2575km (1600 miles)
Weights:	empty 2437kg (5373lb); normal take-off 3492kg (7699lb); maximum take-off 3742kg (8249lb)
Dimensions:	span 10.97m (36ft); length 7.77m (25ft 6in); height 2.92m (9ft 7in)
Armament:	two 20mm fixed forward-firing cannon and four 0.303in fixed forward-firing machine guns in the leading edges of the wing, plus an external bomb load of 227kg (500lb)

Consolidated PBY-1 to PBY-5 Catalina

The PBY series, now almost universally known as the Catalina after its British designation, was built in larger numbers than all other flying boats combined, and was manufactured over a period of 10 years on no fewer than six production lines. The type was extremely slow, even by the standards of flying boats in World War II, but it was also extremely reliable and possessed very good endurance. The XP3Y-1 prototype made its maiden flight in March 1934, and there followed 60, 50, 66, 33 and 1024 examples respectively of the PBY-1, improved PBY-2, PBY-3 with uprated engines, PBY-4 with further uprated engines, and PBY-5 with still more power and with waist blisters rather than hatches. The type was also built in Canada as the Boeing PB2B (290 machines) and in the USSR (considerably more than 400 aircraft). The PBY-5 pictured here was supplied to the RAAF as part of an order for 18 and assigned to No 11 Squadron. Note the ASV.II radar aerials ahead of the struts.

Country of origin:	USA
Type:	(PBY-5) nine-seat maritime reconnaissance and bomber flying boat
Powerplant:	two 1200hp (895kW) Pratt & Whitney R-1830-82 Twin Wasp 14-cylinder two-row radial engines
Performance:	maximum speed 322km/h(200mph); maximum rate of climb 302m (990ft) per minute; ceiling 6585m (21,600ft); range 3050km (1895 miles)
Weights:	empty 7893kg (17,400lb); maximum take-off 15,145kg (33,389lb)
Dimensions:	span 31.70m (104ft); length 19.45m (63ft 10in); height 5.76m (18ft 11in)
Armament:	two 0.3in trainable forward-firing machine guns in bow turret, one 0.3in trainable rearward-firing machine gun in ventral tunnel position, and one 0.5in trainable lateral-firing machine gun in each 'blister' beam position, plus an external load of 4500lb (2041kg)

Consolidated PBY-5A and PBY-6A Catalina

The XPBY-5A prototype first flew in November 1939, improving the versatility of the PBY series by the introduction of retractable tricycle landing gear. This new amphibian flying boat type entered production as the PBY-5A of which 794 were delivered to the US Navy. The Royal Air Force received 225 generally similar PBY-5B 'boats. Further development of the amphibian resulted in the PBY-6A (235 machines) with revised armament and an enlarged tail, and the Naval Aircraft Factory PBN-1 Nomad (156 machines) to a PBY-5A standard improved with a larger tail unit, greater fuel capacity and revised armament. The PBY-5A was also built in Canada as the Canadian Vickers PVB-1A, and numbers of aircraft were transferred to the US Army Air Forces with designations in the OA-10 series. Pictured here is one of the last of all Catalinas, a PBY-6A with US Navy number 46648. Note the pylon-mounted radar and nose turret housing two 0.5in machine guns.

Country of origin:	USA
Type:	(PBY-5A) nine-seat maritime reconnaissance and bomber amphibian flying boat
Powerplant:	two 1200hp (895kW) Pratt & Whitney R-1830-92 Twin Wasp 14-cylinder two-row radial engines
Performance:	maximum speed 288km/h (179mph); climb to 3050m (10,000ft) in 19 minutes 18 seconds; service ceiling 4480m (14,700ft); range 5713 km (3550 miles)
Weights:	empty 9485kg (20,910lb); maximum take-off 16,067kg (35,420lb)
Dimensions:	span 31.70m (104ft); length 19.45m (63ft 10in); height 5.76m (18ft 11in)
Armament:	two 0.3 in trainable forward-firing machine guns in bow turret, one 0.3in trainable rearward-firing machine gun in ventral tunnel position, and one 0.5in trainable lateral-firing machine gun in each 'blister' position, plus an external load of 2041kg (4500lb)

Consolidated B-24D Liberator

Produced in a number of variants for a host of operational and training tasks, the Liberator was built in larger numbers (18,431 machines) than any other US warplane of World War II and was delivered in greater quantities than any other bomber in aviation history. First flown in December 1939, the single XB-24 prototype paved the way for seven YB-24 service test aircraft, and then nine B-24A initial production machines with heavier defensive armament. The XB-24 was then upgraded to the XB-24B standard that led to the nine B-24C bombers and then the first major production models, the B-24D (2738 aircraft), generally similar B-24E (791 aircraft) and B-24G (430 aircraft with a power-operated nose turret). The B-24 made its operational debut in June 1942 with the long-range raids from Egypt against Hitler's Romanian oilfields. Pictured here is B-24D-85-CO *Teggie Ann*, the Group Lead Ship of the 47th Bomb Wing, 376th BG, painted in desert pink.

Country of origin:	USA
Type:	(B-24D) ten-seat long-range heavy bomber
Powerplant:	four 1200hp (895kW) Pratt & Whitney R-1830-43 or -65 14-cylinder two-row radial engines
Performance:	maximum speed 488km/h (303mph); climb to 6095m (20,000ft) in 22 minutes 0 seconds; service ceiling 9755m (32,000ft); range 4586km (2850 miles)
Weights:	empty 14,490kg (32,605lb); maximum take-off 27,216kg (60,000lb)
Dimensions:	span 33.53m (110ft); length 20.22m (66ft 4in); height 4.46m (17ft 11in)
Armament:	two 0.5in trainable forward-firing machine guns in the nose, two 0.5in trainable machines guns in each of the dorsal, ventral and tail turrets, and one 0.5in trainable lateral-firing machine gun in each of the waist positions, plus an internal bomb load of 3992kg (8800lb)

89

Consolidated Liberator B.Mk VI

The Royal Air Force and its Commonwealth allies were the largest recipients of Liberator aircraft transferred from the USA under the terms of the Lend-Lease Act. The overall total of later Liberator variants included 1302 B-24J, 437 B-24L and 47 B-24M aircraft. The B-24J machines served as Liberator B.Mk VI bombers with a ball turret or as Liberator GR.Mk VI long-range maritime reconnaissance aircraft with air-to-surface search radar in place of the ball turret, while the equivalent marks based on the B-24L and B-24M were the Liberator B.Mk VIII and Liberator GR.Mk VIII. The Liberator bombers served mainly in South-East Asia, where they equipped 14 squadrons, and their maritime reconnaissance counterparts served in virtually every British and Commonwealth theatre, undertaking valuable work. Pictured is a Liberator B.Mk VI (B-24H) of No 356 Squadron, part of No 184 (Salbani) Wing in India.

Country of origin:	USA
Type:	(Liberator B.Mk VI) eight-seat long-range heavy bomber
Powerplant:	four 1200hp (895kW) Pratt & Whitney R-1830-65 14-cylinder two-row radial engines
Performance:	maximum speed 435km/h (270mph); climb to 6095m (20,000ft) in 40 minutes; service ceiling 9755m (32,000ft); range 1593km (990 miles) with maximum bomb load
Weights:	empty 16,783kg (37,000lb); maximum take-off 28,123kg (62,000lb)
Dimensions:	span 33.53m (110ft); length 20.47m (67ft 2in); height 5.49m (18ft)
Armament:	two 0.5in trainable machine guns each in the nose, dorsal, ventral and tail turrets, and one 0.5in trainable lateral-firing machine gun in each of the waist positions, plus an internal bomb load of 5806kg (12,800lb)

Consolidated B-24J Liberator

The B-24G, equipped with a nose turret, paved the way for further Liberator development, which included the B-24H (738 built by Consolidated with a Consolidated nose turret, and 2362 made by Douglas and Ford with an Emerson turret), the B-24J that was an improved B-24H with an autopilot and other operational enhancements including a more capable bomb sight (6678 made by Consolidated, Douglas, Ford and North American), the B-24L with two manually operated tail guns rather than a turret (1667 aircraft from Consolidated and Ford), and the B-24M improved version of the B-24J (2593 aircraft from Consolidated and Ford). As with the earlier models, there were also LB-30, C-87 and RY transport, AT-22 trainer, F-7 long-range photo-reconnaissance and PB4Y-1 maritime reconnaissance variants. Seen here in the markings of VP-110, one of the US Navy anti-submarine squadrons, this PB4Y-1 operated from Dunkeswell, Devon.

Country of origin:	USA
Type:	(B-24J) eight/12-seat long-range heavy bomber
Powerplant:	four 1200hp (895kW) Pratt & Whitney R-1830-65 14-cylinder two-row radial engines
Performance:	maximum speed 483km/h (300mph); climb to 6095m (20,000ft) in 25 minutes; service ceiling 8535m (28,000ft); range 3380km (2100 miles)
Weights:	empty 16,556kg (36,500lb); maximum take-off 29,484kg (65,000lb)
Dimensions:	span 33.53m (110ft); length 20.47m (67ft 2in); height 5.49m (18ft)
Armament:	two 0.5in trainable machine guns each in the nose, dorsal, ventral and tail turrets, and one 0.5in trainable lateral-firing machine gun in each of the waist positions, plus an internal bomb load of 3992kg (8800lb)

Consolidated Liberator Mk II

The first British use of the Liberator was in its LB-30 unarmed transport form, but armed models soon followed in the form of 20 Liberator Mk I machines that were equivalents of the B-24A (some used for maritime reconnaissance with radar and a ventral gun tray), 139 Liberator Mk II aircraft (including 79 repossessed by the USA) for maritime reconnaissance, 260 Liberator Mk III aircraft delivered under Lend-Lease arrangements for the maritime reconnaissance role, and 112 B-24G aircraft also delivered as Lend-Lease machines for service as Liberator B.Mk V bombers and Liberator GR.Mk V maritime reconnaissance aircraft. There were also 24 Liberator C.Mk VII transport aircraft based on the C-87 transport derivative of the B-24D. AL 504, *Commando*, was the personal transport of Prime Minister Winston Churchill. It was converted from a Mk II for VIP use in early 1941, and in late 1943 returned to Covair for modification to RY-3 standard.

Country of origin:	USA
Type:	(Liberator Mk III) ten-seat long-range heavy bomber
Powerplant:	four 1200hp (895kW) Pratt & Whitney R-1830-43 or -65 14-cylinder two-row radial engines
Performance:	maximum speed 488km/h (303mph); climb to 6095m (20,000ft) in 22 minutes; service ceiling 9755m (32,000ft); range 4586km (2850 miles)
Weights:	empty 14,490kg (32,605lb); maximum take-off 27,216kg (60,000lb)
Dimensions:	span 33.53m (110ft); length 20.22m (66ft 4in); height 4.46m (17ft 11in)
Armament:	two 0.5in trainable forward-firing machine guns in the nose, two 0.5in trainable machine guns in each of the dorsal, ventral and tail turrets, and one 0.5in trainable lateral-firing machine gun in each of the waist positions, plus internal bomb load of 3992kg (8800lb)

Consolidated TBY Sea Wolf

In 1939 the US Navy issued a requirement for a carrierborne torpedo and level bomber to succeed the Douglas TBD Devastator, and the best of 13 design submissions were made by Brewster, Grumman and Vought. The Brewster type was then discarded, the Grumman type matured as the TBF Avenger, and the Vought type was ordered as the XTBU-1 prototype that first flew in December 1941. This offered better performance than the TBF and was ordered into production. Vought was hard pressed to meet current orders and the contract therefore passed to Consolidated, resulting in a change of designation to TBY. An order for 1100 aircraft was placed in September 1943, these gaining the name Sea Wolf. The first aircraft flew in August 1944, but production was slow and the contract was terminated after the delivery of 180 aircraft that were used only for training. Pictured here is a TBY-2 in US Navy markings.

Country of origin:	USA
Type:	(TBY-2) three-seat carrierborne torpedo and level bomber
Powerplant:	one 2100hp (1566kW) Wright R-2600-22 Cyclone 14 14-cylinder two-row radial engine
Performance:	maximum speed 502km/h (312mph); initial climb rate 539m (1770ft) per minute; service ceiling 8960m (29,400ft); range 1650km (1025 miles)
Weights:	empty 5142kg (11,336lb); maximum take-off 8591kg (18,940lb)
Dimensions:	span 17.35m (56ft 11in); length 11.94m (39ft 2in); height 4.72m (15ft 6in)
Armament:	three 0.5in fixed forward-firing machine guns in leading edges of the wing and in the forward fuselage, one 0.5in trainable rearward-firing machine gun in the dorsal turret, and one 0.3in trainable rearward-firing machine gun in the ventral position, plus a torpedo and bomb load of 726kg (1600lb)

Curtiss Model 77 (SBC Helldiver)

In response to their need for a new-two seat fighter the US Navy ordered a prototype from Curtiss in 1932 of their Model 73, in the form of a two-seat parasol wing monoplane with retractable landing gear. It was later decided to use this aircraft in a scout capacity and later still in the role of scout bomber. Dive-bombing trials highlighted serious structural deficiencies in the design of the wing, and the aircraft was redesigned as the XSBC-2 (Model 77) with a bi-plane wing and a 700hp (522-kW) Wright R-1510-12 Whirlwind 14 engine. This engine was changed in March 1936 to the Pratt & Whitney R-1535-82 Twin Wasp Junior and the aircraft was redesignated XSBC-3. In August 1936 the aircraft was ordered into production as SBC-3 for the US Navy, and the first of 83 aircraft was delivered to VS-5 in July 17, 1937. These were followed by 174 improved SBC-4s with a more powerful Wright engine, and were still in service with two squadrons in December 1941.

Country of origin:	USA
Type:	two-seat carrier based scout-bomber
Powerplant:	(SBC-4) one 900hp (671-kW) Wright R-1820-34 Cyclone 9 radial engine
Performance:	maximum speed 377km/h (234 mph) at 4365m (15,200ft); service ceiling 7315m (24,000ft); range with 227kg (500lb) load 652km (405 miles)
Weights:	empty 2065kg (4,552lb); maximum take-off 3211kg (7,080lb)
Dimensions:	span 10.36m (34ft); length 8.57m (28ft 1 1/2in); height 3.17m (10ft 5in)
Armament:	one forward firing 0.3in machine gun; one trainable 0.3 machine gun in rear cockpit, plus bomb load of 227kg (500lb)

Curtiss SB2C Helldiver

The SB2C Helldiver, schemed as successor to the SBD Dauntless, first flew in XSB2C-1 prototype form in December 1940. The aircraft was never fully effective but, for lack of anything better, was built to the extent of 7200 aircraft including the A-25 land-based version for the US Army as well as the Canadian-built SBF and SBW (300 and 894 respectively) by Canadian Fairchild and Canadian Car & Foundry. The type made its operational debut in November 1943. The main models were the SB2C-1 baseline variant (978 aircraft in two subvariants), SB2C-3 (1112 aircraft) with the 1900hp (1417kW) R-2600-20 engine, SB4C-4 (2045 aircraft in two subvariants) with provision for additional underwing stores, and SB2C-5 (970 aircraft) with increased fuel tankage. Pictured here is an SB2C-1, which by November 1943 was aboard USS *Bunker Hill* with squadron VB-17. The unit was heavily involved in attacks against the Japanese stronghold at Rabaul.

Country of origin:	USA
Type:	(SB2C-1C) two-seat carrierborne and land-based scout and dive-bomber
Powerplant:	one 1700hp (1268kW) Wright R-2600-8 Cyclone 14 14-cylinder two-row radial engine
Performance:	maximum speed 452km/h (281mph); climb to 3050m (10,000ft) in 7 minutes 42 seconds; ceiling 7375m (24,200ft); range 2213 km (1375 miles)
Weights:	empty 4588kg (10,114lb); maximum take-off 7626kg (16,812lb)
Dimensions:	span 15.15m (49ft 8.26in); length 11.18m (36ft 8in); height 4.00m (13ft 1.5in)
Armament:	two 20mm fixed forward-firing cannon in the leading edges of the wing, and two 0.3in trainable rearward-firing machine guns in the rear of the cockpit, plus an internal and external torpedo, bomb and depth charge load of 1361kg (3000lb)

Curtiss P-36 and Mohawk

Anticipating the US Army's need for such an aeroplane, Curtiss designed and built the Model 75 – the USA's first 'modern' monoplane fighter – as a private venture. The prototype made its maiden flight in May 1935 with a Wright SGR-1670-G5 radial engine that was soon replaced by an uprated Wright R-1820-F Cyclone radial engine. The US Army then ordered three YP-36 aircraft for service trials, and this paved the way for 209 production aircraft in the form of 178 P-36A fighters that entered service from April 1938 and 31 P-36C fighters with two additional 0.3in machine guns in the wing. The type was also exported in Model 75A form to several countries including the UK, where the type was known as the Mohawk, and in downgraded Model 75 (or Hawk 75) form with fixed and spatted main landing gear units. The aircraft shown here wears the standard wartime olive-drab colour scheme of the US Army Air Force and early 1942 type national insignia.

Country of origin:	USA
Type:	(P-36C) single-seat fighter
Powerplant:	one 1200hp (895kW) Pratt & Whitney R-1830-17 14-cylinder two-row radial engine
Performance:	maximum speed 500km/h (311mph); climb to 4570m (15,000ft) in 4 minutes 54 seconds; service ceiling 10,270m (33,700ft); range 1320km (820 miles)
Weights:	empty 2096kg (4620lb); maximum take-off 2726kg (6010lb)
Dimensions:	span 11.37m (37ft 3.5in); length 8.79m (28ft 10in); height 2.82m (9ft 3in)
Armament:	one 0.5in fixed forward-firing machine gun and one 0.3in fixed forward-firing machine gun in the upper part of the forward fuselage, and two 0.3in fixed forward-firing machine guns in the leading edges of the wing

Curtiss P-40 and Tomahawk

The R-1830 engine was reliable and powerful by the standards of the 1930s, but when it became clear that it lacked the potential for development into more powerful forms full exploitation of the Model 75 airframe was schemed on the basis of the Allison V-1710 Vee engine. The installation of this engine into a converted P-36A created the Model 81 that first flew in October 1938 as the XP-40 . The first production model was the P-40 of which 199 were delivered with the 1150hp (976kW) V-1710-33 engine for service from May 1940. There followed 131, 193, 22 and 2320 examples of the P-40B, P-40C, P-40D and P-40E as well as 2060 Tomahawk Mk I aircraft for the UK. The P-40 was an adequate fighter by the standards prevailing early in World War II, but really made its mark as a capable fighter-bomber in the close support role. Pictured here is the personal aircraft of Henry Geselbracht, one of the pilots of the 2nd Squadron, American Volunteer Group.

Country of origin:	USA
Type:	(P-40B) single-seat fighter
Powerplant:	one 1040hp (775kW) Allison V-1710-33 (C15) 12-cylinder Vee engine
Performance:	maximum speed 567km/h (352mph); climb to 4570m (15,000ft) in 5 minutes 6 seconds; service ceiling 9875m (32,400ft); range 1513km (940 miles)
Weights:	empty 2536kg (5590lb); maximum take-off 3447kg (7600lb)
Dimensions:	span 11.37m (37ft 3.5in); length 9.66 m (31ft 8.5in); height 3.22m (10ft 7in)
Armament:	two 0.5in fixed forward-firing machine guns in the upper part of the forward fuselage, and two 0.3in fixed forward-firing machine guns in the leading edges of the wing

Curtiss P-40 Warhawk and Kittyhawk

Further development of the Model 81 resulted in the Model 87, which featured the Packard V-1650 (Rolls-Royce Merlin) engine and a lengthened fuselage. The XP-40F prototype conversion (from a standard P-40D airframe) and the three YP-40F service test aircraft paved the way for 1311 P-40F fighter-bombers. The other main variants included the P-40K version of the P-40F with the V-1710-73 engine (1300 short-fuselage aircraft), P-40L with two wing guns removed (700 aircraft), P-40M with the V-1710-81 engine (600 aircraft), P-40N (a lightened version of the P-40L/M —5219 aircraft built), and finally the P-40R re-engined conversions of 300 P-40F/L aircraft. The British also purchased, or received under the Lend-Lease scheme, Kittyhawk Mk II to IV variants of the P-40F, K/M and N. Some 2097 of the American aircraft were shipped to the USSR. Shown here is a Kittyhawk Mk III of No 250 (Sudan) Squadron, RAF, based in southern Italy during late 1943.

Country of origin:	USA
Type:	(P-40M) single-seat fighter and fighter-bomber
Powerplant:	one 1200hp (895kW) Allison V-1710-81 12-cylinder Vee engine
Performance:	maximum speed 552km/h (343mph); climb to 6095m (20,000ft) in 8 minutes 48 seconds; service ceiling 9450m (31,000ft); range 1207km (750 miles)
Weights:	empty 2812kg (6200lb); maximum take-off 5171kg (11,400lb)
Dimensions:	span 11.37m (37ft 3.5in); length 10.16m (33ft 4in); height 3.23m (10ft 7in)
Armament:	six 0.5in fixed forward-firing machine guns in the leading edges of the wing, plus an external bomb load of 680kg (1500lb)

de Havilland Mosquito Mk IV

One of the most successful warplanes ever built, and rivalled only by the Junkers Ju 88 in terms of versatility, the Mosquito was developed as a private venture to provide the Royal Air Force with a bomber that possessed such oustanding performance that no defensive armament would be required. Built largely of a ply/balsa/ply sandwich material, the Mosquito Mk I prototype first flew in November 1940 and paved the way for a mass of variants. The bombers were the Mk IV (273 aircraft with a 2000lb/907kg bomb load), the Mk VII (25 Canadian-built aircraft), the Mk IX (54 aircraft with an uprated powerplant and, in some machines, the ability to carry a 4000lb/1814kg bomb load), the Mk XVI (1200 aircraft to a Mk IX standard upgraded with a pressurised cockpit), the Mk XX (145 Canadian-built aircraft with American equipment), and Mk 25 (400 Canadian-built aircraft). Pictured here is a Mk IV of No 139 Squadron, RAF, based at Marham in 1942-43.

Country of origin:	United Kingdom
Type:	(Mosquito B.Mk XVI) two-seat light bomber
Powerplant:	two 1680hp (1253kW) Rolls-Royce Merlin 72/73 or 76/77 12-cylinder Vee engines
Performance:	maximum speed 668km/h (415mph); climb to 4570m (15,000ft) in 7 minutes 30 seconds; service ceiling 11,280m (37,000ft); range 2888km (1795 miles) with a 907kg (2000lb) bomb
Weights:	empty 7031kg (15,500lb); maximum take-off 11,766kg (25,917lb)
Dimentions:	span 16.51m (54ft 2in); length 13.56m (44ft 6in); height 4.65m (15ft 3in)
Armament:	an internal and external bomb load of up to 1814kg (4000 lb)

de Havilland Mosquito F.Mk II.

The Mosquito's versatility and high performance meant that the type was developed in forms other than the originally planned bomber. The night-fighter, which became the first operational variant after the Mosquito NF.Mk II entered squadron service from December 1941 and operational service from May 1942 with four 20mm cannon and four 0.303in machine guns as well as AI.Mk IV radar. Production of the Mosquito NF.Mk II totalled 467 aircraft, equipped with Merlin 21, 22, or 23 engines in long nacelles and with flat windscreen. Pictured here is aircraft W4082, one of the first Mosquito NF.MK IIs, and delivered in the first week of 1942. With a loaded weight similar to the empty weight of the final NF marks (around 8165kg/18,000lb), the Mk II was slowed by its matt non-reflective paint and AI.IV radar. The unit markings are those of No 157 Squadron, based at Castle Camps, Essex, in mid-1942.

Country of origin:	United Kingdom
Type:	(Mosquito NF.Mk II) two-seat long-range night-fighter with intruder capability
Powerplant:	two 1480hp (1103.5kW) Rolls-Royce Merlin 21 or 23 12-cylinder Vee engines
Performance:	maximum speed 595km/h (370mph); climb to 4570m (15,000ft) in 6 minutes 45 seconds; service ceiling 10,515m (34,500ft); range 2744km (1705 miles)
Weights:	empty 6492kg (14,300lb); maximum take-off 9072kg (20,000lb)
Dimentions:	span 16.51m (54ft 2in); length 13.08m (42ft 11in); height 5.31m (17ft 5in)
Armament:	four 20mm fixed forward-firing cannon and four 0.303in fixed forward-firing machine guns in the nose

de Havilland Mosquito FB.Mk VI

By far the most important of all the Mosquito variants was the FB.Mk VI, the standard fighter version for the RAF. Some 2,584 of these were built with various armament fits, normally four 0.303in machine guns and four 20mm cannon. The first aircraft flew in June 1942, with single stage engines, the guns of the NF.Mk II, and a short bomb bay for two 250lb bombs and wing racks for two more 250lb bombs. With the series VI aircraft this potential bomb/rocket load was doubled to 2000lb. This made the Mk VI series a hugely effective ground attack aircraft and for the rest of the war the versatile FB.Mk VI ranged across Europe on low-level raids, hitting targets such as the Gestapo HQ in the Hague and V-weapon sites, and in the hands of Coastal Command was used to deadly effect against Axis shipping. Pictured here is one of the 38 FB.Mk VIs exported to Australia and assigned to No 1 Squadron, RAAF.

Country of origin:	United Kingdom
Type:	(Mosquito FB.Mk VI) two-seat long-range fighter bomber
Powerplant:	two 1480hp (1103.5kW) Rolls-Royce Merlin 21 or 23 12-cylinder Vee engines
Performance:	maximum speed 595km/h (370mph); climb to 4570m (15,000ft) in 6 minutes 45 seconds; service ceiling 10,515m (34,500ft); range 2744km (1705 miles)
Weights:	empty 6492kg (14,300lb); maximum take-off 9072kg (20,000lb)
Dimentions:	span 16.51m (54ft 2in); length 13.08m (42ft 11in); height 5.31m (17ft 5in)
Armament:	four 20mm fixed forward-firing cannon and four 0.303in fixed forward-firing machine guns in the nose, plus an internal and external bomb, rocket or drop tank load of 907kg (2000lb)

de Havilland Mosquito NF.Mk XIX

First flown in April 1944, the Mosquito NF.Mk XIX was a Mosquito NF.Mk XIII development with Merlin 25 engines and the so-called 'universal' radome able to accommodate the antennae of the British-designed AI.Mk VIII or American-designed AI.Mk X radars. Production totalled 280 aircraft, and these were followed by the NF.Mk 30 (530 aircraft with 1650hp/1230kW Merlin 72, 76 or 113 engines optimised for high-altitude performance), NF.Mk 36 (163 post-war aircraft to an NF.Mk 30 standard improved with AI.Mk IX radar and Merlin 113/114 or 113A/114A engines), and NF.Mk 38 (101 aircraft to an improved NF.Mk 36 standard with AI.Mk IX radar and Merlin 114A engines). Some 60 of the NF.Mk 38 aircraft, built up to 1950, were sold to Yugoslavia. Pictured here is one of the NF MIX aircraft built by the Leavesden factory, and operated by No 157 Squadron from Swannington and West Malling during the invasion of Europe.

Country of origin:	United Kingdom
Type:	(Mosquito NF.Mk XIX) two-seat long-range night-fighter with intruder capability
Powerplant:	two 1635hp (1219kW) Rolls-Royce Merlin 25 12-cylinder Vee engines
Performance:	maximum speed 608km/h (378mph); initial climb rate 823m (2700ft) per minute; service ceiling 8535m (28,000ft)
Weights:	empty 6622kg (14,598lb), maximum take-off 10,260kg (22,620lb)
Dimentions:	span 16.51m(54ft 2in); length 12.34m (40ft 6in); height 5.31m (17ft 5in)
Armament:	four 20mm fixed forward-firing cannon in the nose

Dewoitine D.500 series

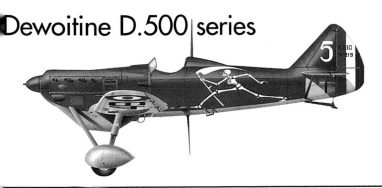

In 1930 the French air ministry issued a requirement for a Nieuport Ni-D.62 replacement, and Dewoitine decided to break away from its previous pattern of parasol-wing monoplane fighters by designing a cantilever low-wing monoplane of all-metal construction. The resulting D.500.01 prototype first flew in June 1932, and there followed for export sales as well as French service 101 D.500C.1 production aircraft with the 690hp (515kW) Hispano-Suiza 12Xbrs engine, 157 D.501C.1 aircraft with the 12Xcrs engine, and finally 120 D.510C.1 aircraft with an uprated engine in a lengthened nose. Together with older D.500 and D.501 aircraft serving with second-line units, 60 D.510 fighters were still operational with the French Air Force in 1939 but were rapidly relegated to training service or redeployed to North Africa. Pictured is a D.510 of the 1st Escadrille, Groupe de Chasse I/8, Armeé de l'Air, based at Marignane in September 1939.

Country of origin:	France
Type:	(D.510C.1) single-seat fighter
Powerplant:	one 860hp (641kW) Hispano-Suiza 12Ycrs 12-cylinder Vee engine
Performance:	maximum speed 375km/h (233mph); climb to 5000m (16,405ft) in 7 minutes 30 seconds; service ceiling 10,200m (33,465ft); range 840km (522 miles)
Weights:	empty 1378kg (3038lb); maximum take-off 1823kg (4019lb)
Dimensions:	span 11.48m (37ft 8in); length 7.56m (24ft 9.63in); height 2.70m (8ft 10.5in)
Armament:	one 20mm fixed forward-firing cannon in the nose and two 7.5mm fixed forward-firing machine guns in the leading edges of the wing

Dewoitine D.520

The D.520 resulted from a 1934 requirement for an advanced single-seat fighter to replace types such as the Dewoitine D.510, which had been rendered obsolete by the advent of the first 'modern' fighters such as the Hawker Hurricane. The aircraft was developed via the indifferent D.513 to meet a revised 1936 requirement, and incorporated features such as cantilever low-set flapped wing, enclosed cockpit, landing gear with retractable main units and engine delivering about 1000 hp (746kW) driving a variable-pitch propeller The D.520 prototype first flew in October 1938, and only 36 D.520C.1 fighters had been delivered before the German invasion of May 1940. Further deliveries were made during the German offensive, and the D.520 acquitted itself very well. Production eventually reached 905 aircraft for service mainly with the Vichy French Air Force and were also passed to Germany's allies.

Country of origin:	France
Type:	(D.520C.1) single-seat fighter
Powerplant:	one 930hp (693kW) Hispano-Suiza 12Y-45 12-cylinder Vee engine
Performance:	maximum speed 540km/h (336mph); climb to 4000m (13,125ft) in 5 minutes 49 seconds; service ceiling 11,000m (36,090ft); range 1540km (957 miles)
Weights:	empty 2125kg (4685lb); maximum take-off 2790kg (6151lb)
Dimensions:	span 10.20m (33ft 5.5in); length 8.76m (28ft 8.75in); height 8ft 2.57m (5.25in)
Armament:	one 20mm fixed forward-firing cannon in the nose, and four 7.5mm fixed forward-firing machine guns in the leading edges of the wing

Dornier Do 17Z

Development of the Do 17E/F led to the Do 17M/P medium bomber/-reconnaissance types with Bramo 323 radial engines. These were followed by the Do 17S/U reconnaissance/pathfinder types that reverted to liquid-cooled engines but introduced a revised, shortened and enlarged forward fuselage of the glazed 'beetle eye' type. The 18 Do 17S/U pre-production types were followed by the definitive Do 17Z radial-engined model of which 522 were built. The three new-build variants were the Do 17Z-1 with a 1102lb (500 kg) bomb load, Do 17Z-2 with an uprated powerplant and greater bomb load, and Do 17Z-3 reconnaissance bomber, while conversions included the Do 17Z-4 dual-control trainer, Do 17Z-5 maritime reconnaissance, Do 17Z-6 long-range night-fighter with the distinctive nose of the Junkers Ju 88C-2, and Do 17Z-10 night-fighter with a redesigned nose. Pictured is a Do-17Z-2 of III/KG2.

Country of origin:	Germany
Type:	(Do 17Z-2) four/five-seat medium bomber
Powerplant:	two 1000hp (746kW) BMW Bramo 323P Fafnir nine-cylinder single-row radial engines
Performance:	maximum speed 410km/h (255mph); service ceiling 8200m (26,905ft); range 1500km (932 miles)
Weights:	empty 5200kg (11,464lb); maximum take-off 8590kg (18,937lb)
Dimensions:	span 18.00m (59ft 0.5in); length 15.80m (51ft 9.67in); height 4.60m (15ft 1in)
Armament:	one or two 7.92mm trainable machine guns each in the windscreen, nose, dorsal and ventral positions, plus an internal bomb load of 1000kg (2205lb)

Dornier Do 17E

Designed as a fast mailplane for Deutsche Lufthansa and first flown in 1934, the Do 17 was rejected in its planned role after the delivery of three single-finned aircraft and was then developed via 12 prototypes as a high-speed bomber with twin vertical tail surfaces. Entering service in the first months of 1937 and soon receiving the nickname 'The Flying Pencil' as a result of their very slender fuselage, the first two military variants were the Do 17E-1 and Do 17F-1 intended for the high-speed bomber and long-range photo-reconnaissance roles respectively, the latter with additional fuel and the internal bomb bay revised for the carriage of two cameras. The two types offered good performance and adequate all-round capabilities by the standards of the day, but were soon seen as obsolescent. Pictured is one of the Do 17Es operated by KG 40 under the command of Fliegerführer Atlantik from March 1941 onwards.

Country of origin:	Germany
Type:	(Do 17E-1) three/four-seat light bomber
Powerplant:	two 750hp (559kW) BMW VI 7,3 12-cylinder Vee engines
Performance:	maximum speed 355km/h (221mph); service ceiling 5100m (16,730ft); radius 500km (311 miles) with maximum bomb load
Weights:	empty 4500kg (9921lb); maximum take-off weight 7040kg (15,520lb)
Dimensions:	span 18.00m (59ft 0.67in); length 16.25m (53ft 3.5in); height 4.32m (14ft 2in)
Armament:	one 7.92mm trainable forward-firing machine gun in the starboard side of the cockpit, provision for one 7.92mm trainable forward-firing machine gun in the lower nose, one 7.92mm trainable rearward-firing machine gun in the rear of the cockpit, one 7.92mm rearward-firing machine gun; internal bomb load of 750kg (1653lb)

Dornier Do 217E-5

Ｏne of the ulimate subvariants of the basic D0 217E series was the E-5, built from the start with wing pylons for the Hs 293A stand-off radio-guided anti-shipping missile, together with the associated Kehl/Strassburg guidance system. This model entered service with II/KG 100, one of the specialised anti-shipping units of the Luftwaffe, in April 1943. Operating in the area around the Bay of Biscay and further out into the North Atlantic the aircraft soon made its mark against Allied shipping, sinking a substantial amount of vessels, though there were never enough aircraft to pose a serious threat to convoys. The first attack was made against British destroyers on August 25, 1943. This Do 217E-5, from 6/KG 100, is unusual in retaining its fixed MG 151 cannon under the nose; normally this was removed when the 20mm MG FF hand-aimed cannon was added in the glazed part of the nose. Note the size of the missile in comparison with the aircraft.

Country of origin:	Germany
Type:	(Do 217E-5) four-seat anti-shipping aircraft
Powerplant:	two 1580hp (1178kW) BMW 801ML 14-cylinder radial engines
Performance:	maximum speed 515km/h (320mph); initial climb rate 216m (740ft) per minute; service ceiling 9000m (29,530ft); range 2800km (1740 miles)
Weights:	empty 10,535kg (23,225lb); maximum take-off 16,465kg (36,299lb)
Dimensions:	span 19.00m (62ft 4in); length 18.20m (59ft 8.5in); height 5.03m (16ft 6in)
Armament:	one 20mm cannon in lower port side of nose, one 13mm machine gun in dorsal turret, one 13mm machine gun in ventral step position, 7.92mm forward-firing machine gun in nose, one 7.92mm machine gun in each cockpit side window; plus a bomb load of 4000kg (8818lb)

Dornier Do 18

The Do 18 was designed as a medium-range maritime reconnaissance type to supersede the Dornier Wal 33 (from 1934 Do 15) and as a mailplane flying boat for service with Deutsche Lufthansa. The first of four prototypes made its maiden flight in March 1935. Only six civil flying boats were completed, the majority of the approximately 148 production 'boats going to the military for service from 1938. The primary military variants were the Do 18D (three subvariants to a total of about 75 machines) with 600hp (447.5kW) Junkers Jumo 205D Diesel engines, the Do 18G improved Do 18D with revised armament and provision for RATO units, and the Do 18H six-seat trainer. Do 18G and Do-18H production was 71 'boats, and many Do 18G machines were converted to Do 18N standard as air/sea rescue flying boats. Pictured here is a Do 18D of 3./Küstenfliegergruppe 406, based at List on the island of Sylt in August 1939.

Country of origin:	Germany
Type:	(Do 18G-1) four-seat maritime reconnaissance flying boat
Powerplant:	two 880hp (656kW) Junkers Jumo 205D six-cylinder horizontally opposed Diesel engines
Performance:	maximum speed 267km/h (166mph); climb to 2000m (6560ft) in 17 minutes 30 seconds; service ceiling 4200m (13,780ft); range 3500 km (2175 miles)
Weights:	empty 5980kg (13,183lb); normal take-off 10,000kg (22,046lb); maximum take-off 10,800kg (23,809lb)
Dimensions:	span 23.70m (77ft 9.25in); length 19.37m (63ft 7in); height 5.32m (17ft 5.5in)
Armament:	one 20mm trainable rearward-firing cannon in the dorsal turret, and one 13mm trainable forward-firing machine gun in the bow position, plus an external bomb load of 100kg (220lb)

Dornier Do 217

The Do 217 was Dornier's response to a 1937 requirement for a long-range warplane optimised for the heavy level and dive bombing roles. The Do 217 was essentially a scaled-up version of the Do 215 version of the Do 17, and first flew in August 1938. The first operational model was the Do 217E of which some 800 aircraft were built in Do 217E-0 to Do 217E-4 subvariants with BMW 801 radial engines. These were followed by 950 examples of the Do 217K night bomber with a revised and unstepped nose, and finally the Do 217M development of the Do 217K with DB 603 inverted-Vee engines. Prototype and pre-production variants were the Do 217C bomber, Do 217P high-altitude reconnaissance, and Do 217R missile launching aircraft. There were also Do 217E and Do 217K subvariants armed with Hs 293 anti-ship missiles and *Fritz-X* guided bombs respectively. Do 217s sank the Italian ship *Roma* as she steamed to the Allies after Italy's surrender.

Country of origin:	Germany
Type:	(Do 217E-2) four-seat heavy bomber
Powerplant:	two 1580hp (1178kW) BMW 801ML 14-cylinder radial engines
Performance:	maximum speed 515km/h (320mph); initial climb rate 216m (740ft) per minute; ceiling 9000m (29,530ft); range 2800km (1740 miles)
Weights:	empty 10,535kg (23,225lb); maximum take-off 16,465kg (36,299lb)
Dimensions:	span 19.00m (62ft 4in); length 18.20m (59ft 8.5in); height 5.03m (16ft 6in)
Armament:	one 15mm cannon in lower port side of nose, one 13mm machine gun in dorsal turret, one 13mm machine gun in ventral step position, 7.92mm forward-firing machine gun in nose, one 7.92mm machine gun in each cockpit side window; in the Do 217E-2/R19 subvariant, one remotely-controlled 7.92mm rearward-firing machine gun in the tail cone, plus a bomb load of 4000kg (8818lb)

Dornier Do 215

A Yugoslav order for the Do 17K derivative of the Do 17M (70 or more German- and Yugoslav-built aircraft with the Gnome-Rhône 14N radial engine) led to the development of the Do 215 as an export variant. This was ordered by Sweden but none had been delivered when World War II started. Production totalled 112 aircraft, of which four and two were delivered to Hungary and the USSR respectively, the remainder entering German service. The variants were the Do 215A-1 ordered by Sweden with DB 601A engines, Do 215B-3 for the USSR, and Do 215B-4 reconnaissance bomber. The only other significant model was the Do 215B-5 night-fighter and intruder, which was created as a small number of conversions based on the Do 17Z-10 with an infra-red sensor and a fixed forward-firing armament of two 20mm cannon and four 7.92mm machine guns. This D0-215B-5 Kauz III served with Stab II/NJG 2 based at Leeuwarden in the summer of 1942.

Country of origin:	Germany
Type:	(Do 215B-4) four-seat medium reconnaissance bomber
Powerplant:	two 1100hp (820kW) Daimler-Benz DB 601Aa 12-cylinder engines
Performance:	maximum speed 470km/h (292mph); climb to 1000m (3280ft) in 2 minutes 18 seconds; ceiling 9000m (29,530ft); range 2445km (1519 miles)
Weights:	empty 5775kg (12,731lb); maximum take-off 8800kg (19,400lb)
Dimensions:	span 18.00m (59ft 0.33in); length 15.80m (51ft 9.67in); height 4.55m (14ft 11.5in)
Armament:	two 7.92mm forward-firing machine guns in windscreen, one or two 7.92mm trainable forward-firing machine guns in nose position, two 7.92mm trainable lateral-firing machine guns in side windows, one 7.92mm trainable machine gun in dorsal position, one 7.92mm gun in ventral position; internal bomb load of 1000kg (2205lb)

Douglas A-20

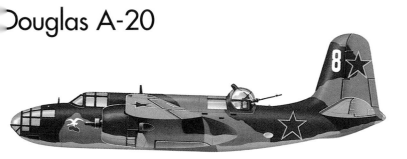

First ordered in June 1939, the A-20 was the American version of the light bomber initially bought by France and the UK as the DB-7 and Boston. The first US orders were for the A-20 and A-20A (63 and 143 aircraft) with supercharged and normally aspirated engines, the former being converted to P-70 night-fighters and the latter entering service in 1941. There followed 999 A-20Bs equivalent to the DB-7A, 948 A-20Cs with British equipment, 17 A-20E conversions from A-20A standard with the powerplant of the A-20B, 2,850 A-20G attack bombers with a 'solid' nose and considerably heavier forward-firing armament, 412 A-20Hs with an uprated powerplant, and 450 and 413 A-20Js and A-20Ks based on the A-20G and A-20H with a frameless transparent nose. The F-3 was a photo-reconnaissance conversion. Pictured here is one of the A-20B aircraft, fitted with a Russian dorsal turret, that served with the Black Sea Fleet Air Force in the spring of 1944.

Country of origin:	USA
Type:	(A-20G) three-seat light attack bomber
Powerplant:	two 1700hp (1268kW) Wright R-2600-23 14-cylinder two-row radial engines
Performance:	maximum speed 546km/h (339mph); climb to 3050m (10,000ft) in 8 minutes 48 seconds; ceiling 7225m (23,700ft); range 3380km (2100 miles)
Weights:	empty 7708kg (16,993lb); normal take-off 10,964kg (24,127lb); maximum take-off 12,338kg (27,200lb)
Dimensions:	span 18.69m (61ft 4in); length 14.63m (47ft 11.88in); height 5.36m (17ft 7in)
Armament:	six 0.5in fixed forward-firing machine guns, two 0.5in trainable machine guns in the dorsal turret, and one 0.5 in trearward-firing machine gun in the ventral position; bomb load of 1814kg (4000lb)

Douglas DB-7

Designed by 'Ed' Heinemann under the supervision of 'Jack' Northrop, the Northrop N-7A light attack bomber concept paved the way – after Northrop's take-over by Douglas – for the Model 7B that first flew in October 1938. The type soon drew the attention of a French purchasing mission, which ordered an initial 270 examples of the revised DB-7 bomber with a transparent nose and two 1100hp (820kW) Pratt & Whitney R-1830-SC3G Twin Wasp radial engines. The 100 DB-7A bombers that followed switched to a pair of 1500hp (1118kW) Wright R-2600-A5B radial engines, and the DB-7B differed mainly in its enlarged vertical tail surface. The first DB-7 flew in August 1939, but only a comparatively small number had entered service before France's defeat in June 1940, when the others passed to the UK or were repossessed by the USA. Pictured is a DB-7B-3 serving with Groupe de Bommbardment I/19, Armée de l'Air d'Armistice, in autumn 1940.

Country of origin:	USA
Type:	(DB-7B) three-seat light attack bomber
Powerplant:	two 1600hp (1193kW) Wright GR-2600-A5B Double Cyclone radial engines
Performance:	maximum speed 515km/h (320mph); initial climb rate 609m (2000ft) per minute; ceiling 7470m (24,500ft); range 845km (525 miles)
Weights:	empty 5534kg (12,200lb); normal take-off 8959kg (19,750lb); maximum take-off 9789kg (21,580lb)
Dimensions:	span 18.69m (61ft 4in); length 14.48m (47ft 6in); height 5.36m (17ft 7in)
Armament:	four 0.303in fixed forward-firing machine guns on the sides of the forward fuselage, two 0.303in trainable machine guns in the dorsal position, and one 0.303in trainable machine gun in the ventral position, plus an internal bomb load of 907kg (2000lb)

Douglas C-47 Skytrain/Dakota

The DC-3 was developed from the DC-2 with greater power and accommodation increased to 21, and first flew in December 1935. Some 445 aircraft were built to civil orders, but the DC-3 remains better known in its military forms as the C-47 Skytrain, R4D and Dakota for the US Army Air Corps, US Navy and Royal Air Force respectively. Production of these and other military variants in the USA totalled some 10,050 aircraft, excluding major production in Japan and the USSR. These aircraft were truly war-winning weapons, providing the Western Allies with an unparalleled transport capability that expanded into paratroop and glider-towing capabilities as World War II progressed. Related developments were the C-48 to C-52 and C-68 impressments, and the C-53 and C-117 personnel transports. Pictured here is a Douglas Dakota III of No 24 Squadron, RAF. The squadron was actually a communications unit, and flew Dakotas to Malta from 1943 onwards.

Country of origin:	USA
Type:	(C-47) two/three-seat transport with accommodation for 28 troops, or 14 litters plus three attendants or 10,000lb (4536kg) of freight
Powerplant:	two 1200hp (895kW) Pratt & Whitney R-1830-92 14-cylinder two-row radial engines
Performance:	maximum speed 370km/h (230mph); climb to 3050m (10,000ft) in 9 minutes 36 seconds; service ceiling 7315m (24,000ft); range 2575km (1600 miles)
Weights:	empty 8103kg (17,865lb); maximum take-off 14,061kg (31,000lb)
Dimensions:	span 28.90m (95ft 0in); length 19.63m (64ft 5.5in); height 5.20m (16ft 11in)
Armament:	none

Douglas A-26 Invader

Though only produced in small numbers by World War II standards, the A-26 has the distinction of having flown in more conflicts than any other warplane. The type was ordered in XA-26, XA-26A and XA-26B prototype forms, the first as a three-seat attack bomber a potential 2268kg (5000lb) bomb load, the second as a two-seat night-fighter and intruder with radar and cannon in a 'solid' nose, and the third as a three-seat heavy attack fighter with a 75mm cannon in the 'solid' nose. The type first flew in July 1942, and the A-26B (1355 built) entered service in Europe during November 1944, and at the same time became operational in the Pacific. Powered by two 1491kw (2000hp) Pratt & Whitney radial engines that conferred a maximum speed of 571km/h (377 mph) the A-26B was the fastest US bomber of the war. Pictured here is A-26B-15-DT 'Stinky' of the 552nd Bomb Squadron, 386th Bomb Group, US 9th Air Force, based at Beaumont-sur-Oise, France, in April 1945.

Country of origin:	USA
Type:	(A-26B) three-seat light attack and reconnaissance bomber
Powerplant:	two 2000hp (1491kW) Pratt & Whitney R-2800-27 or -71 18-cylinder two-row radial engines
Performance:	maximum speed 571km/h (355mph); climb to 3050m (10,000ft) in 7 minutes 0 seconds; service ceiling 6735m (22,100ft); range 2092km (1300 miles) with a 1361kg (3000lb) bomb load
Weights:	empty 10,147kg (22,370lb); maximum take-off 12,893kg (42,300lb)
Dimensions:	span 21.34m (70ft); length 15.42m (50ft 7in); height 5.64m (18ft 6in)
Armament:	six 0.5in fixed forward-firing machine guns, two 0.5in trainable machine guns in dorsal barbette, two 0.5in trainable rearward-firing machine guns in optional ventral barbette, and provision for eight 0.5in fixed forward-firing machine guns in four underwing packs, plus a bomb load of 2722kg (6000lb)

Douglas A-26C Invader

The only other production model of the A-26 to see service during World War II was the A-26C, of which 1091 were delivered with a transparent nose for a bomb aimer's position and nose armament reduced to two guns. The type remained in service long after the war; the first conversion was for 150 JD-1 target-towing aircraft form A-26Cs for the US Navy. Some were later converted to launch and control missile test vehicles and drones, under the designation JD-1D. In 1948 USAF A-26B and A-26C aircraft were redesignated and became B-26B and B-26C respectively. Both versions were heavily employed in the air war over Korea and, during the Vietnam War, some 70 aircraft were converted to B-26K standard for counter-insurgency operations. The RAF took possession of 140 Invader Mk 1s (A-26C) under the Lend-Lease scheme. Many other models were produced for a variety of roles, including photoreconnaissance and even executive transport.

Country of origin:	USA
Type:	(A-26B) three-seat light attack and reconnaissance bomber
Powerplant:	two 2000hp (1491kW) Pratt & Whitney R-2800-27 or -71 18-cylinder two-row radial engines
Performance:	maximum speed 571km/h (355mph); climb to 3050m (10,000ft) in 7 minutes 0 seconds; service ceiling 6735m (22,100ft); range 2092km (1300 miles) with a 1361kg (3000lb) bomb load
Weights:	empty 10,147kg (22,370lb); maximum take-off 12,893kg (42,300lb)
Dimensions:	span 21.34m (70ft); length 15.42m (50ft 7in); height 5.64m (18ft 6in)
Armament:	two 0.5in fixed forward-firing machine guns, two 0.5in trainable machine guns in dorsal barbette, two 0.5in trainable rearward-firing machine guns in optional ventral barbette, and provision for eight 0.5in fixed forward-firing machine guns in four underwing packs, plus a bomb load of 2722kg (6000lb)

Douglas SBD Dauntless

The Dauntless was one of World War II's decisive warplanes, particularly in terms of the part it played in the Battle of Midway, and despite the fact that it possessed only indifferent performance and poor manoeuvrability. As a result of these shortcomings the type was phased out of first-line service well before the end of the war despite having only entered service in 1940. The first flight of the XBT-2 (converted Northrop BT-1) prototype was made in April 1938. The main production models were the SBD-1 (57) with the 1000hp (746kW) R-1820-32 engine, SBD-2 (87) with heavier armament and more fuel, SBD-3 (584) with 0.5in rather than 0.3in machine guns, self-sealing fuel tankage and 24- rather than 12-volt electrics, SBD-4 (780) with detail improvements, SBD-5 (3025) with greater power, and SBD-6 (451) with the 1350hp (1007kW) R-1820-66 engine. Illustrated is an SBD-5 Dauntless of Escuadron Aéreo de Pelea 200, Fuerza Aérea Mexicana, in 1946.

Country of origin:	USA
Type:	(SBD-5) two-seat carrierborne and land-based scout and dive bomber
Powerplant:	one 1200hp (895kW) Wright R-1820-60 Cyclone nine-cylinder single-row radial engine
Performance:	maximum speed 410km/h (255mph); climb to 3050m (10,000ft) in 8 minutes; service ceiling 7780m (25,530ft); range 2519km (1565 miles)
Weights:	empty 2905kg (6404lb); maximum take-off 4853kg (10,700lb)
Dimensions:	span 12.66m (41ft 6.38in); length 10.09m (33ft 1.25in); height 4.14m (13ft 7in)
Armament:	two 0.5in fixed forward-firing machine guns in the upper part of the forward fuselage, and two 0.3in trainable rearward-firing machine guns in the rear of the cockpit, plus an external bomb load of 1021kg (2250lb)

Douglas A-24

When it began to receive intelligence information about the Germans' successful employment of the Junkers Ju 87 dive-bomber in the early European campaigns, the US Army Air Corps decided to develop a similar capability. After evaluation of borrowed aircraft in 1940 the USAAC opted for the Douglas Dauntless already in service with the US Navy as the SBD. The first model ordered was the A-24 (eventually 178 aircraft) that was essentially similar to the SBD-3A; the first aircraft were delivered between July and October 1942. Combat experience in the South-West Pacific theatre highlighted some fundamental deficiencies, however, and later aircraft were used mainly for training. These later models were the A-24A and A-24B (170 and 615 aircraft to SBD-4A and SBD-5 standards respectively. More than 40 A-24Bs were transferred to France in 1944. This aircraft wears the markings of the Free French air force.

Country of origin:	USA
Type:	(A-24) two-seat dive-bomber
Powerplant:	one 1000hp (746kW) Wright R-1820-52 nine-cylinder single-row radial engine
Performance:	maximum speed 402km/h (250mph); climb to 3050m (10,000ft) in 7 minutes; service ceiling 7925m (26,000ft); range 2092 km (1300 miles)
Weights:	empty 2804kg (6181lb); maximum take-off 4627kg (10,200lb)
Dimensions:	span 12.66m (41ft 6.38in); length 9.96m (32ft 8in); height 4.14m (13ft 7in)
Armament:	two 0.5in fixed forward-firing machine guns in the upper part of the forward fuselage, and two 0.3in trainable rearward-firing machine guns in the rear of the cockpit, plus an external bomb load of 544kg (1200lb)

Douglas DB-7

The Douglas DB-7 light attack bomber was a shoulder-wing monoplane of basically all-metal construction with a semi-monocoque fuselage, cantilever wing and retractable tricycle landing gear, and was initially bought by France. With the fall of Belgium and France by June 1940, however, the UK took over the outstanding orders for DB-7 warplanes intended for those countries. These were allocated the name Boston Mk 1. The first 20 machines to arrive were powered by two Pratt & Whitney R-1830-SC3G radial engines with single-speed superchargers. Four of them were in such poor condition that they were immediately struck off charge. The other 16 were ex-Belgian aircraft and, after a minimal modification programme (including a reversal of the throttle action to the British system of forward to open), were pressed into service as Boston Mk I conversion trainers. Pictured here is a DB-7B of GB I/19, French Vichy air force, Algeria, in autumn 1940.

Country of origin:	USA
Type:	three-seat light attack bomber
Powerplant:	two 1100hp (820kW) Pratt & Whitney R-1830-SC3G Twin Wasp 14-cylinder two-row radial engines
Performance:	maximum speed 475km/h (295mph); climb to 3660m (12,000ft) in 8 minutes; service ceiling 7835m (25,800ft)
Weights:	empty 5171kg (11,400lb); maximum take-off 8636kg (19,040lb)
Dimensions:	span 18.67m (61ft 3in); length 14.32m (46ft 11.75in); height 4.83m (15ft 10in)
Armament:	generally none, though provision was retained for 7.5mm fixed forward-firing machine guns on the sides of the forward fuselage, one 7.5mm trainable machine gun in the dorsal position, and one 7.5mm trainable machine gun in the ventral position, plus an internal bomb load of 800kg (1764lb)

Douglas Boston Mk III

The DB-7 bombers taken over from French contracts (and powered by two R-1830-S3C4G radial engines with two-speed superchargers) were originally to have become Boston Mk II light bombers in British service but in the event were adapted as Havoc Mk I night-fighters. The type entered service in April 1941 with No 85 Squadron. The next light bomber was thus the Boston Mk III, a designation applied to a total of 753 aircraft including 452 DB-7Bs taken over from France. The Boston Mk III had improved self-sealing fuel tanks, additional armour protection, a number of strengthening features to cater for a significantly increased maximum take-off weight, a slightly longer fuselage, and increased fuel capacity. The aircraft were delivered to the UK from the summer of 1941, and entered service in October of the same year. Some aircraft were adapted as Boston Mk III (Intruder) machines with four 20mm cannon in a ventral pack.

Country of origin:	USA
Type:	four-seat light attack bomber
Powerplant:	two 1600hp (1193kW) Wright GR-2600-A5B Double Cyclone radial engines
Performance:	maximum speed 515km/h (320mph); initial climb rate 609m (2000ft) per minute; service ceiling 7470m (24,500ft); range 1996km (1240 miles) with reduced bomb load
Weights:	empty 5534kg (12,200lb); normal take-off 8959kg (19,750lb); maximum take-off 9789kg (21,580lb)
Dimensions:	span 18.69m (61ft 4in); length 14.48m (47ft 6in); height 5.36m (17ft 7in)
Armament:	four 0.303in fixed forward-firing machine guns on the sides of the forward fuselage, two 0.303in trainable machine guns in the dorsal position, and one 0.303in trainable machine gun in the ventral position, plus an internal bomb load of 907kg (2000lb)

Douglas Boston Mk111A

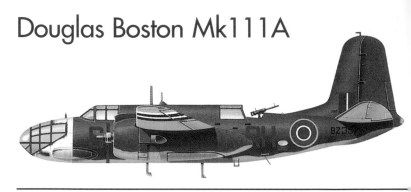

The Boston served in all theatres of the war and earned a well-deserved reputation for toughness and reliability. Pictured here is one of the many variants, the Boston Mk IIIA, in the colours of No 88 (Hong Kong) Squadron, Royal Air Force, at Hartford Bridge, Hampshire, on the eve of D-Day, June 1944. The aircraft wears USAAF olive-drab and grey camouflage with soluble white paint on the nose. The two under-fuselage smoke pipes were used to eject smokescreen trails to cover Allied movements during the Normandy landings. The Mk IIIA was the RAF designation for the Douglas A-20C Havoc, 140 of which were supplied to the RAF under the Lend-Lease scheme. This aircraft differed from the DB-7B previously mentioned in minor details, such as individual exhaust stacks to replace the collector rings. This helped to boost maximum speed by 24km/h (15 mph). A total of 958 A-20Cs were built, 808 by Douglas and 150 by Boeing.

Country of origin:	USA
Type:	four-seat light attack bomber
Powerplant:	two 1600hp (1193kW) Wright GR-2600-A5B Double Cyclone radial engines
Performance:	maximum speed 539km/h (335mph); initial climb rate 609m (2000ft) per minute; service ceiling 7470m (24,500ft); range 1996km (1240 miles) with reduced bomb load
Weights:	empty 5534kg (12,200lb); normal take-off 8959kg (19,750lb); maximum take-off 9789kg (21,580lb)
Dimensions:	span 18.69m (61ft 4in); length 14.48m (47ft 6in); height 5.36m (17ft 7in)
Armament:	four 0.303in fixed forward-firing machine guns on the sides of the forward fuselage, two 0.303in trainable machine guns in the dorsal position, and one 0.303in trainable machine gun in the ventral position, plus an internal bomb load of 907kg (2000lb)

Douglas DC-2

The DC-1 was the aeroplane that truly ushered in the era of the 'modern' cantilever low-wing monoplane transport with an all-metal structure, enclosed accommodation, retractable landing gear, nicely cowled engines and other features It was designed to a requirement of Transcontinental and Western Air and first flew in July 1933 but was then developed as the more capable DC-2 that first took to the air in May 1934. The US forces were highly interested in the type but could not afford large-scale purchases, so of the total production of 208 aircraft only 64 were directly purchased by the US forces as the military C-32, C-33, C-34, C-39, C-41, C-42 and C-43 as well as the naval R2D. Of these, the variants procured in largest numbers were the C-33 and C-39 (18 and 35 machines). Some 24 civil DC-2s were also impressed for wartime service as C-32A aircraft. Pictured here is a KLM DC-2, based at Whitchurch in England throughout most of World War II.

Country of origin:	USA
Type:	(R2D-1) two-seat transport with accommodation for 14 passengers
Powerplant:	two 710hp (529.5kW) Wright R-1820-12 Cyclone nine-cylinder single-row radial engines
Performance:	maximum speed 338km/h (210mph); initial climb rate 305m (1000ft) per minute; service ceiling 6845m (22,450ft); range 1609km (1000 miles)
Weights:	maximum take-off 8256kg (18,200lb)
Dimensions:	span 25.91m (85ft); length 18.82m (61ft 9in); height 4.97m (16ft 4in)
Armament:	none

Fairey Albacore

The Albacore was designed to supersede the Fairey Swordfish as the primary torpedo bomber of the Fleet Air Arm. In fact the Albacore was only able to complement the Swordfish in this role; the older aircraft outlived the Albacore by more than one year. Resulting from a 1936 requirement, the Albacore was in effect a modernised and technically somewhat improved development of the Swordfish with enclosed accommodation, a higher-rated engine, hydraulically operated flaps, and a number of aerodynamic revisions designed to reduce drag. The first of two Albacore prototypes made its maiden flight in December 1938, and the first of 798 Albacore Mk I production aircraft entered service in March 1940, initially as a land-based type and only from 1941 on board aircraft carriers. The Albacore spawned no improved models, and was withdrawn from first-line service in 1944. Pictured here is an AlbacoreTB.Mk 1 of No 826 Squadron, Fleet Air Arm.

Country of origin:	United Kingdom
Type:	(Albacore Mk I) three-seat carrierborne and land-based torpedo bomber and reconnaissance aeroplane
Powerplant:	one 1130hp (843kW) Bristol Taurus XII 14-cylinder two-row radial engine
Performance:	maximum speed 257km/h (161mph); climb to 1830m (6000ft) in 8 minutes; service ceiling 6310m (20,700ft); range 1497km (930 miles)
Weights:	empty 3269kg (7200lb); maximum take-off 5670kg (12,500lb)
Dimensions:	span 15.23m (49ft 11.75in); length 12.18m (39ft 11.75in); height 3.81m (12ft 6in)
Armament:	one 0.303in fixed forward-firing machine gun in the leading edge of the starboard lower wing, and one or two 0.303in trainable rearward-firing machine guns in the rear cockpit, plus an external torpedo and bomb load of 907kg (2000lb)

Fairey Battle

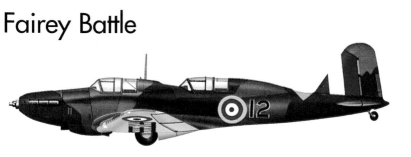

The Battle was an advance over the Hawker light bomber biplanes that it was designed to replace in Royal Air Force service. Nonetheless it was technically and tactically obsolescent by the time it entered service in March 1937, as a result of the rapid pace of aeronautical development during the approach to World War II. This is unsurprising considering the aeroplane was designed to meet a 1932 requirement but did not fly until March 1936. Production of the Battle light bomber totalled 1818 from two British manufacturers for RAF service (subsequently redesignated as the Battle Mks I to V depending on the mark of engine installed) and 18 Belgian-built aircraft for Belgian service. The type was relegated to second-line service in 1940 as the Battle (T) trainer and Battle (TT) target-tug, of which 100 and 266 were built to supplement conversions. Shown here is one of the Battle trainer aircraft in September 1940.

Country of origin:	United Kingdom
Type:	(Battle Mk II) two/three-seat light day bomber
Powerplant:	one 1030hp (768kW) Rolls-Royce Merlin II 12-cylinder Vee engine
Performance:	maximum speed 406km/h (252mph); climb to 4570m (15,000ft) in 16 minutes 12 seconds; service ceiling 7925m (26,000ft); range 1931km (1200 miles) with a 644kg (1420lb) bomb load
Weights:	empty 3361kg (7410lb); normal take-off 4944kg (10,900lb); maximum take-off 5307kg (11,700lb)
Dimentions:	Span 16.45m (54ft); length 12.93m (42ft 5in); height 4.57m (15ft)
Armament:	one 0.303in fixed forward-firing machine gun in the leading edge of the starboard wing, and one 0.303in trainable rearward-firing machine gun in the rear cockpit, plus an internal and external bomb load of 680kg (1500lb)

Fairey Fox

Fairey produced two types of Fox day bombers in the 1920s, namely the two-seat Fox Mk I with the Curtiss D-12 engine and the three-seat Fox Mk II with the Rolls-Royce Kestrel engine. Two-seat developments of the Fox Mk II, produced mainly by Fairey's Belgian subsidiary, served with the Belgian air force in the first part of World War II. The main variants were the Kestrel-engined Fox Mk II bomber mentioned previously, Fox Mk III reconnaissance fighter, Fox Mk IIIC with an enclosed cockpit and Fox Mk IIIS dual-control trainer. These were followed by the Hispano-Suiza-engined Fox Mk VI reconnaissance fighter, Fox Mk VII single-seat fighter, and Fox Mk VIII improved version of the Mk VI. The type entered service in 1932, was wholly obsolete by the beginning of World War II, and the 50 surviving aircraft suffered heavy losses at German hands. A seaborne reconnaissance version of similar design was the Fairey Seafox.

Country of origin:	Belgium (from a British design)
Type:	(Fox Mk VIR) two-seat reconnaissance fighter and light bomber
Powerplant:	one 860hp (641kW) Hispano-Suiza 12-cylinder Vee engine
Performance:	maximum speed 365km/h (227mph); climb to 5000m (16,405ft) in 6 minutes 30 seconds; service ceiling 10,000m (32,810ft); range 600km (373 miles)
Weights:	empty 1325kg (2920lb); normal take-off 2245kg (4950lb); maximum take-off 2345kg (5170lb)
Dimensions:	span 11.58m (38ft); length 9.17m (30ft 1in); height 3.35m (11ft)
Armament:	two 7.62mm fixed forward-firing machine guns in the upper part of the forward fuselage, and one or two 7.62mm trainable rearward-firing machine guns in the rear of the cockpit, plus an external bomb load of 100 kg (220lb)

Fairey Swordfish Mk I

The Swordfish has an enduring reputation as one of the finest warplanes of World War II. This reputation resulted from its anachronistic biplane airframe and a combination of ruggedness, reliability, versatility in terms of weapons and equipment, and such completely viceless handling characteristics that it could be flown in most weather conditions from aircraft carriers ranging in size from the largest fleet carriers to the smallest of escort carriers. The type, universally known as the 'Stringbag', resulted from a 1930 requirement for a carrierborne aeroplane to serve in the spotter, reconnaissance and torpedo attack roles. The first of four prototype and pre-production aircraft flew in March 1933. Successful trials led to orders for an eventual 989 aircraft. Fairey built 689 and the remainder were Blackburn-built machines. Service deliveries began in July 1936 and by the beginning of World War II the FAA had 13 operational Swordfish squadrons.

Country of origin:	United Kingdom
Type:	(Swordfish Mk I) three-seat carrierborne and land-based torpedo bomber, level bomber and reconnaissance aeroplane
Powerplant:	one 775hp (578kW) Bristol Pegasus IIIM3 nine-cylinder single-row radial engine
Performance:	maximum speed 224km/h (139mph); climb to 1525m (5000ft) in 10 minutes 30 seconds; ceiling 3780m (12,400ft); range 1657km (1030 miles)
Weights:	empty 2359kg (5200lb); maximum take-off 4196kg (9250lb)
Dimensions:	span 13.87m (45ft 6in); length 11.07m (36ft 4in) with the tail up; height 4.11m (13ft 5.75in) with the tail up
Armament:	one 0.303in fixed forward-firing machine gun in the starboard side of the forward fuselage, and one 0.303in trainable rearward-firing machine in the rear cockpit; external bomb load of 726kg (1600lb)

Fairey Swordfish Mk II

Built by Blackburn to the total of 1080 aircraft, the Swordfish Mk II was a development of the Swordfish Mk I with a strengthened lower wing skinned on its lower surfaces with metal rather than the fabric of the Mk I to permit the carriage and firing of up to eight 3in (76mm) air-to-surface rockets. These could be of two types, differentiated by their warheads. The 60lb (27.2kg) high explosive rocket was notably effective against coastal shipping, while the 25lb (11.3kg) armour-piercing rocket was used mainly against submarines and coastal fortifications. A number of Swordfish Mk II aircraft, which could be operated on floats as alternatives to the standard wheeled landing gear, were converted to Swordfish Mk IV standard with enclosed accommodation for use in Canadian waters. The Swordfish achieved some notable victories during the war, including the first U-boat sinking and the decimation of the Italian fleet at Taranto in November 1940.

Country of origin:	United Kingdom
Type:	(Swordfish Mk II) three-seat carrierborne and land-based torpedo bomber, level bomber and reconnaissance aeroplane
Powerplant:	one 775hp (578kW) Bristol Pegasus IIIM3 or 750hp (559kW) Pegasus XXX nine-cylinder single-row radial engine
Performance:	maximum speed 224km/h (139mph); climb to 1525m (5000ft) in 10 minutes 30 seconds; ceiling 3780m (12,400ft); range 1657km (1030 miles)
Weights:	empty 2132kg (4700lb); maximum take-off 4196kg (9250lb)
Dimensions:	span 13.87m (45ft 6in); length 11.07m (36ft 4in) with the tail up; height 4.11m (13ft 5.75in) with the tail up
Armament:	one 0.303in fixed forward-firing machine gun in the starboard side of the forward fuselage, and one 0.303in trainable rearward-firing machine in the rear cockpit, plus an external torpedo, bomb and rocket load of 1600lb (726kg)

126

Fairey Swordfish Mk III

Built by Blackburn to a total of 320 aircraft, the Swordfish Mk III was a development of the Swordfish Mk II with improved anti-submarine capability bestowed by the addition of ASV.Mk X air-to-surface search radar with its antenna in a large radome between the main landing gear legs. In all other respects the Swordfish Mk III was similar to the Swordfish Mk I and Mk II with the exception of a higher all up weight, and like its Mk II stablemate rendered excellent service while operating from small escort carriers charged with protecting Atlantic and Arctic convoys from German submarine attack. The last of the great torpedo attacks made by these aircraft came in 1942, when an attempt was made to prevent the German battleships *Gneisenau* and *Prinz Eugen* passing through the English Channel. The Fleet Air Arm's last Swordfish unit was No 836 Squadron, which was disbanded in May 1945 just after the surrender of Germany.

Country of origin:	United Kingdom
Type:	(Swordfish Mk II) three-seat carrierborne and land-based torpedo bomber, level bomber and reconnaissance aeroplane
Powerplant:	one 775hp (578kW) Bristol Pegasus IIIM3 or 750hp (559kW) Pegasus XXX nine-cylinder single-row radial engine
Performance:	maximum speed 224km/h (139mph); climb to 1525m (5000ft) in 10 minutes 30 seconds; ceiling 3780m (12,400ft); range 1657km (1030 miles)
Weights:	empty 2132kg (4700lb); maximum take-off 4196kg (9250lb)
Dimensions:	span 13.87m (45ft 6in); length 11.07m (36ft 4in) with the tail up; height 4.11m (13ft 5.75in) with the tail up
Armament:	one 0.303in fixed forward-firing machine gun in the starboard side of the forward fuselage, and one 0.303in trainable rearward-firing machine in the rear cockpit, plus an external torpedo, bomb and rocket load of 726kg (1600lb)

Farman F.221 and F.222

The F.220.01 bomber prototype was first flown in May 1932, and was then converted as a long-range mailplane. This was followed by the F.221.01 prototype that differed mainly in its redesigned vertical tail surface, fully enclosed nose and ventral gunner's positions, a semi-retractable 'dustbin' in place of the previous hatch position for the ventral gunner, and a considerably uprated powerplant. Next were 10 F.221BN.5 bombers with enhanced defensive armament, and then the F.222BN.5 that was produced in two variants as 11 F.222.1BN.5 machines with retractable main landing gear units and 24 F.222.2BN.5 machines with a lengthened nose and dihedralled outer wing panels. Some 29 aircraft were in service in 1939, and before the fall of France operated in the bomber role before being relegated to transport use up to 1944. Pictured here is an F.222.1 of the 2nd Escadrille, GB I/15, based at Reims-Courcy in May 1940.

Country of origin:	France
Type:	(F.222.2BN.5) five-seat heavy night bomber
Powerplant:	four 970hp (723kW) Gnome-Rhòne 14N-11/15 radial engines
Performance:	maximum speed 320km/h (199mph); climb to 4000m (13,125ft) in 13 minutes 30 seconds; service ceiling 8000m (26,245ft); range 2000km (1243 miles) with a 2500kg (5511lb) bomb load
Weights:	empty 10,500kg (23,148lb); normal take-off 15,200kg (33,510lb); maximum take-off 18,700kg (41,226lb)
Dimensions:	span 36.00m (118ft 1.33in); length 21.45m (70ft 4.5in); height 5.19m (17ft 0.33in)
Armament:	one 7.5mm trainable forward-firing machine gun in the nose turret, one 7.5mm trainable machine gun in the dorsal turret, and one 7.5mm trainable rearward-firing machine gun in the ventral 'dustbin' position, plus an internal bomb load of 4200kg (9259lb)

Farman NC.223

The NC.223 (originally F.223) was a completely new aeroplane that retained a conceptual affinity to its F.222 predecessor, and in overall terms was a blend of ancient and modern. In addition to the obsolete configuration retained from the F.222 bomber, the F.223 was also designed with the rectangular-section fuselage of the F.222. A revised tail unit with two vertical surfaces was added, but in contrast to these drag-producing features an excellent wing of modern stressed-skin concept with braced outer ends was used. The F.223.1.01 was a mailplane prototype and was followed into the air during January 1938 by the NC.223.01 bomber prototype. This was followed by eight or possibly more NC.223.3BN.5 production aircraft that entered service during the Battle of France. The aircraft were then converted as transports. Shown here is *Jules Verne*, one of the NC.223.4 aircraft operated as a long-range bomber by the French Air Force in the opening months of the war.

Country of origin:	France
Type:	(NC.223.3BN.5) five-seat heavy night bomber
Powerplant:	four 920hp (686kW) Hispano-Suiza 12Y-29 12-cylinder Vee engines
Performance:	maximum speed 400km/h (249mph); climb to 4000m (13,125ft) in 10 minutes; absolute ceiling 8000m (26,245ft); range 2400km (1491 miles)
Weights:	empty 10,550kg (23,258lb); maximum take-off 19,200kg (42,329lb)
Dimensions:	span 33.58m (110ft 2in); length 22.00m (72ft 2in); height 5.08m (16ft 8in)
Armament:	one 20mm trainable cannon in the dorsal turret, one 20mm trainable rearward-firing cannon in the ventral turret, and one 7.5mm trainable forward-firing machine gun in the nose position, plus an internal bomb load of 4200kg (9259lb)

Fiat BR.20 Cicogna

The BR.20 Cicogna (stork) was the first 'modern' medium bomber produced in Italy during the period leading up to World War II, and first flew in prototype form during February 1936 for service from the autumn of the same year. Delivery of 320 aircraft, including 85 for Japan and one for Venezuela, was followed by production of 264 improved BR.20M bombers. This model featured improved nose contours, revised armament and increased armour protection. The final variant was the BR.20bis (15 aircraft) with two 1250hp (932kW) Fiat A.82 RC.42S radial engines, a redesigned nose, two 7.7mm machine guns in waist positions, and a power-operated dorsal turret. More than 160 Cicogna bombers were available when Italy entered World War II, and all but a handful were lost in extensive operations before Italy's September 1943 armistice with the Allies. Pictured here is a BR.20M of the 4th Squdriglia, 11th Gruppo, 13th Stormo, based in Belgium during late 1940.

Country of origin:	Italy
Type:	(BR.20M) five-seat medium bomber
Powerplant:	two 1030hp (768kW) Fiat A.80 RC.41 14-cylinder two-row radial engines
Performance:	maximum speed 430km/h (267mph); climb to 5000m (16,405ft) in 17 minutes 56 seconds; service ceiling 7200m (23,620ft); range 1240km (770.5 miles) with a 1000kg (2205lb) bomb load
Weights:	empty 6740kg (14,859lb); maximum take-off 10,340kg (22,795lb)
Dimensions:	span 21.56m (70ft 8.8in); length 16.17m (53ft 0.5in); height 4.30m (14ft 1.25in)
Armament:	one 7.7mm trainable forward-firing machine gun in the nose turret, two 7.7mm or one 12.7mm trainable rearward-firing machine guns in the dorsal turret, and one 7.7mm trainable machine gun in the ventral hatch position, plus an internal bomb load of 1600kg (3527lb)

Fieseler Fi 156 Storch

One of the most remarkable aircraft produced by the German aero industry during the Nazi regime, the Storch (stork) remains a vivid example of Gerhard Fieseler's interest in STOL aircraft with powerful high-lift devices. This is borne out by some remarkable statistics: the Storch could take-off in 71 yards (65m), land in 22 yards (20m) and virtually hover in a 25mph (40km/h) wind without any loss of control. Resulting from a 1935 requirement for an army co-operation, casualty evacuation and liaison aeroplane, the Fi 156 first flew in the spring of 1936 and entered service in 1937. Production totalled about 2900 aircraft, and the main variants were the initial, unarmed Fi 156A model, Fi-156C armed model in four main subvariants, and Fi 156D air ambulance model in two subvariants. Pictured here is an Fi 156C Storch of the *Kurierstaffel Oberkommando de Luftwaffe*, operating on the Don section of the Eastern Front in August 1942.

Country of origin:	Germany
Type:	(Fi 156C-2) three-seat army co-operation, battlefield reconnaissance, liaison and casualty evacuation aeroplane
Powerplant:	one 240hp (179kW) Argus As 10C-3 eight-cylinder inverted-Vee engine
Performance:	maximum speed 175km/h (109mph); climb to 1000 m (3280ft) in 3 minutes 24 seconds; service ceiling 5200m (17,060ft); range 1015km (631 miles)
Weights:	empty 940kg (2072lb); maximum take-off 1320kg (2910lb)
Dimensions:	span 14.25m (46ft 9in); length 9.90m (32ft 5.75in); height 3.05m (10ft)
Armament:	one 7.92mm trainable rearward-firing machine gun in the rear of the cockpit

Fieseler Fi 167

In 1936 the German navy laid down its first aircraft carrier, which was launched in 1938 but never completed. Shortly after the keel of the new ship had been laid, the German air ministry issued to selected companies a requirement for a multi-role carrierborne warplane with excellent STOL capability, a folding biplane wing cellule, and the strength to make dive-bombing attacks at high speeds. Only Arado and Fieseler responded, and the two Fi 167 prototypes revealed good handling (including the ability to land at very low speeds), performance and payload. Fieseler received an order for 12 Fi 167A-0 pre-production aircraft with jettisonable main landing gear units but the abandonment of the carrier programme made the Fi 167 superfluous and nine aircraft were passed to Romania for coastal operations over the Black Sea. Shown here is an Fi 167A-0 of *Erprobungsstaffel* 167, based in the Netherlands during 1940-42.

Country of origin:	Germany
Type:	Fi 167A-0) two-seat torpedo bomber and reconnaissance aeroplane
Powerplant:	one 1100hp (820kW) Daimler-Benz DB 601B 12-cylinder inverted-Vee engine
Performance:	maximum speed 325km/h (202mph); climb to 1000m (3280ft) in 2 minutes 42 seconds; service ceiling 8200m (26,905ft); range 1500km (932 miles)
Weights:	empty 2800kg (6173lb); maximum take-off 4850kg (10,692lb)
Dimensions:	span 13.50m (44ft 3.5in); length 11.40m (37ft 4.75in); height 4.80m (15ft 9in)
Armament:	one 7.92mm fixed forward-firing machine gun in the starboard upper side of the forward fuselage, and one 7.92mm trainable rearward-firing machine gun in the rear cockpit, plus an external torpedo and bomb load of 1000kg (2205lb)

Focke-Wulf Fw 187 Falke

Early in 1936 Kurt Tank began work on the design of a twin-engined heavy fighter which, he estimated, would attain a maximum speed of 560km/h (348mph) with two 960hp (716kW) Daimler-Benz DB 600 engines. Work later began on two initial prototypes, and the first of these made its maiden flight in the summer of 1937 with two 680hp (507kW) Junkers Jumo 210Da engines. There followed four more prototypes armed with two 7.92mm machine guns and a pair of 20mm cannon, a lengthened cockpit canopy, revised engine nacelles and, in the sixth machine, two DB 600A engines. The final order was for three Fw 187A-0 pre-production aircraft with heavier armament, and these were used by a unit protecting the Focke-Wulf factory in summer 1940 before undergoing fruitless trials with 13. (Zerstörer) Staffel of JG 77 in Norway. The aircraft pictured was part of the unit tasked with defending the Focke-Wulfe factory.

Country of origin:	Germany
Type:	(Fw 187A-0) two-seat heavy fighter
Powerplant:	two 700hp (522kW) Junkers Jumo 210Ga 12-cylinder inverted-Vee engines
Performance:	maximum speed 529km/h (329mph); climb to 6000m (19,685ft) in 5 minutes 48 seconds; service ceiling 10,000m (32,810ft)
Weights:	empty 3700kg (8157lb); maximum take-off 5000kg (11,023lb)
Dimensions:	span 15.30 m (50ft 2.25in); length 11.10m (36ft 5in); height 3.85m (12ft 7.5in)
Armament:	two 20mm fixed forward-firing cannon and four 7.92mm fixed forward-firing machine guns in the nose

Focke-Wulf Fw 189 Eule

Given the fact that the Luftwaffe was designed primarily as a tactical air force for the support of the army, it is an unusual reflection on the service's overall thinking that during World War II it used only two main types of short-range reconnaissance aircraft, one of them Focke-Wulf Fw 189 Eule (owl) twin-boom monoplane with the crew in an extensively glazed central nacelle. This first flew in July 1938 and entered service late in 1940. Production totalled 848 excluding 16 prototype and pre-production aircraft. The main model was the Fw 189A in subvariants such as the baseline Fw 189A-1, Fw 189A-2 with twin rather than single defensive machine guns, Fw 189A-3 dual-control trainer, and Fw 189A-4 tactical support model with ventral armour and 20mm cannon rather than machine guns in the wing roots. Pictured here is an Fw 189A-2 of 1.(H) Staffel, Aufklärungsgruppe 32, based on the Eastern Front in 1943.

Country of origin:	Germany
Type:	(Fw 189A-2) three-seat short-range tactical reconnaissance aeroplane with limited close-support and night fighter capabilities
Powerplant:	two 465hp (347kW) Argus As 410A-1 12-cylinder engines
Performance:	maximum speed 350km/h (217mph); climb to 4000m (13,125ft) in 8 minutes 18 seconds; service ceiling 7300m (23,950ft); range 670km (416 miles)
Weights:	empty 3245kg (7154lb); maximum take-off 4170kg (9193lb)
Dimensions:	span 18.40m (60ft 4.5in); length 12.03m (39ft 5.5in); height 3.10m (10ft 2in)
Armament:	two 7.92mm fixed forward-firing machine guns in wing roots, one 7.92mm two-barrel machine gun in dorsal position, and one 7.92mm two-barrel machine gun in the tailcone turret, plus a bomb load of 200kg (441lb)

Focke-Wulf Fw 189 Uhu

Despite the apparent fragility of the design the success of the Fw 189 Eule on the Eastern Front led to its adaptation to a wide variety of roles. In addition to the close-support role the Fw 189 was adapted for use as a night-fighter. At least 30 A-1s were modified to serve in this role. Conversion involved removing reconnaissance equipment and various other items, adding FuG 212 *Lichtenstein* C-1 interception radar, with the usual quad array of dipole aerials mounted ahead of the nose, and replacing the mid-upper MG 81Z guns by a fixed, oblique forward/upwards-firing MG 151/15 (sometimes this was replaced by an MG 15/20). This armament arrangement was commonly known as 'schräge Musik'. Night fighter Fw 189s were operated by I/NJG 100 and NJG 5. Pictured here is one of the aircraft on the strength of Stab/Nachtjagdgeschwader 100, operating from Greifswald in February 1945 towards the end of the war.

Country of origin:	Germany
Type:	(Fw 189A-1) three-seat night fighter
Powerplant:	two 465hp (347kW) Argus As 410A-1 12-cylinder engines
Performance:	maximum speed 350km/h (217mph); climb to 4000m (13,125ft) in 8 minutes 18 seconds; service ceiling 7300m (23,950ft); range 670km (416 miles)
Weights:	empty 3245kg (7154lb); maximum take-off 4170kg (9193lb)
Dimensions:	span 18.40m (60ft 4.5in); length 12.03m (39ft 5.5in); height 3.10m (10ft 2in)
Armament:	two 7.92mm fixed forward-firing machine guns in wing roots, one 15mm obliquely forward/upward-firing cannon, and one 7.92mm two-barrel machine gun in the tailcone turret, plus a bomb load of 200kg (441lb)

Focke-Wulf Fw 190A-1 to A-4

The Fw 190 was the only German fighter to enter service and large-scale production during the course of the war, and despite being designed for a radial engine was developed to a definitive standard as the Fw 190D with a Vee engine. The first Fw 190 prototype flew in June 1939 and, after intensive development concentrated on the alternative BMW 139 or BMW 801 engines and a shorter- or longer-span wing, the Fw 190A entered production with the BMW 801 and larger wing. The 40 Fw 190A-0 pre-production aircraft were followed by 100 Fw 190A-1 fighters, and the type entered service in the autumn of 1941. There followed 426 longer-span Fw 190A-2 fighters with heavier armament, 509 Fw 190A-3 fighter-bombers with revised armament, and 894 Fw 190A-4 fighter-bombers with a methanol/water power boost system. Pictured here is a Fw 190A-4/U3 of the Gefechtsverband Druschel (II/SchG-1), during the battle for Kursk in July 1943.

Country of origin:	Germany
Type:	(Fw 190A-3) single-seat fighter-bomber
Powerplant:	one 1700hp (1267.5kW) BMW 801D-2 14-cylinder two-row radial engine
Performance:	maximum speed 605km/h (382mph); initial climb rate 863m (2830ft) per minute; service ceiling 10,600m (34,775ft); range 800km (497 miles)
Weights:	empty 2900kg (6393lb); maximum take-off 3980kg (8770lb)
Dimentions:	span 10.50m (34ft 5.5in); length 8.80m (28ft 10.5in); height 3.95m (12ft 11.5in)
Armament:	four 20mm fixed forward-firing cannon in the leading edges of the wing, and two 7.92mm fixed forward-firing machine guns in the upper part of the forward fuselage

Focke-Wulf Fw 190A-5/A-6

Introduced to service early in 1943, the Fw 190A-5 was an Fw 190A-4 development with the engine relocated some 5.9in (0.15m) farther forward. This restored the centre of gravity to the location it had occupied before its alteration by the addition of extra equipment in the rear fuselage, and the 723 aircraft were delivered or adapted for a number of roles including heavy, night, ground-attack, torpedo and bomber destroyer fighting. The Fw 190A-6, of which 569 were completed, was the production-line version of the Fw 190A-5/U10 fighter with a lightened wing structure that was nonetheless able to accommodate a fixed armament of four 20mm cannon. There were different types of A-6 subvariants, one being a fighter-bomber with provision for 1000kg (2205lb) of bombs and others being bomber-destroyers with 30mm cannon. The aircraft shown here is an Fw 190A-6/R11 of 1./NJG 10 flown by Oberleutenant Hans Krause from Werneuchen in August 1944.

Country of origin:	Germany
Type:	(Fw 190A-6) single-seat fighter-bomber
Powerplant:	one 1700hp (1267.5kW) BMW 801D-2 14-cylinder two-row radial engine
Performance:	maximum speed 605km/h (382mph); initial climb rate 863m (2830ft) per minute; service ceiling 10,600m (34,775ft); range 800km (497 miles)
Weights:	normal take-off 3900kg (8598lb); maximum take-off 4140kg (9127lb)
Dimensions:	span 10.50m (34ft 5.5in); length 8.80m (28ft 10.5in); height 3.95m (12ft 11.5in)
Armament:	four 20mm fixed forward-firing cannon in the leading edges of the wing, and two 7.92mm fixed forward-firing machine guns in the upper part of the forward fuselage

Focke-Wulf Fw 190A-7/A-8

Entering production in December 1943, the Fw 190A-7 was the production derivative of the Fw 190A-5/U9 with a maximum take-off weight of 8818lb (4000kg) and the revised armament of two 20mm cannon in the wing roots and two 13mm machine guns in the forward fuselage. Production totalled only 80 aircraft before the advent of the Fw 190A-8 that was the last new-build variant of the Fw 190A series. Manufactured from December 1943 to the extent of 1334 aircraft, the Fw 190A-8 had a nitrous oxide power boost system and additional fuel capacity in a small rear-fuselage tank. A small number of the aircraft were modified to Fw 190S-8 dual-control trainers in the fashion of the Fw 190S-5 conversion of the Fw 190A-5. Further development of the Fw 190 fighter was centred on the Fw 190D with the Junkers Jumo 211 Vee engine. The aircraft pictured wears the black-white-black 'Defence of the Reich' bands of JG/4's I Gruppe, based at Delmenhorst in 1945.

Country of origin:	Germany
Type:	(Fw 190A-8) single-seat fighter
Powerplant:	one 1700hp (1267.5kW) BMW 801D-2 14-cylinder two-row radial engine
Performance:	maximum speed 656km/h (408mph); climb to 6000m (19,685ft) in 9 minutes 6 seconds; service ceiling 11,400m (37,400ft); range 1470km (915 miles)
Weights:	empty 3470kg (7652lb); maximum take-off 4900kg (10,802lb)
Dimentions:	span 10.51m (34ft 5.5in); length 8.95m (29ft 4.25in); height 3.95m (12ft 11.5in)
Armament:	two 20mm fixed forward-firing cannon in the wing roots, two 20mm fixed forward-firing cannon in the leading edges of the wing, and two 13mm fixed forward-firing machine guns in the upper part of the forward fuselage

Focke-Wulf Fw 190F

Though schemed as a fighter, the Fw 190 was so adaptable that it was readily developed as the Fw 190F series for the dedicated ground-attack role, in which it was preceded by the long-range Fw 190G interim model. Entering service at the end of 1942, the Fw 190F-1 (about 30 aircraft) was the production-line version of the Fw 190A-5/U3 fighter based on the Fw 190A-4 with strengthened landing gear, more armour protection, and a combination of one ETC 501 bomb rack under the fuselage and four ETC 50 bomb racks under the wings. There followed 271 Fw 190F-2s with an improved canopy, about 250 Fw 190F-3s with a revised wing structure, 385 Fw 190F-7s based on the Fw 190A-7, and an unknown number of Fw 190F-9s with the 2270hp (1692.5kW) BMW 801TS/TH turbocharged engine. There were also numerous subvariants. Shown here is 'Blue Eight', and Fw 190F-8 of Schlachtgeschwader 4 during Unternehmen 'Bodenplatte' of January 1st, 1945.

Country of origin:	Germany
Type:	(Fw 190F-3) single-seat ground-attack and close-support fighter
Powerplant:	one 1700hp (1267.5kW) BMW 801D-2 14-cylinder two-row radial engine
Performance:	maximum speed 635km/h (395mph); initial climb rate 642m (2106ft) per minute; service ceiling 10,600m (34,780ft); range 750km (466 miles)
Weights:	empty 3325kg (7328lb); maximum take-off 4925kg (10,858lb)
Dimensions:	span 10.5m (34ft 5.5in); length 8.95m (29ft 4.25in); height 3.95m (12ft 11.5in)
Armament:	two 20mm fixed forward-firing cannon in the wing roots and two 13mm fixed forward-firing machine guns in the upper part of the forward fuselage, plus an external bomb load of 1200kg (2646lb)

Focke-Wulf Fw 200 Condor

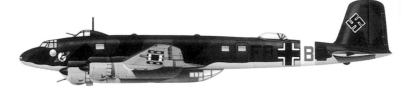

The Condor is best remembered as the long-range reconnaissance aeroplane that searched for Allied convoys in the North Atlantic during World War II and then either attacked them directly with bombs/missiles or vectored-in packs of German U-boats. The type was designed as a transatlantic airliner, however, and first flew in this form during July 1937. The first of 259 Fw 200C military aircraft entered service in September 1939. A few of these aircraft were used as VIP transports, but the majority of the machines were long-range reconnaissance bombers in seven subvariants, some of which spawned their own subvariants with different armament fits, radar fits and provision for missile carriage and guidance, as well as stripped-down forms for special transport tasks. Pictured here is F8-BB, one of the first few 200C-1 Condors with a ventral gondola and full maritime and bombing equipment. It was assigned to Stab I/KG 40 and took part in the invasion of Norway.

Country of origin:	Germany
Type:	(Fw 200C-3/U4) six-seat maritime reconnaissance bomber
Powerplant:	four 1200hp (895kW) BMW-Bramo 323R-2 Fafnir nine-cylinder single-row radial engines
Performance:	maximum speed 360km/h (224mph); service ceiling 6000m (19,685ft); range 4440km (2759 miles)
Weights:	empty 12,950kg (28,549lb); maximum take-off 22,700kg (50,044lb)
Dimensions:	span 32.84m (107ft 8in); length 23.46m (76ft 11.5in); height 6.30m (20ft 8in)
Armament:	one 20mm trainable cannon in forward ventral gondola position, one 13mm trainable machine gun in rear dorsal position, one 13mm trainable machine gun in each beam position, one 7.92mm machine gun in rear ventral position, and one 7.92mm machine gun in forward dorsal turret, plus a bomb load of 2100kg (4630lb)

Fokker C.V

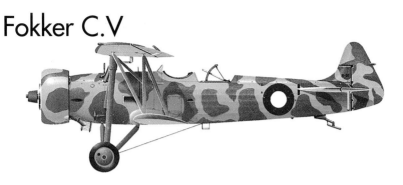

In 1923 Fokker flew the prototype of its C.IV reconnaissance biplane, and in May 1924 followed with the first flight of the C.V that was a development with a slimmer fuselage. The C.V was one the most successful general-purpose aircraft of the 1920s and 1930s, and numbers were still in service with smaller air forces in the first part of World War II. Production exceeded 750 aircraft built in the Netherlands and under licence with a number of air- and water-cooled engine types and wing cellules of different span and area. The two most important models were sesquiplanes with tapered rather than constant-chord wing panels, and were the C.V-D used mainly in the escort fighter and reconnaissance roles, and the C.V-E with an enlarged wing cellule for greater lifting power and therefore used mainly for the bombing role. Pictured is a Fokker C.V of the 3. Eskadrille of Danish army aviation during the mid-1930s.

Country of origin:	Netherlands
Type:	(C.V-D) two-seat reconnaissance and artillery-spotting aeroplane with secondary light bombing and escort capabilities
Powerplant:	one 450hp (335.5kW) Hispano-Suiza 12 12-cylinder Vee engine
Performance:	maximum speed 225km/h (140mph); initial climb rate not available; service ceiling 5500m (18,045ft); range 770km (478 miles)
Weights:	empty 1250kg (2756lb); normal take-off 1850kg (4078lb); maximum take-off 1915kg (4222lb)
Dimentions:	span 12.50m (41ft 0.25in); length 9.50m (31ft 2in); height 3.50m (11ft 5.75in)
Armament:	one or two 7.92mm fixed forward-firing machine guns in forward fuselage, one or two 7.92mm trainable rearward-firing machine guns in the rear cockpit, and provision for one 7.92mm rearward-firing machine gun in the ventral position; bomb load of 200kg (441lb)

Fokker C.X

In 1933 Fokker decided that the time was ripe for the development of a successor to its C.V two-seat warplane, and the resulting C.X was first flown in 1934 as a development of the C.V-E, and thus a trim biplane with fixed landing gear and its predecessor's mixed metal and wood construction. Production totalled 71 aircraft, the later aircraft with an enclosed cockpit, and comprised 32 aircraft for the Netherlands and Dutch East Indies with the 650hp (485kW) Rolls-Royce Kestrel V Vee engine, and 39 aircraft (including 35 built under licence) for Finland with a radial engine. Some 10 aircraft were still in Dutch service in 1940 and were destroyed, but the Finnish aircraft served with modest success throughout the Finnish involvement in World War II and the last was written off only in 1958. Shown here is a Fokker C.X of TLeLV 12, Suomen Ilmavoimat (Finnish Air Force) based at Suur-Merijoki in the winter of 1939-40.

Country of origin:	Netherlands
Type:	(C.X) two-seat tactical reconnaissance and army co-operation warplane
Powerplant:	one 890hp (663.5kW) Tammerfors-built Bristol Pegasus XII or XXI nine-cylinder single-row radial engine
Performance:	maximum speed 335km/h (208mph); climb to 3000m (9845ft) in 6 minutes ; service ceiling 8100m (26,575ft); range 900km (559 miles)
Weights:	empty 1550kg (3417lb); maximum take-off 2900kg(6393lb)
Dimensions:	span 12.00m (39ft 4.5in); length 9.20m (30ft 2.25in); height 3.30m (10ft 10in)
Armament:	one 7.62mm fixed forward-firing machine gun in the upper part of the forward fuselage, and one 7.62mm trainable rearward-firing machine gun in the rear cockpit, plus an external bomb load of 500kg (1102lb)

Fokker D.XXI

Designed to meet a requirement of the Netherlands East Indies Army Air Service, the D.XXI was a moderately advanced fighter in Fokker's traditional mixed metal and wood construction with fixed landing gear but advanced features such as a cantilever low-set wing, an enclosed cockpit and trailing-edge flaps. The D.XXI-1 prototype flew in March 1936, and the type was ordered for Dutch rather than Dutch East Indies service (35 aircraft), with Denmark and Finland taking two and seven aircraft, the former then building another 10 aircraft and the latter 85 (50 with the 825hp/615kW Pratt & Whitney R-1535-SB4 engine) to complement five assembled for spares. most of the Dutch aircraft were destroyed in the German invasion of May 1940, but the Finnish aircraft were moderately successful and the last were not retired until 1948. Shown here is a Fokker D.XXI of TLeLV 12, Suomen Ilmavoimat (Finnish Air Force) in June 1941.

Country of origin:	Netherlands
Type:	(D.XXI-2) single-seat fighter
Powerplant:	one 830hp (619kW) Bristol Mercury VIII nine-cylinder single-row radial engine
Performance:	maximum speed 460km/h (286mph); climb to 6000m (19,685ft) in 7 minutes 30 seconds; service ceiling 11,000m (36,090ft); range 930km (578 miles)
Weights:	empty 1450kg (3197lb); maximum take-off 2050kg (4519lb)
Dimensions:	span 11.00 m (36ft 1in); length 8.20m (26ft 10.75in); height 2.95m (9ft 8in)
Armament:	two 7.92mm fixed forward-firing machine guns in the upper part of the forward fuselage, and two 7.92mm fixed forward-firing machine guns in the leading edges of the wing

Fokker G.I

During the mid-1930s there was considerable interest in the concept of the twin-engined heavy fighter that would offer, in the opinion of many analysts, speed and climb performance comparable with that of single-engined fighters, together with longer range, heavier firepower and all the reliability advantages of a twin-engined powerplant. Among the countries that essayed such a type was the Netherlands with the G.I that first flew in two-seat prototype form during March 1937. About 36 of the two/three-seat G.IA initial production model followed, and orders were placed by six countries for the G.IB export model. Three of these were pressed into Dutch service in May 1940, when virtually all the aircraft were destroyed, and about 20 more were later completed for German use as trainers. Shown here is one of the G.IB aircraft that was thrown into battle against the German invaders by the Luchtvaartafdeling (Dutch Air Force) in May 1940.

Country of origin:	Netherlands
Type:	(G.IA) two/three-seat heavy fighter and close-support warplane
Powerplant:	two 830hp (619kW) Bristol Mercury VIII nine-cylinder single-row radial engines
Performance:	maximum speed 475km/h (295mph); climb to 6000m (19,685ft) in 8 minutes 54 seconds; service ceiling 9300m (30,510ft); range 1500km (932 miles)
Weights:	empty 3330kg (7341lb); maximum take-off 5000kg (11,023lb)
Dimensions:	span 17.16m (56ft 3.6in); length 10.87m (35ft 7.9in); height 3.80m (12ft 5.6in)
Armament:	eight 7.92mm fixed forward-firing machine guns in the nose, and one 7.92mm trainable rearward-firing machine gun in the nacelle tailcone position, plus an external bomb load of 400kg (882lb)

Fokker T.VIII-W

In 1936 the Dutch naval air service issued a requirement for a modern floatplane to replace the wholly obsolete Fokker T.IV-W floatplanes operated by itself and the air arm of the Netherlands East Indies Navy in the torpedo-bombing and reconnaissance roles, and Fokker responded with the T.VIII-W design. This type was first delivered in 1939, and was produced in three forms. The first was the T.VIII-W/G of which 19 were delivered with a mixed metal and wood structure including a rear fuselage of wood, the second was the T.VIII-W/M of which 12 were delivered with a mixed structure including a light alloy rear fuselage, and the third was the somewhat enlarged T.VIII-W/C of which five were delivered to Finland (one of them with wheeled landing gear) with two 890hp (663.5kW) Bristol Mercury XI radial engines. Pictured here is a Fokker T.VIII-Wg of Groep Vliegtuigen 4, Luchtvaartafdeling (Dutch Air Force) operating from Westeindermeer.

Country of origin:	Netherlands
Type:	(T.VIII-W/G) three-seat maritime reconnaissance and torpedo bomber floatplane
Powerplant:	two 450hp (335.5kW) Wright R-975-E3 Whirlwind nine-cylinder single-row radial engines
Performance:	maximum speed 285km/h (177mph); climb to 3000m (9845ft) in 7 minutes 48 seconds; ceiling 6800m (22,310ft); range 2750 km (1709 miles)
Weights:	empty 3100kg (6834lb); maximum take-off 5000kg (11,023lb)
Dimentions:	span 18.00m (59ft 0.33in); length 13.00m (42ft 7.75in); height 5.00m (16ft 4.75in)
Armament:	one 7.92mm fixed forward-firing machine gun in the port side of the forward fuselage, and one 7.92mm trainable rearward-firing machine gun in the rear of the cockpit, plus provision for an internal torpedo and bomb load of 600kg (1323lb)

Gloster Gladiator

The last and finest biplane British fighter, the Gladiator was a conceptual development of the Gauntlet with improved features such as an enclosed cockpit, trailing-edge flaps and cantilever main landing gear legs. The prototype flew in September 1934, and the first of 378 Gladiator Mk I fighters entered service in 1937 pending the large-scale advent of more advanced monoplane fighters. The Gladiator Mk I was supplemented by the Gladiator Mk II, of which 311 were delivered with the Mercury VIIIA or VIIIAS engine. Some 38 of the aircraft were converted to Interim Sea Gladiator standard, paving the way for the carrierborne Sea Gladiator of which 60 were completed. The Gladiator saw first-line service in the northern European and Mediterranean theatres to 1940 and the middle of 1941, and numbers of the aircraft were also exported. Pictured here is a Gladiator Mk II of the Arma de Aeronautica (Portugese Air Force) in 1940.

Country of origin:	United Kingdom
Type:	(Gladiator Mk I) single-seat fighter
Powerplant:	one 830hp (619kW) Bristol Mercury IX nine-cylinder single-row radial engine
Performance:	maximum speed 407km/h (253mph); climb to 4570m (15,000ft) in 5 minutes 40 seconds; service ceiling 9995m (32,800ft); range 689km (428 miles)
Weights:	empty 1633kg (3600lb); maximum take-off 2083kg (4592lb)
Dimensions:	span 9.83m (32ft 3in); length 8.36m (27ft 5in); height 3.22m (10ft 7in)
Armament:	two 0.303in fixed forward-firing machine guns in the sides of the forward fuselage, and two 0.303in fixed forward-firing machine guns in the leading edges of the lower wing

Gotha Go 244

The Go 242 was the German Air Force's standard transport glider in the second half of World War II, deliveries totalling 1526 Go 242A and Go 242B gliders with skid and wheeled landing gear respectively. The success of the latter paved the way for the Go 244 that was in essence a powered version of the glider and evaluated with low-powered German or captured Soviet and French engines. The last were preferred, and deliveries totalled 174 aircraft including 133 Go 242B conversions. These were completed in forms corresponding to the five Go 242B production versions, and were the Go 244B-1 freighter with torsion-bar shock absorption, Go 244B-2 freighter with wider-track main units and oleo shock absorption, Go 244B-3 and B-4 paratroop transport versions of the Go 244B-1 and B-2, and Go 244B-5 with dual controls and balanced rudders. Shown here is a Gotha Go 244B-1 of an unidentified Luftwaffe transport unit.

Country of origin:	Germany
Type:	(Go 244B-2) two-seat transport with accommodation for 23 troops or freight
Powerplant:	two 700hp (522kW) Gnome-Rhône 14M-4/5 14-cylinder two-row radial engines
Performance:	maximum speed 290km/h (180mph); climb to 5000m (16,405ft) in 18 minutes 30 seconds; ceiling 7650m (25,100ft); range 740km (460 miles)
Weights:	empty 5225kg (11,517lb); maximum take-off 7800kg (17,196lb)
Dimensions:	span 24.50m (80ft 4.5in); length 15.80m (51ft 10.25in); height 4.60m (15ft 1in)
Armament:	one 7.92mm machine gun in cockpit roof position, one 7.92mm machine gun in tail of central nacelle, one 7.92mm machine gun in each side of central nacelle, and provision for the troops to fire up to four 7.92mm machine guns from hold windows

Grumman TBF Avenger

Making a disastrous combat debut in the Battle of Midway (June 1942), the TBF rapidly matured as the classic torpedo bomber of World War II. The first of two XTBF-1 prototypes made the type's maiden flight in August 1941. Grumman then built only the TBF-1 model, whose total of 2289 aircraft completed by March 1945 included subvariants such as the baseline TBF-1, winterised TBF-1J Avenger, TBF-1P photo-reconnaissance type, TBF-1B (402 aircraft) delivered to the UK, TBF-1C (764 aircraft) with two 0.5in machine guns in the leading edges of the wing, TBF-1CP photo-reconnaissance type, TBF-1D for the anti-submarine role with radar and underwing rockets, TBF-1E with podded air-to-surface radar, and TBF-1L with a retractable searchlight for night illumination of surfaced submarines. The Royal Navy's wartime Avengers were mostly TBF-1Bs (404 received). In Fleet Air Arm service they were designated Tarpon Mk I and then Avenger Mk I in January 1944.

Country of origin:	USA
Type:	(TBF-1C) three-seat carrierborne and land-based torpedo bomber
Powerplant:	one 1700hp (1268kW) Wright R-2600-8 Cyclone 14 14-cylinder two-row radial engine
Performance:	maximum speed 414km/h (257mph); climb to 3050m (10,000ft) in 13 minutes; service ceiling 6525m (21,400ft); range 4321km (2685 miles)
Weights:	empty 4788kg (10,555lb); maximum take-off 7876kg (17,364lb)
Dimensions:	span 16.51m (54ft 2in); length 12.42m (40ft 9in); height 4.19m (13ft 9in)
Armament:	two 0.5in fixed forward-firing machine guns in the leading edges of the wing, one 0.5in Browning trainable rearward-firing machine gun in the dorsal turret, and one 0.3in rearward-firing machine gun in ventral position, plus torpedo, bomb and rocket load of 1134kg (2500lb)

Grumman TBM Avenger

With Avenger requirements far exceeding Grumman's production capabilities, the bulk of production was undertaken by the Eastern Aircraft Division of the General Motors Corporation, which produced the TBM model to the extent of 7546 aircraft up to September 1945. These were 550 TBM-1 and 2332 TBM-1C analogues of the TBF-1 and TBF-1C, and then 4657 examples of the TBM-3 series with the more powerful R-2600-20 engine. The TBM-3 was produced in a number of subvariants similar to those of the TBM-1 but also including the TBM-3D with anti-submarine radar and the TBM-3E with podded anti-submarine radar. Many aircraft were transferred under Lend-Lease, and numerous other subvariants appeared after the war for a number of increasingly important tasks. Pictured is one of the General Motors-built TBM-3 aircraft, operating from USS *Randolph*, part of Task Force 58 in January 1945.

Country of origin:	USA
Type:	(TBM-3E) three-seat carrierborne and land-based torpedo bomber
Powerplant:	one 1900hp (1417kW) Wright R-2600-20 Cyclone 14 14-cylinder two-row radial engine
Performance:	maximum speed 444km/h (276mph); initial climb rate 628m (2060ft) per minute; service ceiling 9175m (30,100ft); range 3090km (1920 miles)
Weights:	empty 4783kg (10,545lb); maximum take-off 8117kg (17,895lb)
Dimensions:	span 16.51m (54ft 2in); length 12.48m (40ft 11.5in); height 5.00m (16ft 5in)
Armament:	two 0.5in fixed forward-firing machine guns in leading edges of the wing, one 0.5in Browning machine gun in dorsal turret, and provision for one 0.3in machine gun in ventral position, plus a torpedo, bomb and rocket load of 1134kg (2500lb)

Grumman F3F

This G-11 design was evolved by Grumman as a slightly enlarged version of the G-8 (F2F) fighter with changes to correct the earlier warplane's lack of directional stability and tendency to spin. The US Navy ordered a single XF3F-1 prototype, and this made its maiden flight in March 1935 with the Pratt & Whitney R-1535-72 Twin Wasp Junior engine. Two other prototypes followed before the US Navy contracted for 54 examples of the F3F-1 production version that differed from the third XF3F-1 only in a slight increase in fuselage length. The aircraft were delivered between January and September 1936, and were initially flown by three squadrons, namely VF-5B and VF-6B (later VF-4 and VF-3) on the aircraft carriers USS *Ranger* and USS *Saratoga,* and VF-4M (later VMF-2) of the US Marine Corps shore-based at San Diego. These aircraft were the forerunners of the famous 'Cat' series of fleet fighters that formed the basis of US Navy air strength during the Pacific campaign.

Country of origin:	USA
Type:	(F3F-1) single-seat carrierborne and land-based fighter and fighter-bomber
Powerplant:	one 700hp (522kW) Pratt & Whitney R-1535-84 Twin Wasp Junior 14-cylinder two-row radial engine
Performance:	maximum speed 372km/h (231mph); initial climb rate 579m (1900ft) per minute; service ceiling 8685m (28,500ft); range 1609km (1000 miles)
Weights:	empty 1339kg (2952lb); maximum take-off 1997kg (4403lb)
Dimensions:	span 9.75m (32ft); length 7.09m (23ft 3.1in); height 2.77m (9ft 1in)
Armament:	one 0.5in fixed forward-firing machine gun and one 0.3in fixed forward-firing machine gun in the upper part of the forward fuselage, plus an external bomb load of 105kg (232lb)

Grumman F3F-2

In June 1936 Grumman proposed an F3F-1 development with the Wright R-1820-22 engine. The US Navy ordered an XF3F-2 prototype that made its initial flight in July 1936. This prototype also featured an increase in the internal fuel capacity, and this was retained for the 81 F3F-2 production aircraft that were delivered between July 1937 and May 1938 and supplemented by the XF3F-2 upgraded to production standard. Delivered between December 1938 and May 1939, the 27 F3F-3 aircraft differed only in their low-drag engine cowlings, revised cockpit enclosure, and modified wing leading edges. Some 76 F3F aircraft were in service with training units and another 101 were on the verge of transfer to other such units in December 1941, and the last of these aircraft was finally retired in November 1943. Pictured here is an F2F-1 of VF-2B, operating from USS *Lexington*. This unit was the first and last to operate the F2F-1, from February 1935 to September 1940.

Country of origin:	USA
Type:	(F3F-2) single-seat carrierborne and land-based fighter and fighter-bomber
Powerplant:	one 950hp (708kW) Wright R-1820-22 Cyclone nine-cylinder single-row radial engine
Performance:	maximum speed 418km/h (260mph); initial climb rate 853m (2800ft) per minute; service ceiling 9845m (32,300ft); range 1819km (1130 miles)
Weights:	empty 1476kg (3254lb); maximum take-off 2155kg (4750lb)
Dimensions:	span 9.75m (32ft); length 7.01m (23ft); height 9ft 4in (2.84m)
Armament:	one 0.5in fixed forward-firing machine gun and one 0.3in fixed forward-firing machine gun in the upper part of the forward fuselage, plus an external bomb load of 105kg (232lb)

Grumman F6F-3 Hellcat

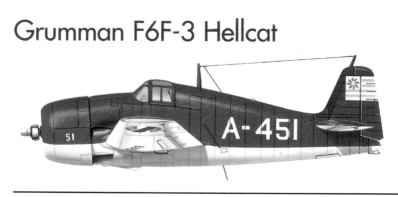

The most successful fighter of the Pacific campaign, shooting down 5156 Japanese aircraft for the loss of only 270 of its own number in air-to-air combat; the F6F was designed from the spring of 1941 as an F4F successor. The F6F was in effect an enlarged and better streamlined F4F with a considerably more potent engine, and the XF6F-3 first prototype flew in June 1942. The F6F-3 initial production model (4402 aircraft including 205 F6F-3N night-fighters and 18 radar-equipped F6F-3E night intruders) entered combat in August 1943, and soon revealed a superb balance of high performance, hard-hitting firepower, great strength and adequate agility. Some 252 of the standard fighters were transferred under Lend-Lease to the UK for service with the Fleet Air Arm with the designation Gannet Mk I soon changed to Hellcat Mk I. Pictured here is one of F6F-5 Hellcats supplied to the Aviacion Navale Uruguaya.

Country of origin:	USA
Type:	(F6F-3): single-seat carrierborne fighter and fighter-bomber
Powerplant:	one 2000hp (1491kW) Pratt & Whitney R-2800-10 or -10W Double Wasp 18-cylinder two-row radial engine
Performance:	maximum speed 603km/h (375mph); initial climb rate 1067m (3500ft) per minute; service ceiling 11705m (38,400ft); range 2559km (1590 miles)
Weights:	empty 4128kg (9101lb); maximum take-off 7025kg (15,487lb)
Dimensions:	span 13.06m (42ft 10in); length 10.24m (33ft 7in); height 3.99m (13ft 1in)
Armament:	six 0.5in fixed forward-firing machine guns in the leading edges of the wing, plus an external bomb load of 454kg (1000lb)

Grumman F6F-5 Hellcat

The F6F-3 was essentially 'right', so the succeeding F6F-5 was little more than a product-improved F6F-3 with a redesigned and closer-fitting engine cowling, strengthened airframe, flat windscreen, spring-tab ailerons, and improved fighter-bomber capability with two 1000lb (454kg) bombs or 11.75in (298mm) 'Tiny Tim' rockets and six 5in (127mm) rockets. The first F6F-5 flew in April 1944, and production totalled 7868 aircraft including 1432 F6F-5N night-fighters with radar and, in later aircraft, two of the machine guns replaced by 20mm cannon. The only other World War II variant was the F6F-5P unarmed photo-reconnaissance conversion. Under the terms of the Lend-Lease Act, the UK received 930 F6F-5 and F6F-5N fighters for service as the Hellcat F.Mk II and Hellcat NF.Mk II. Pictured is JZ999, one of the Fleet Air Arm's Hellcat NF.Mk II night-fighters, built as F6F-5N with 3cm radar, showing to good effect the overall midnight blue paint scheme.

Country of origin:	USA
Type:	(F6F-5N) single-seat carrierborne night-fighter
Powerplant:	one 2000hp (1491kW) Pratt & Whitney R-2800-10W Double Wasp 18-cylinder two-row radial engine
Performance:	maximum speed 589km/h (366mph); initial climb rate 866m (2840ft) per minute; service ceiling 11,185m (36,700ft); range 2028km (1260 miles)
Weights:	empty 4273kg (9421lb); maximum take-off 6464kg (14,250lb)
Dimensions:	span 13.06m (42ft 10in); length 10.24m (33ft 7in); height 3.99m (13ft 1in)
Armament:	six 0.5in fixed forward-firing machine guns or two 20mm fixed forward-firing cannon and four 0.5in fixed forward-firing machine guns in the leading edges of the wing

Grumman F4F Wildcat

The F4F was the US Navy's most important fighter at the time of the USA's entry into World War II in December 1941 after the Japanese attack on Pearl Harbor, and it remained in production right through the war. The aircraft was originally schemed as the XF4F-1 biplane, before being revised as the XF4F-2 monoplane that first flew in September 1937. This was followed by the XF4F-3 that paved the way for the 284 F4F-3 initial production aircraft with the R-1830-76 engine. Later variants were the F4F-3A with the R-1830-90 engine (95 aircraft), F4F-4 with manually folding wing tips (1144 aircraft) and unarmed photo-reconnaissance F4F-7 (21 aircraft). General Motors also built 1140 FM-1 (F4F-4) aircraft and 4467 FM-2 aircraft with the R-1830-56 engine and a taller fin. The 1082 F4Fs were delivered to the UK, where the type was initially known as the Martlet and then as the Wildcat in variants up to the Mk VI.

Country of origin:	USA
Type:	(F4F-4 and Wildcat Mk II) single-seat carrierborne fighter and fighter-bomber
Powerplant:	one 1200hp (895kW) Pratt & Whitney R-1830-86 Twin Wasp 14-cylinder two-row radial engine
Performance:	maximum speed 512km/h (318mph); initial climb rate 594m (1950ft) per minute; service ceiling 10,365m (34,000ft); range 2012km (1250 miles)
Weights:	empty 2612kg (5758lb); maximum take-off 3607kg (7952lb)
Dimentions:	span 11.58m (38ft 0in); length 8.76m (28ft 9in); height 2.81m (9ft 2.5in)
Armament:	six 0.5in fixed forward-firing machine guns in the leading edges of the wing, plus an external bomb load of 91kg (200lb)

Handley Page Hampden

One of the most important medium bombers available to the British at the start of World War II, the Hampden was in many ways a good warplane but was hampered by its narrow fuselage, which prevented crew members from taking over the task of another should he be injured. The Hampden prototype first flew in June 1937, and deliveries of the Hampden Mk I started in September 1938. Deliveries of this model amounted to 1,430 aircraft from two British and one Canadian manufacturers, the last contributing 160 machines. Further capability came from the availability for training purposes of 100 Hereford aircraft that differed only in its powerplant of two 1000hp (746kW) Napier Dagger engines. Nine Herefords were converted to Hampden standard, and from 1942 some 141 surviving Hampden bombers were adapted as Hampden TB.Mk I torpedo bombers for the anti-shipping role. Pictured is a TB.Mk 1 of an Operational Training Unit in Scotland during 1942.

Country of origin:	United Kingdom
Type:	(Hampden Mk I) four-seat medium bomber
Powerplant:	two 1000hp (746kW) Bristol Pegasus XVIII nine-cylinder single-row radial engines
Performance:	maximum speed 426km/h (255mph); climb to 4570m (15,000ft) in 18 minutes 54 seconds; service ceiling 6920m (22,700ft); range 3034km (1885 miles) with a 907kg (2000lb) bomb load
Weights:	empty 5343kg (11,780lb); maximum take-off 10,206kg (22,500lb)
Dimensions:	span 21.08 m (69ft 2in); length 16.33m (53ft 7in); height 4.55m (14ft 11in)
Armament:	one 0.303in fixed forward-firing machine gun in port side of the forward fuselage, one 0.303in forward-firing machine gun in nose position,two 0.303in machine guns in dorsal position, two 0.303in machine guns in ventral position; bomb load of 1814kg (4000lb)

Handley Page Halifax

The Halifax was the main, but ultimately less glamorous partner to the Lancaster in the RAF heavy bomber force during the second half of World War II. It proved to be a highly versatile warplane and also undertook maritime reconnaissance, transport and airborne forces roles. The two prototypes, of which the first flew in October 1939, were followed by the Halifax Mk I (84 aircraft in three series) that entered service in November 1940 with 1280hp (954kW) Rolls-Royce Merlin X Vee engines, and the Halifax Mk II (1977 aircraft in three sub-series) with 1390hp (1036kW) Merlin XX or XXII engines. The Halifax Mk III saw a switch to Bristol Hercules radial engines; 2091 aircraft were made by five manufacturers. The Halifax Mk V, of which 904 were completed by two manufacturers in three sub-series, was an improved Mk II and was delivered in both bomber and maritime reconnaissance forms. The aircraft pictured has the markings of a Pathfinder unit.

Country of origin:	United Kingdom
Type:	(Halifax Mk III) seven-seat heavy bomber
Powerplant:	four 1615hp (1204kW) Bristol Hercules VI or XVI 14-cylinder two-row radial engines
Performance:	maximum speed 454km/h (282mph); climb to 6095m (20,000ft) in 37 minutes 30 seconds; service ceiling 7315m (24,000ft); range 3194km (1985 miles) with a 3175kg (7000lb) bomb load
Weights:	empty 19,278kg (42,500lb); maximum take-off 29,484kg (65,000lb)
Dimensions:	span 30.07m (98ft 8in) or in later aircraft 31.59 m (103ft 8in); length 21.74m (71ft 4in); height 6.12m (20ft 1in)
Armament:	one 0.303in trainable forward-firing machine gun in the nose position, four 0.303in trainable machine guns in the dorsal turret, and four 0.303in trainable machine guns in the tail turret, plus an internal bomb load of 6577kg (14,500lb)

Handley Page Halifax (electronic countermeasures)

The slight superiority of the Lancaster over the Halifax in the night bomber role meant that a number of comparatively early Halifax aircraft were made available for other roles. Halifax A.Mk III, for example, was the designation of Mk III bombers converted for the glider-towing role, while Halifax C.Mk III was the designation of Mk III bombers adapted as troop transports with fuselage accommodation for up to 24 men. The Halifax Mk III was also used for clandestine operations, two special duties squadrons (Nos 138 and 161) operating the type for the delivery of agents and equipment by parachute into German-held territory. No.100 Group of Bomber Command operated Halifax bombers converted for the increasingly important electronic countermeasures role to degrade the capabilities of the Germans' radar and radio systems as an aid to other more conventional operations.

Country of origin:	United Kingdom
Type:	seven-seat electronic countermeasures aircraft
Powerplant:	four 1615hp (1204kW) Bristol Hercules VI or XVI 14-cylinder two-row radial engines
Performance:	maximum speed 454km/h (282mph); climb to 6095m (20,000ft) in 37 minutes 30 seconds; service ceiling 7315mt (24,000f); range 3194km (1985 miles)
Weights:	empty 19,278kg (42,500lb); maximum take-off 29,484kg (65,000lb)
Dimentions:	span 31.59 m (103ft 8in); length 21.74m (71ft 4in); height 6.12m (20ft 1in)
Armament:	one 0.303in trainable forward-firing machine gun in the nose position, four 0.303in trainable machine guns in the dorsal turret, and four 0.303in trainable machine guns in the tail turret

Handley Page Halifax B Mk VI

First flown in October 1944 and built to the extent of 467 aircraft, the Halifax B.Mk VI was an improved Halifax Mk III intended for South-East Asian operations and therefore fitted with an uprated powerplant and an enlarged fuel capacity. A number of the aircraft were later converted as Halifax C.Mk VI 24-passenger transports as well as Halifax GR.Mk VI and Met.Mk VI maritime and meteorological reconnaissance machines. Another 193 aircraft were completed to Hercules B.Mk VII standard with 1615hp (1204kW) Hercules XVI engines, and many of these machines were later converted as Halifax C.Mk VII 24-passenger transports. The Halifax A.Mk VII (234 aircraft) was a glider tug, and some of these were also later converted as Halifax C.Mk VII 24-passenger transports, while the Halifax C.Mk VIII (96 aircraft) were 11-passenger transports. Further models were introduced following the end of World War II.

Country of origin:	United Kingdom
Type:	(Halifax B.Mk VI) seven-seat heavy bomber
Powerplant:	four 1675hp (1249kW) Bristol Hercules 100 14-cylinder two-row radial engines
Performance:	maximum speed 502km/h (312mph); climb to 6095m (20,000ft) in 50 minutes; service ceiling 6705m (22,000ft); range 1260 miles (2028km) with maximum bomb load
Weights:	empty 17,690kg (39,000lb); maximum take-off 30,845kg (68,000lb)
Dimensions:	span 31.75m (104ft 2in); length 21.82m (71ft 7in); height 6.32m (20ft 9in)
Armament:	one 0.303in trainable forward-firing machine gun in the nose position, four 0.303in trainable machine guns in the dorsal turret, and four 0.303in trainable machine guns in the tail turret, plus an internal and external bomb load of 6577kg (14,500lb)

Hawker Fury Mk I/II

The Fury Mk I entered service in 1931 as the first British fighter capable of more than 200mph (322km/h). As a private venture Hawker then produced the Intermediate Fury and the High-Speed Fury for the evaluation of improved features. These two aircraft paved the way to the Fury Mk II that was a Fury Mk I development with spatted wheels and the uprated Kestrel VI engine whose 20 per cent greater power provided eight per cent and 34 per cent increases in speed and climb rate respectively. The Fury Mk II was accepted as an interim type, and 98 aircraft were completed for service from early 1937 with five RAF squadrons. After they were retired in 1939, most of the aircraft were stored. The previous year 24 had been shipped to South Africa, where they equipped three squadrons that were deployed to East Africa in 1940-41 for possible operations against the Italians. Pictured is a Fury Mk I of No I(F) Squadron, based at Tangmere in 1936-37.

Country of origin:	United Kingdom
Type:	(Fury Mk II) single-seat fighter
Powerplant:	one 640hp (477kW) Rolls-Royce Kestrel VI 12-cylinder Vee engine
Performance:	maximum speed 359km/h (223mph); climb to 3050m (10,000ft) in 3 minutes 50 seconds; service ceiling 8990m (29,500ft); range 434.5km (270 miles)
Weights:	empty 1240kg (2734lb); maximum take-off 1637kg (3609lb)
Dimensions:	span 9.14m (30ft); length 8.15m (26ft 9in); height 3.10m (10ft 2in)
Armament:	two 0.303in fixed forward-firing machine guns in the upper part of the forward fuselage

Hawker Hart

Aclassic warplane that emerged in the late 1920s and resulted in more aircraft of the basic and derived series than any other British aeroplane of the period between the two world wars, the Hart was the result of a 1926 requirement for a fast day bomber to replace the Airco (de Havilland) D.H.9A and Fairey Fawn. The design was based on the concept of maximum aerodynamic efficiency, and the prototype made its maiden flight in June 1928. There followed 450 Hart Bomber, nine Hart Communications and 507 Hart Trainer aircraft for British service, as well as a number of export machines. These included ten dual control trainers that were built for the Royal Australian Air Force, which designated them Demon Mk II. The Hart was withdrawn from first-line service in the UK during 1938 but was still significant as a trainer after this time. A small number of the aircraft were operational in the Middle East and East Africa up to 1943.

Country of origin:	United Kingdom
Type:	(Hart Bomber) two-seat light day bomber
Powerplant:	one 525hp (391kW) Rolls-Royce Kestrel IB or XDR 12-cylinder Vee engine
Performance:	maximum speed 296km/h (184mph); climb to 3050m (10,000ft) in 8 minutes; service ceiling 6510m (21,350ft); range 756km (470 miles)
Weights:	empty 1148kg (2530lb); maximum take-off 2066kg (4554lb)
Performance:	span 11.35m (37ft 3in); length 8.94m (29ft 4in); height 3.17m (10ft 5in)
Armament:	one 0.303in fixed forward-firing machine gun in the port side of the forward fuselage, and one 0.303in trainable rearward-firing machine gun in the rear cockpit, plus an external bomb load of 263kg (580lb)

Hawker Hurricane Mk I

Although the Spitfire has come to be remembered as the fighter that 'won' the Battle of Britain, it was in fact the sturdy and stable Hurricane that served in larger numbers and destroyed more German aircraft than the rest of the defences combined. The Hurricane was the first monoplane fighter to enter British service in the 1930s. Sidney Camm's design was not as advanced technically as the Spitfire and it had an unstressed covering largely of fabric. The prototype first flew in November 1935, and the Hurricane Mk I entered service late in 1937 with a two-blade fixed-pitch propeller that later gave way to a three-blade constant-speed unit. Equipping 19 squadrons on the outbreak of World War II, the type flew with some 29 squadrons in August 1940, and production totalled about 3650 aircraft including 40, 489 and 150 examples of the Canadian-built Mks I, X and XI. Nearly 200 of the RAF Hurricanes were lost in the spring of 1940.

Country of origin:	United Kingdom
Type:	(Hurricane Mk I) single-seat fighter
Powerplant:	one 1030hp (768kW) Rolls-Royce Merlin III 12-cylinder Vee engine
Performance:	maximum speed 521km/h (324mph); climb to 5670m (15,000ft) in 6 minutes 18 seconds; service ceiling 10,120m (33,200ft); range 716km (445 miles)
Weights:	empty 2308kg (5085lb); maximum take-off 3024kg (6661lb)
Dimensions:	span 12.19m (40ft); length 9.55m (31ft 4in); height 4.07m (13ft 4.5in)
Armament:	eight 0.303in fixed forward-firing machine guns in the leading edges of the wing

Hawker Hurricane Mk II

In 1939 Hawker turned to the creation of an improved Hurricane Mk II with an uprated powerplant, heavier armament and enhancements such as metal-skinned wings, three-blade propeller and better protection. These features were also incorporated on later Mk I aircraft. Mk II production reached more than 7500 aircraft for service from September 1940 in variants such as the Mk IIA with eight 0.303in machine guns, the Mk IIB with 12 0.303in machine guns, the Mk IIC with four 20mm cannon and 454kg (1000lb) of external stores, and the anti-tank Mk IID produced in small numbers. The Mk II thus marked the Hurricane's transition to the fighter-bomber role, and many of the aircraft were tropicalised for North African and Far Eastern service with a special chin air filter to prevent sand being ingested into the carburettor. Canadian production added Mk IIB and Mk IIC equivalents as 248 Mk XII and 150 Mk XIIA aircraft.

Country of origin:	United Kingdom
Type:	(Hurricane Mk IID) single-seat anti-tank warplane
Powerplant:	one 1460hp (1088.5kW) Rolls-Royce Merlin XX 12-cylinder Vee engine
Performance:	maximum speed 518km/h (322mph); climb to 6095m (20,000ft) in 12 minutes 24 seconds; service ceiling of 9785m (32,100ft); range 1448km (900 miles)
Weights:	empty 2586kg (5700lb); normal take-off 3493kg (7700lb); maximum take-off 3674kg (8100lb)
Dimensions:	span 12.19m (40ft 0in); length 9.81m (32ft 2.25in); height 3.98m (13ft 1in)
Armament:	two 40mm fixed forward-firing cannon under the wing, and two 0.303in fixed forward-firing machine guns in the leading edges of the wing

Hawker Hurricane Mk IV

Making its debut in 1943 with the designation Hurricane Mk IIE that was used for the first 270 of the 794 aircraft, the Hurricane Mk IV was the final British production model and was basically the Hurricane Mk II with the Merlin 24 or 27 engine, 350lb (159kg) of additional armour protection, and with the so-called Universal Wing that allowed the optimisation of the warplane for a number of ground-attack roles. The wing incorporated two 0.303in machine guns and had undersurface provision for either two 40mm cannon, two bombs of up to 500lb (227kg) in weight, two small bomb carriers, eight 3in (76mm) air-to-surface rocket projectiles each carrying a 60lb (27kg) warhead, or two smoke-laying installations. The Hurricane Mk IV was the last model in British service, the final aircraft being retired in 1946. The aircraft pictured is a Mk IV with heavy underwing anti-tank guns, powerful enough to slow the aircraft significantly in the air when fired.

Country of origin:	United Kingdom
Type:	(Hurricane Mk IV) single-seat ground-attack fighter
Powerplant:	one 1620hp (1208kW) Rolls-Royce Merlin 24 or 27 12-cylinder Vee engine
Performance:	maximum speed 531km/h (330mph); climb to 6095m (20,000ft) in 9 minutes 18 seconds; service ceiling 9935m (32,600ft); range 1464.5km (910 miles)
Weights:	empty 2790kg (6150lb); maximum take-off 3833kg (8450lb)
Dimensions:	span 12.19m (40ft); length 9.81m (32ft 2.25in); height 3.98m (13ft 1in)
Armament:	two 0.303in fixed forward-firing machine guns in the leading edges of the wings, plus an external bomb or rocket load of 454kg (1000lb)

Hawker Tempest Mk II

As the Tempest Mk V was entering production, Hawker was pressing ahead with the development of improved models, most especially the Tempest Mk II with the altogether different Centaurus radial engine. This first flew in prototype form during June 1943 with the original type of Typhoon tail unit but the newer type of one-piece sliding canopy. Powerplant development proved difficult, and the first of an eventual 472 Tempest Mk II aircraft was completed only in October 1944 after production had been switched from Gloucester to Bristol. Later production was undertaken by Hawker, and the last 300 or so aircraft were completed after World War II to a fighter-bomber rather than fighter standard. The aircraft entered service shortly after the end of World War II. Pictured here is a Tempest Mk II of No 54 Squadron, Royal Air Force, based at Chilbolton in 1946. India and Pakistan took delivery of 89 and 24 similar aircraft during 1947-48.

Country of origin:	United Kingdom
Type:	(Tempest Mk II) single-seat fighter and fighter-bomber
Powerplant:	one 2590hp (1931kW) Bristol Centaurus V 18-cylinder two-row radial engine
Performance:	maximum speed 708km/h (440mph); climb to 6095m (20,000ft) in 6 mins 20 seconds; range 1700 miles (2736km)
Weights:	empty 4218kg (9300lb); normal take-off 5352kg (11,800lb); maximum take-off 6305kg (13,900lb)
Dimensions:	span 12.49m (41ft); length 10.49m (34ft 5in); height 4.42m (14ft 6in)
Armament:	four 20mm fixed forward-firing cannon in the leading edges of the wing, plus an external bomb and rocket load of 907kg (2000lb)

Hawker Tempest Mk V

The Tempest was the third Hawker fighter to enjoy operational status in World War II, and while not as well known as the preceding Hurricane and Typhoon, was nonetheless an excellent warplane that proved highly adaptable in terms of its production in variants with air-cooled and liquid-cooled engines. Planned as an advanced fighter to undertake the interceptor role in which the Typhoon had failed, the Tempest was a generally similar aeroplane except for its significantly thinner wing and longer fuselage. It first flew in prototype form during September 1942, retaining the chin radiator of the Typhoon. The type entered service as the Tempest Mk V in April 1944. The Tempest Mk V Series 1 (100 aircraft) had protruding cannon muzzles, but the Tempest Mk V Series 2 (700 aircraft) had cannon muzzles flush with the wing's leading edges. After the war some were converted for use as target tugs and designated Tempest TT.Mk 5.

Country of origin:	United Kingdom
Type:	(Tempest Mk V) single-seat fighter and fighter-bomber
Powerplant:	one 2260hp (1685kW) Napier Sabre IIA, IIB or IIC 24-cylinder H-type engine
Performance:	maximum speed 700km/h (435mph); climb to 6095m (20,000ft) in 6 minutes 6 seconds; service ceiling 10,975m (36,000ft); range 2092km (1300 miles)
Weights:	empty 4854kg (10,700lb); normal take-off 5221kg (11,510lb); maximum take-off 6187kg (13,640lb)
Dimensions:	span 12.50m (41ft); length 10.26m (33ft 8in); height 4.90m (16ft 1in)
Armament:	four 20mm fixed forward-firing cannon in the leading edges of the wing, plus an external bomb and rocket load of 907kg (2000lb)

Hawker Typhoon Mk IA

The Typhoon was possibly the Western Allies' finest ground-attack fighter of World War II. In another light it may be regarded as a distinct failure, as it had been planned as a heavily armed interceptor to succeed the Hawker Hurricane and Supermarine Spitfire, the RAF's first-generation monoplane fighters. A cantilever low-wing monoplane of basically all-metal stressed-skin construction with retractable tail wheel landing gear, the Typhoon was finally planned in two forms with the Napier Sabre liquid-cooled H-type engine and the Bristol Centaurus air-cooled radial engine, the latter becoming the Tempest. First flown in prototype form on 24 February 1940, the Typhoon did not fly in Mk IA production form (105 aircraft) until May 1941 and entered service in June of the same year, initially proving a failure as a result of a structural weakness in the tail and wholly indifferent performance at altitude as a result of its thick wing.

Country of origin:	United Kingdom
Type:	(Mk 1a) single-seat interceptor
Powerplant:	one 2100hp (1566kW) Napier Sabre I 24-cylinder H-type engine
Performance:	maximum speed about 663km/h (412mph); climb to 4570m (15,000ft) in 5 minutes 50 seconds; service ceiling 10,730m (35,200ft); range 510 miles (821km) with standard fuel
Weights:	empty 4445kg (9800lb); normal take-off 5171kg (11,400lb)
Dimensions:	span 12.67m (41ft 7in); length 9.73m (31ft 11in); height 4.67m (15ft 4in)
Armament:	twelve 0.303in fixed forward-firing machine guns with 500 rounds per gun in the wing

Hawker Typhoon Mk IB

The Typhoon Mk IB was the definitive version of the Typhoon. The fixed forward-firing armament was revised to four 20mm cannon with 140 rounds per gun in the wing, the original type of framed canopy with a side door was replaced (from 1943)by a clear-view bubble canopy with a rearward-sliding access section, and the highly unreliable Sabre I engine replaced by the uprated and slightly less troublesome Sabre II generally driving a four- rather than three-blade propeller. These changes coincided with the realisation that the Typhoon would make a superb low-level fighter well able to defeat the fast fighter-bombers with which the German were harassing southern England, and the Typhoon Mk IB could also take the offensive role after being fitted with two underwing hardpoints for bombs or drop tanks. A night-fighter version of the Typhoon designated Nf.Mk IB was produced, together with a small number of FR.Mk IB reconnaissance aircraft.

Country of origin:	United Kingdom
Type:	single-seat ground-attack and close air support fighter-bomber
Powerplant:	one 2180hp (1625.5kW) Napier Sabre IIA, or 2200hp (1640kW) Sabre IIB or 2260hp (1685kW) Sabre IIC 24-cylinder H-type engine
Performance:	maximum speed 663km/h (412mph); climb to 4570m (15,000ft) in 5 minutes 50 seconds; service ceiling 10,730m (35,200ft); range 1577km (980 miles) with drop tanks
Weights:	empty 4445kg (9800lb); normal take-off 5171kg (11,400lb); maximum take-off 6010kg (13,250lb)
Dimentions:	Span 12.67m (41ft 7in); length 9.73m (31ft 11in); height 4.67m (15ft 4in)
Armament:	four 20mm fixed forward-firing cannon in the leading edges of the wing, plus an external bomb load of 907kg (2000lb)

Hawker Typhoon Mk IB

The effective employment of the Typhoon Mk IB in the ground-attack role became possible only with the introduction of disposable weapons carried under the wing. Here there were two hardpoints for the carriage initially of two 454 or 227kg (1000 or 500lb) bombs, or alternatively of two drop tanks for additional range. During 1943 these hardpoints were qualified for rail units for the carriage of four 3in unguided air-to-surface rockets fitted with a 60lb (27kg) warhead. These rockets were truly devastating in attacks on trains, armoured vehicles and light shipping, and in the fighting that followed the Allies' June 1944 invasion of North-West Europe the Typhoon became a decisive weapon when operated in the 'Cab Rank' system of standing patrols. Typhoon production totalled 3315 aircraft that served with 32 squadrons. Some production aircraft were allocated to Royal Canadian Air Force and Royal New Zealand Air Force units operating in Europe.

Country of origin:	United Kingdom
Type:	single-seat ground-attack and close air support fighter-bomber
Powerplant:	one 2180hp (1625.5kW) Napier Sabre IIA, or 2200hp (1640kW) Sabre IIB or 2260hp (1685kW) Sabre IIC 24-cylinder H-type engine
Performance:	maximum speed 663km/h (412mph); climb to 4570m (15,000ft) in 5 minutes 50 seconds; service ceiling 10,730m (35,200ft); range 1577km (980 miles) with drop tanks
Weights:	empty 4445kg (9800lb); normal take-off 5171kg (11,400lb); maximum take-off 6010kg (13,250lb)
Dimensions:	span 12.67m (41ft 7in); length 9.73m (31ft 11in); height 4.67m (15ft 4in)
Armament:	four 20mm fixed forward-firing cannon in the leading edges of the wing, plus an external bomb or rocket load of 907kg (2000lb)

Heinkel He 59

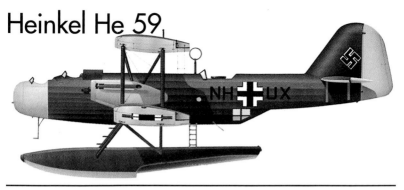

Designed in 1930, the He 59 resulted from a requirement for a torpedo bomber and reconnaissance warplane able to operate with equal facility on wheeled landing gear or twin-float alighting gear. The He 59b landplane prototype was the first to fly, an event that took place in September 1931, but it was the He 59a floatplane prototype that paved the way for the He 59B initial production model, of which 142 were delivered in three variants. Later developments were the He 59C-1 unarmed trainer, He 59C-2 air/sea rescue model, He 59D-1 combined trainer and ASR model, He 59E-1 torpedo bomber trainer, He 59E-2 reconnaissance trainer, and He 59N navigation trainer produced as He 59D-1 conversions. The trainer models survived slightly longer in service than the operational models, but all had been retired by 1944. Some aircraft were operated by Legion Condor in Spain in 1936. Pictured here is a Heinkel He 59 D-1 of the Luftwaffe in 1940.

Country of origin:	Germany
Type:	(He 59B-2) four-seat coastal reconnaissance and torpedo bomber floatplane with navigational training and air/sea rescue capabilities
Powerplant:	two 660hp (492kW) BMW VI 6,0 ZU 12-cylinder Vee engines
Performance:	maximum speed 220km/h (137mph); climb to 2000m (6560ft) in 11 minutes 12 seconds; service ceiling 3500m (11,480ft); range 1530km (950 miles)
Weights:	empty 5000kg (11,023lb); maximum take-off 9100kg (20,062lb)
Dimentions:	span 23.70m (77ft 9in); length 17.40m (57ft 1in); height 7.10m (23ft 3.5in)
Armament:	one 7.92mm trainable forward-firing machine gun in the nose position, one 7.92mm trainable rearward-firing machine gun in the dorsal position, and one 7.92mm rearward-firing machine gun in the ventral position, plus torpedo and bomb load of 1000kg (2205lb)

Heinkel He 70 Blitz

Designed to meet a 1932 requirement by Deutsche Lufthansa for a high-speed passenger and mail transport, the He 70 first flew in prototype form during December 1932. The programme was then taken over by the German air forces, which saw in the He 70 a type ideal for conversion as an interim communications aeroplane and high-speed bomber. As a result the fourth and fifth prototypes were completed to military standards. This paved the way for the production models, of which 287 were completed. The communications type was the He 70D, but the majority of the aircraft were He 70E bombers and, most importantly, He 70F reconnaissance bombers. The He 70 made its operational debut as a bomber in Spain during August 1936, but by the start of World War II the surviving aircraft had been relegated to communications and training duties. Shown here in the markings of a Luftwaffe Kurierstaffel is an He 70F.

Country of origin:	Germany
Type:	(He 70F-2) three-seat reconnaissance bomber generally used in the communications role
Powerplant:	one 750hp (559kW) BMW VI 7,3 Z 12-cylinder Vee engine
Performance:	maximum speed 360km/h (223mph); climb to 1000m (3280ft) in 2 minutes 30 seconds; service ceiling 5485m (18,000ft); range 1250km (776 miles)
Weights:	empty 2530kg (5579lb); maximum take-off 3640kg (7629lb)
Dimensions:	span 14.79m (48ft 6.75in); length 12.00m (39ft 4.5in); height 3.10m (10ft 2in)
Armament:	one 7.92mm trainable rearward-firing machine gun in the dorsal position, plus an internal bomb load of 300kg (661lb)

Heinkel He 100

Bitterly disappointed that its He 112 had failed to secure a production order over the rival Messerschmitt Bf 109 as the Luftwaffe's first monoplane fighter, Heinkel started work on the design of a more advanced fighter. The result was the He 100, and the first of its 10 prototypes flew in January 1938. There were considerable technical problems to be overcome with the evaporative cooling system, and it was only in September 1939 that the first of three He 100D-0 pre-production and 12 He 100D-1 production aircraft flew with a larger vertical and horizontal tail surfaces respectively. Shortages of the DB 601 engine meant that there was no German requirement for the type, so six prototypes and the three pre-production aircraft were sold to the USSR and Japan, while the production aircraft were used for defence of the Heinkel factory. The He 100D-1aircraft shown here wears spurious Lufwaffe markings.

Country of origin:	Germany
Type:	(He 100D-1) single-seat interceptor fighter
Powerplant:	one 1175hp (876kW) Daimler-Benz DB 601M 12-cylinder inverted-Vee engine
Performance:	maximum speed 670km/h (416mph); climb to 6000m (19,685ft) in 7 minutes 48 seconds; service ceiling 11,000m (36,090ft); range 1010km (627 miles)
Weights:	empty 2010kg (4431lb); maximum take-off 2500kg (5511lb)
Dimensions:	span 9.40m (30ft 10in); length 8.20m (26ft 10.75in); height 3.60m (11ft 9.75in)
Armament:	one 20mm fixed forward-firing cannon in an engine installation, and either two 20mm fixed forward-firing cannon or two 7.92mm fixed forward-firing machine guns in the wing roots

Heinkel He 111P

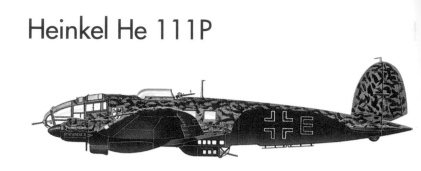

The Heinkel He 111 was Germany's most important medium bomber of World War II, and although ostensibly designed as a civil transport had entered air force service by 1936 as the He 111B bomber with Daimler-Benz DB 601 engines and a conventional forward fuselage with a stepped cockpit. These 300 aircraft were followed by some 190 He 111E bombers with Junkers Jumo 211 engines, and the next significant model, entering service in the spring of 1939, was the He 111P with the asymmetric fully glazed nose typical of all subsequent He 111 models. Built to the extent of some 400 aircraft in bomber and trainer subvariants between the He 111P-1 and He 111P-6, the He 111P was a useful type whose production was curtailed only by the reallocation of DB 601 engine supplies to fighters. Many He 111P-6 aircraft were later adapted as glider tugs. Spanish aircraft manufacturers built 236 He 111Hs under licence during and after the war as the CASA 2.111.

Country of origin:	Germany
Type:	(He 111P-2) four-seat medium bomber
Powerplant:	two 1100hp (820kW) Daimler-Benz DB 601A-1 12-cylinder engines
Performance:	maximum speed 398km/h (247mph); climb to 4500m (14,765ft) in 31 minutes 18 seconds; service ceiling 8000m (26,245ft); range 2400km (1491 miles)
Weights:	empty 8015kg (17,670lb); maximum take-off 13,500kg (29,762lb)
Dimentions:	span 22.60m (74ft 1.75in); length 16.40m (53ft 9.5in); height 3.40m (13ft 1.5in)
Armament:	one 7.92mm fixed machine gun in the nose, one 7.92mm machine gun in the nose position, one 7.92mm machine gun in dorsal position, one 7.92mm machine gun in rear of ventral gondola, two 7.92mm machine guns in two beam positions, and provision for one 7.92mm fixed machine gun in the tail cone; bomb load of 2000kg (4409lb)

Heinkel He 111H and He 111Z

The definitive model of the He 111 series was the He 111H, which was in essence the He 111P with the revised powerplant of two Junkers Jumo 211 engines. The He 111H entered service in 1939, and production totalled about 6150 aircraft in major variants between the He 111H-1 and He 111H-23. These aircraft were characterised by a progressively uprated powerplant, increased fuel capacity, improved defensive as well as offensive armament, additional armour protection, and provision for use in alternative roles such as anti-shipping attack, pathfinding, missile carrying and launching, paratroop delivery and glider towing. The introduction of the huge Messerschmitt Me 321 Gigant glider necessitated the development of the final variant, the He 111Z (Zwilling, or twin), of which small numbers were produced as two He 111H-6 or -16 airframes joined by a new centre section carrying a fifth engine.

Country of origin:	Germany
Type:	(He 111H-16): five-seat medium bomber
Powerplant:	two 1350hp (1007kW) Junkers Jumo 211F-2 12-cylinder engines
Performance:	maximum speed 405km/h (252mph); climb to 4000m (13,125ft) in 23 minutes 30 seconds; service ceiling 8500m (27,890ft); range 1930km (1199 miles) with maximum bomb load
Weights:	empty 8680kg (19,136lb); maximum take-off 14,000kg (30,865lb)
Dimensions:	span 22.60m (74ft 1.75in); length 16.40m (53ft 9.5in); height 3.40m (13ft 1.5in)
Armament:	one 7.92mm fixed machine gun in the nose, one 7.92mm machine gun in a nose position, one 7.92mm machine gun in dorsal position, one 7.92mm machine gun in rear of ventral gondola, two 7.92mm machine guns in each of two beam positions, and one 7.92mm fixed machine gun in the tail cone, plus a bomb load of 2500kg (5511lb)

Heinkel He 112

The He 112 was the Bf 109's rival for the contract as the German Air Force's first monoplane fighter. The Heinkel was comparatively advanced, and the first of an eventual 12 prototypes flew in the summer of 1935. During the programme a number of powerplant, fuselage, wing and tail unit configurations were investigated. The Luftwaffe then selected the Bf 109, but the German air ministry was sufficiently impressed with the Heinkel fighter to order 43 He 112B-0 pre-production aircraft that operated with a fighter wing during 1938. Seventeen of the aircraft were sent to Spain for operational evaluation, after which the 15 survivors were passed to the Nationalist rebel forces. Of the others Germany sold 13 each to Japan and Romania, the latter later also acquiring 11 of the 13 He 112B-1 production aircraft for service up to 1942. Hungary also acquired a few aircraft. Pictured here is an He 112B-0 on the strength of III/JG 132 during August 1938.

Country of origin:	Germany
Type:	(He 112B-1) single-seat fighter and fighter-bomber
Powerplant:	one 680hp (507kW) Junkers Jumo 210Ea 12-cylinder inverted-Vee engine
Performance:	maximum speed 510km/h (317mph); climb to 6000m (19,685ft) in 9 minutes 30 seconds; service ceiling 8500m (27,890ft); range 1100km (683 miles)
Weights:	empty 1620kg (3571lb); maximum take-off 2250kg (4960lb)
Dimentions:	span 9.10m (29ft 10.25in); length 9.30m (30ft 6in); height 3.85m (12ft 7.5in)
Armament:	two fixed forward-firing cannon in the leading edges of the wing and two 7.92mm fixed forward-firing machine guns in the sides of the forward fuselage, plus an external bomb load of 60kg (132lb)

Heinkel He 115A/B

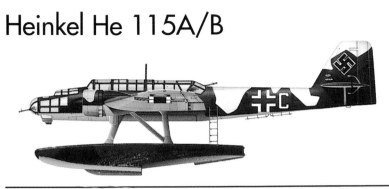

Resulting from a 1935 requirement for an advanced torpedo bomber floatplane that was also to be capable of undertaking a number of other coastal roles such as minelaying and reconnaissance, the He 115 V1 (first of four prototypes) made its maiden flight in August 1937. The He 115 was subsequently ordered into production early in 1938. Some 10 He 115A-0 pre-production aircraft were delivered from the summer of the same year, and paved the way for 137 production machines. The first of these was the baseline He 115A (three subvariants including one for export), and this was followed by the structurally strengthened He 115B. This in turn was operated in two main versions that spawned a number of minor subvariants for the torpedo, bombing, minelaying and reconnaissance roles. Many of these were built under licence by Weser Flugzeugbau. During the course of its career the aircraft served with Germany, Britain and Sweden.

Country of origin:	Germany
Type:	(He 115B-1) three-seat coastal general-purpose and torpedo bomber floatplane
Powerplant:	two 960hp (716kW) BMW 132K nine-cylinder single-row radial engines
Performance:	maximum speed 295km/h (183mph); service ceiling 5200m (17,600ft); range 2600km (1616 miles)
Weights:	empty 6715kg (14,804lb); normal take-off 10,400kg (22,930lb)
Dimentions:	span 22.28m (73ft 1in); length 17.30m (56ft 9.25in); height 6.59m (21ft 7.75in)
Armament:	one 7.92mm trainable forward-firing machine gun in the nose position, and one 7.92mm trainable rearward-firing machine gun in the dorsal position, plus an internal and external torpedo, bomb and mine load of 920kg (2028lb)

Heinkel He 115C/D

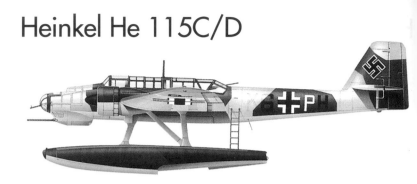

Early experience with the He 115A/B suggested that the variants' gun armament was too light, and early in 1940 one of the prototypes was tested with 20mm fixed cannon in place of the trainable machine gun in the nose for improved offensive capability against light shipping. The trials were not notably successful, but clearly something needed to be achieved in the way of improving the He 115's firepower. This led to the He 115C-1 with a 15mm fixed forward-firing cannon as a supplement to the trainable machine gun in the nose, and a single 7.92mm fixed rearward-firing machine gun in the rear of each engine nacelle to deter pursuing fighters. Companion models were the He 115C-2 with strengthened floats, He 115C-3 minelayer, and He 115C-4 for arctic service. Many of the aircraft were later converted as convoy escorts. The He 115D was the designation of one aircraft with two 1193kW (1600 hp) BMW 801C engines).

Country of origin:	Germany
Type:	(He 115C-1) three-seat coastal and torpedo bomber floatplane
Powerplant:	two 960hp (716kW) BMW 132K nine-cylinder radial engines
Performance:	maximum speed 300km/h (186mph); climb to 3000m (9845ft) in 22 minutes 18 seconds; service ceiling 5165m (16,950ft); range 2800 km (1740 miles)
Weights:	empty 6870kg (15,146lb); normal take-off 10, 680kg (23,545lb)
Dimentions:	span 22.28m (73ft 1in); length 17.30m (56ft 9.25in); height 6.59m (21ft 7.75in)
Armament:	one 15mm fixed forward-firing cannon on lower port side of nose, one 7.92mm fixed rearward-firing machine gun in rear of engine nacelles, one 7.92mm trainable forward-firing machine gun in nose position, and one 7.92mm rearward-firing machine gun in dorsal position; torpedo, bomb and mine load of 2028lb (920kg)

Heinkel He 162 Salamander

The He 162 was in every respect a prodigious effort that confirmed the feats of which German industry was capable in the dire conditions that prevailed in the terminal stage of World War II. A mere 69 days separated the beginning of the He 162 programme from the maiden flight of the first of 30 prototypes in December 1944. Conceived as a turbojet-powered interceptor built largely from readily available supplies of wood for ease and speed of manufacture (a rate of 4000 aircraft per month being envisaged!), the He 162 was notable for the 'piggyback' installation of its engine. More than 240 He 162A production aircraft were completed, but the sole operating unit was created only four days before the war's end. This was perhaps fortunate as the He 162A's structure proved to be highly suspect as a result of poor materials and workmanship. Pictured is an He 162A-2 of 3./JG 1, based at Leck in Schleswig-Holstein during May 1945.

Country of origin:	Germany
Type:	(He 162A-2) single-seat interceptor fighter
Powerplant:	one 1764lb st (7.85kN) BMW 109-003E-1/2 Sturm turbojet
Performance:	maximum speed 905km/h (562mph); initial climb rate 594m (1950ft) per minute; service ceiling 12,000m (39,370ft); range 975km (606 miles)
Weights:	empty 1663kg (3666lb); normal take-off 2485kg (5478lb); maximum take-off 2605kg (5744lb)
Dimensions:	span 7.20m (23ft 7.5in); length 9.05m (29ft 8.5in); height 2.60m (8ft 6.33in)
Armament:	two 20mm fixed forward-firing cannon in the lower sides of the forward fuselage

Heinkel He 177A-1/3 Greif

The Greif (Griffin) was a potentially excellent but ultimately disastrous warplane on which Germany expended enormous and therefore largely wasted resources. The type was schemed as a bomber able to deliver a large bomb load over a considerable range at high speed and high altitude, and in an effort to extract maximum performance from a four-engined powerplant by the minimisation of drag, it was decided that the pair of engines on each wing should be coupled to drive a single propeller. This coupled powerplant was beset by enormous technical problems that were never wholly cured and resulted in numerous inflight fires (the engines had a habit of catching fire without warning). The first of eight He 177 prototypes flew in December 1939, and slow development meant that it was the summer of 1942 before 130 He 177A-1 and 170 He 177A-3 early production aircraft entered service.

Country of origin:	Germany
Type:	(He 177A-1/R1 Greif) five-crew heavy bomber
Powerplant:	two 2700hp (2013kW) Daimler-Benz DB 606 (coupled DB 601) 24-cylinder engines
Performance:	maximum speed 510km/h (317mph); service ceiling 7000m (22,965ft); range 1200km (746 miles) with maximum bomb load
Weights:	empty 18,040kg (39,771lb); maximum take-off 30,000kg (66,139lb)
Dimentions:	span 31.44m (103ft 1.75in); length 20.40m (66ft 11in); height 6.39m (20ft 11.75in)
Armament:	one 7.92mm trainable forward-firing machine gun in nose position, one 20mm trainable forward-firing cannon in ventral gondola, two 7.92mm machine guns in ventral gondola, one 13mm machine gun in remotely controlled dorsal barbette, and one 13mm machine gun in tail position, plus a bomb load of 6000kg (13,228lb)

Heinkel He 177A-5 Greif

The He 177A-4 was an unbuilt high-altitude model, so the next Greif variant after the He 177A-3 was the He 177A-5. This introduced the uprated powerplant of two DB 610 coupled engines, and was optimised for the carriage of external loads such as the LT 50 torpedo, Hs 293 air-to-surface missile and FX-1400 *Fritz X* guided bomb, and thus featured a strengthened wing structure, shortened landing gear legs and the removal of the Fowler flaps along the inboard section of the wings in line with the weapon hardpoints. Production totalled 565 aircraft in subvariants between the He 177A-5/R2 and R8 with different armament fits. Finally came seven He 177A-5 conversions as six He 177A-6 aircraft for the long-range role with additional armament, including a tail turret, and one He 177A-7 with DB 613 engines. The above aircraft served with KG 100, which flew anti-shipping missions over the Baltic Sea.

Country of origin:	Germany
Type:	(He 177A-5/R2) six-seat heavy bomber and anti-ship warplane
Powerplant:	two 3100hp (2311kW) Daimler-Benz DB 610A/1/B-1 24-cylinder engines
Performance:	maximum speed 488km/h (303mph); climb to 6095m (20,000ft) in 39 minutes; service ceiling 8000m (26,245ft); range 5500km (3418 miles) with two Hs 293 missiles
Weights:	empty 16,800kg (37,038lb);maximum take-off 31,000kg (68,343lb)
Dimentions:	span 31.44m (103ft 1.75in); length 22.00m (72ft 2in); height 6.39m (20ft 11.75in)
Armament:	one 7.92mm trainable machine gun in nose position, one 20mm trainable cannon and two 7.92mm trainable machine guns in ventral gondola, two13mm machine guns in remotely controlled dorsal barbettes, one 20mm cannon in tail; bomb load of 13,228lb (6000kg)

Heinkel He 177A-5 Greif

In total Heinkel and Arado together delivered 565 He 177A-5 aircraft, and their operational record was much better than that of earlier versions. The most important Luftwaffe units to use the He 177 were KG 40 and KG 100, both taking part in revenge attacks against London during the early weeks of 1944. The A-6 version, of which six were built, had a pressurised cabin. However, the problems with the engines persisted. On February 1944, for example, 14 A-5s taxied out for a bombing raid on England. By the time the aircraft took off one had already encountered mechanical problems, and eight more soon returned to base with overheated or burning engines. Only four reached England to deliver their bomb loads, and of these one was shot down. The aircraft pictured above is an A-5 of II Gruppe, which features a search radar and Hs 293A missiles under the wings for attacks against shipping.

Country of origin:	Germany
Type:	(He 177A-5/R2) six-seat heavy bomber and anti-ship warplane
Powerplant:	two 3100hp (2311kW) Daimler-Benz DB 610A/1/B-1 24-cylinder engines
Performance:	maximum speed 488km/h (303mph); climb to 6095m (20,000ft) in 39 minutes; service ceiling 8000m (26,245ft); range 5500km (3418 miles) with two Hs 293 missiles
Weights:	empty 16,800kg (37,038lb);maximum take-off 31,000kg (68,343lb)
Dimentions:	span 31.44m (103ft 1.75in); length 22.00m (72ft 2in); height 6.39m (20ft 11.75in)
Armament:	one 7.92mm trainable machine gun in nose position, one 20mm trainable cannon and two 7.92mm trainable machine guns in ventral gondola, two13mm machine guns in remotely controlled dorsal barbettes, one 20mm cannon in tail; bomb load of 13,228lb (6000kg)

Heinkel He 219 Uhu

The Uhu (Owl) was the finest German night-fighter of World War II, but despite its exceptional capabilities was built only in very small numbers as a result of political antipathy to the Heinkel company, which continued to develop and build the type despite orders not to do so. Design of the He 219 began in 1940 as a multi-role warplane, and it was only late in 1941 that the type became a dedicated night-fighter. The first of 10 prototypes flew in November 1942, and by this time there were orders for 300 He 219A initial production aircraft including an initial 130 He 219A-0 pre-production machines. The first production model was the He 219A-2, and more than 150 He 219A aircraft were built in variants up to the He 219A-7 for limited service from the middle of 1943 with various engine and armament fits. On June 11, 1943 Major Werner Streib shot down five Avro Lancasters in a single sortie, and in the first six sorties flown by his unit 20 aircraft were shot down.

Country of origin:	Germany
Type:	(He 219A-7/R1) two-seat night-fighter
Powerplant:	two 1900hp (1417kW) Daimler-Benz DB 603G 12-cylinder inverted-Vee engines
Performance:	maximum speed 670km/h (416mph); initial climb rate 552m (1810ft) per minute; service ceiling 12,700m (41,665ft); range 2000km (1243 miles)
Weights:	empty 11,200kg (24,692lb); maximum take-off 15,300kg (33,730lb)
Dimentions:	span 18.50m (60ft 8.33in); length 15.54m (50ft 11.75in); height 4.10 m (13ft 5.5in)
Armament:	two 30mm fixed forward-firing cannon in the wing roots, two 30mm and two 20mm fixed forward-firing cannon in a ventral tray, and two 30mm obliquely upward/forward-firing in the upper part of the rear fuselage

Henschel Hs 129

The Hs 129 was designed by Henschel in response to a spring 1937 requirement for a *Schlachtflugzeug* (battle aeroplane) that was to be relatively small but heavily armoured for survivability as it provided close air support for the German ground forces. It emerged as a cantilever low-wing monoplane of all-metal construction and first flew in the spring of 1939 with two 465hp (347kW) Argus As 410 inverted-Vee engines. Development was slow as a result of the aeroplane's poor performance and handling in combination with the pilot's woeful fields of vision, and it was only in April 1942 that the type entered service in its Hs 129B-1 form with an uprated powerplant of captured French radial engines. The aeroplane was still underpowered, and the engines were both unreliable and very vulnerable to battle damage, but the demands of the campaign on the Eastern Front resulted in the delivery of 843 Hs 129B warplanes.

Country of origin:	Germany
Type:	(Hs 129B-2) single-seat close-support and anti-tank warplane
Powerplant:	two 700hp (522kW) Gnome-Rhône 14M-4/5 14-cylinder two-row radial engines
Performance:	maximum speed 407km/h (253mph); initial climb rate 486m (1595ft) per minute; service ceiling 9000m (29,530ft); range 560km (348 miles) with an underfuselage pack carrying one 30mm cannon
Weights:	empty 4020kg (8862lb); maximum take-off 5250kg (11,574lb)
Dimensions:	span 14.20m (46ft 7in); length 9.75m (31ft 11.75in); height 3.25m (10ft 8in)
Armament:	two 20mm fixed forward-firing cannon and two 13mm fixed forward-firing machine guns in the upper and lower sides of the fuselage, provision under the fusforward-firing cannon or four 7.92mm forward-firing machine guns; bomb load of 450kg (992lb)

Henschel Hs 129

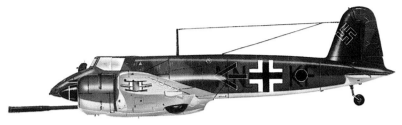

Introduced in 1943, the Hs 129B-2 was a development of the Hs 129B-1 incorporating as standard all the improvements effected individually in the course of the Hs 129B-1 production run. Soon after the type's introduction, provision for add-on weapons kits was replaced by underfuselage attachments for anti-tank weapons. This resulted in the Hs 129B-2/Wa subvariant that could be fitted first with a 30mm MK 103 cannon offering a higher muzzle velocity than the MK 101, and then with the 37mm BK 3,7 cannon whose installation meant the deletion of the machine guns to provide volume for the cannon's ammunition. By the beginning of 1944 the 30mm and 37mm cannon were no longer effective against Soviet tanks, and the designation Hs 129B-3/Wa was adopted for some 25 Hs 129B-2 warplanes adapted on the production line with a 75mm BK 7,5 (converted PaK 40L) anti-tank gun in a jettisonable underfuselage pack.

Country of origin:	Germany
Type:	(Hs 129B-3) single-seat close-support and anti-tank warplane
Powerplant:	two 700hp (522kW) Gnome-RhÙne 14M-4/5 14-cylinder two-row radial engines
Performance:	maximum speed 407km/h (253mph); initial climb rate 486m (1595ft) per minute; service ceiling 9000m (29,530ft); range 690km (429 miles) with no external stores
Weights:	empty 4020kg (8862lb)
Dimentions:	span 14.20m (46ft 7in); length 9.75m (31ft 11.75in); height 3.25m (10ft 8in)
Armament:	two 20mm fixed forward-firing cannon in the upper sides of the fuselage, and provision under the fuselage for a pack accommodating one 75mm fixed forward-firing cannon

Henschel Hs 123

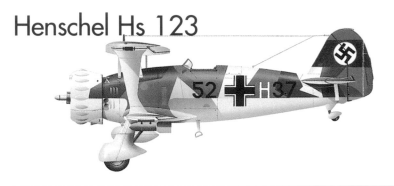

Designed in 1934 and first flown in 1935 for service from 1936, the Hs 123 served in the Spanish Civil War and was technically obsolete by the time World War II started in 1939, but went on to play an important part in Germany's early successes and was still an important anti-partisan weapon in 1945. The Hs 123 was a sturdy single-bay biplane of fabric-covered metal construction with fixed tailwheel landing gear as well as an open cockpit, and although conceived as a dive-bomber was generally operated in the close-support role. Here its great strength, considerable agility and stability as a gun platform offset its limited performance and comparatively light armament. Production of 604 Hs 123A-1 warplanes ended in 1938, but so useful was the type that there were calls in World War II for it to be returned to production. Pictured is an Hs 123A-1 of 7./Stukageschwader 165 'Immelmann' based at Fürstenfeldbruck in October 1937.

Country of origin:	Germany
Type:	single-seat dive-bomber and close-support warplane
Powerplant:	one 730hp (544kW) BMW 132A-3 nine-cylinder radial engine
Performance:	maximum speed 290km/h (180mph); climb to 2000m (6560ft) in 4 minutes 24 seconds; service ceiling 4100m (13,450ft); range 480km (298 miles) with a 200kg (441lb) bomb load
Weights:	empty 1420kg (3131lb); maximum take-off 2350kg (5181lb)
Dimensions:	span 10.50m (34ft 5.33in); length 8.66m (28ft 4.75in); height 3.76m (12ft 4in)
Armament:	two 7.92mm fixed forward-firing machine guns in the upper part of the forward fuselage, plus an external bomb load of 450kg (992lb)

Henschel Hs 126

The older of the two types that provided the Germans with the bulk of their battlefield reconnaissance capability in World War II, the Hs 126 was a parasol-wing aeroplane that first flew in early 1935. Three prototypes and 10 Hs 126A-0 pre-production aircraft paved the way for about 800 examples of the two production variants, which entered service during 1938 with the German forces fighting alongside the Nationalist forces in the Spanish Civil War. These models were the Hs 126A-1 with the 880hp (656kW) BMW 132Dc radial engine, and the Hs 126B-1 with a different engine. The Hs 126 served in a front-line role to 1942, and was thereafter relegated to the glider-towing and night harassment roles, the latter with loads of light bombs in regions such as the Baltic and Balkans. Pictured here is one of the Hs 126B-1 aircraft on the strength of 2.(H)/Aufklärungsgruppe 31, operating on the Eastern Front in 1941/42.

Country of origin:	Germany
Type:	(Hs 126B-1) two-seat tactical reconnaissance and army co-operation warplane
Powerplant:	one 850hp (634kW) BMW-Bramo 323A-1 or Q-1 Fafnir nine-cylinder single-row radial engine
Performance:	maximum speed 355km/h (221mph); climb to 4000m (13,125ft) in 7 minutes 12 seconds; service ceiling 8230m (27,000ft); range 720km (447 miles)
Weights:	empty 2032kg (4480lb); maximum take-off 3270kg (7209lb)
Dimensions:	span 14.50m (47ft 6.75in); length 10.85m (35ft 7in); height 3.75m (12ft 3.5in)
Armament:	one 7.92mm fixed forward-firing machine gun in the starboard upper part of the forward fuselage, and one 7.92mm rearward-firing machine gun in the rear cockpit; external bomb load of 150kg (331lb)

Ilyushin Il-4

Designed as the DB-3f and first flown in January 1940 for service from 1941, the Il-4 was a modernised development of the DB-3M optimised for ease of production and field maintenance. The Il-4 remained in production up to 1944 and with a total of 5256 aircraft was among the Soviets' most important medium bombers of World War II. The first aircraft were powered by two 1000hp (746kW) Tumanskii M-88 radial engines, but these were soon replaced by uprated versions of the same engine. Other changes included during the production run included a four- rather than three-man crew, self-sealing fuel tanks, and larger-calibre defensive weapons: the 7.62mm turret gun was replaced by a 12.7mm machine gun and then a 20mm cannon, and the machine gun in the nose was changed to a 20mm cannon. Shown here is an Illyushin Il-4 (DB-3F) of a Red Air Force *bombardirovoishchnaya aviatsionyyl polk* (bomber regiment) in 1944.

Country of origin:	USSR
Type:	four-seat long-range medium bomber
Powerplant:	two 1100hp (820kW) Tumanskii M-88B 14-cylinder two-row radial engine
Performance:	maximum speed 420km/h (261mph); climb to 5000m (16,405ft) in 12 minutes; service ceiling 9400m (30,840ft); range 2600km (1616 miles) with a 1000kg (2205lb) bomb load
Weights:	empty 5800kg (12,787lb); maximum take-off 10,300kg (22,707lb)
Dimensions:	span 21.44m (70ft 4.5in); length 14.80m (48ft 7in); height 4.10m (13ft 5.5in)
Armament:	one 7.62mm trainable forward-firing machine gun in nose position, one 7.62mm trainable machine gun in dorsal turret, and one 7.62mm trainable rearward-firing machine gun in ventral hatch position, plus an internal bomb load of 2700kg (5952lb)

Ilyushin Il-2

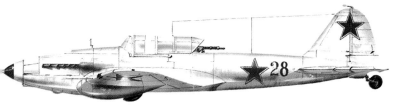

Built in larger numbers (36,150 aircraft) and at a higher rate than any other warplane in history, the Il-2 was instrumental in the Soviet defeat of Germany by 1945. The type entered service as the single-seat Il-2 three months before the German onslaught of June 1941 and was initially an indifferent warplane with the 1660hp (1238kW) AM-38 engine and an armament of two 20mm cannon and two 7.62mm machine guns as well as bombs and 82mm rockets. The aircraft matured into a formidable ground attack aircraft and was much feared by German forces on the ground. The Il-2 was followed by the Il-2M with the AM-38 engine and 23mm cannon, the Il-2M Tip 3 two-seat version of the Il-2M to allow the provision of rearward defence, and the Il-2M Tip 3M with 37mm rather than 23mm cannon for greater anti-tank capability. Shown here in hastily applied winter camouflage for the Stalingrad counter-offensive in February 1943 is an Il-2m3.

Country of origin:	USSR
Type:	(Il-2M Tip 3) two-seat close support and anti-tank warplane
Powerplant:	one 1770hp (1320kW) Mikulin AM-38F 12-cylinder Vee engine
Performance:	maximum speed 415km/h (258mph); climb to 5000m (16,405ft) in 15 minutes; service ceiling 6000m (19,685ft); range 800km (497 miles)
Weights:	empty 4525kg (9976lb); maximum take-off 6360kg (14,021lb)
Dimensions:	span 14.60m (47ft 11in); length 12.00m (39ft 4.5in); height 3.40m (11ft 1.75in)
Armament:	two 23mm fixed forward-firing cannon and two 7.62mm fixed forward-firing machine guns in the leading edges of the wings, and one 12.7mm trainable rearward-firing machine gun in the rear cockpit, plus an internal and external bomb and rocket load of 1000kg (2205lb)

Ilyushin Il-10

The Il-2 was a remarkably successful warplane, but its proven capabilities did not deter the Soviets from deciding in 1942 to press ahead with the creation of an improved ground-attack and anti-tank type. Various Ilyushin prototypes were evaluated before the decision came down in favour of the Il-10. This aircraft was clearly a linear descendant of the Il-2 but featured improved armour protection, a higher-rated engine, slightly smaller overall dimensions, considerably greater manoeuvrability and much enhanced performance. The Il-10 was ordered into production during August 1944, had fully replaced the Il-2 in production by November 1944, and entered service in February 1945. Some 3500 Il-10s were completed by the end of World War II, and the type remained in production and service until well after this time. The aircraft pictured wears the markings of a Polish air assault regiment in 1951.

Country of origin:	USSR
Type:	two-seat close support and anti-tank warplane
Powerplant:	one 2000hp (1491kW) Mikulin AM-42 12-cylinder Vee engine
Performance:	maximum speed 551km/h (342mph); climb to 5000m (16,405ft) in 9 minutes 42 seconds; service ceiling 7250m (23,790ft); range 800km (497 miles)
Weights:	empty 4680kg (10,317lb); maximum take-off 6535kg (14,407lb)
Dimensions:	span 13.40m (43ft 11.5in); length 11.10m (36ft 5in); height 3.50m (11ft 5.75in)
Armament:	two 37mm fixed forward-firing cannon and two 7.62mm fixed forward-firing machine guns or four 23mm fixed forward-firing cannon in the leading edges of the wing, and one 20mm trainable rearward-firing cannon in the dorsal turret, plus an internal and external bomb and rocket load of 1000kg (2205lb)

Junkers Ju 52/3m

Intended as successor to the highly successful W 33 and W 34 transports, the Ju 52 was planned from the late 1920s as an enlarged version of the same basic design concept, and first flew in prototype form during October 1930 with one 725hp (541kW) BMW VII Vee engine. The Ju 52a to Ju 52d initial production models for the civil market differed only in the type of engine used, but with the Ju 52/3m a three-engined powerplant was introduced for greater payload and performance. The series was built to the extent of some 4850 aircraft, the vast majority of them to meet military orders in variants between the Ju 52/3m ge and the Ju 52/3m g14e. The Ju 52/3m served initially as a bomber as well as transport, but in World War II was a transport and airborne forces aeroplane that saw operational use in every German theatre right up to May 1945. The aircraft pictured is a Ju 52/3mg6e equipped with a large magnetic loop for mine clearance operations.

Country of origin:	Germany
Type:	(Ju 52/3m g7e) three-seat transport with accommodation for 18 troops, or 12 litters, or freight
Powerplant:	three 730hp (544kW) BMW 132T-2 nine-cylinder radial engines
Performance:	maximum speed 286km/h (178mph); climb to 3000m (9845ft) in 17 minutes 30 seconds; service ceiling 5900m (19,360ft); range 1305km (811 miles)
Weights:	empty 6500kg (14,328lb); maximum take-off 11,030kg (24,317lb)
Dimensions:	span 29.20m (95ft 10in); length 18.90m (62ft); height 4.52m (14ft 10in)
Armament:	one 13mm or 7.92mm trainable rearward-firing machine gun in rear dorsal position, provision for one 7.92mm trainable machine gun in forward dorsal position, and one 7.92mm trainable lateral-firing machine gun in each of the two beam positions

Junkers Ju 52

The 18-seat Ju 52/3mg7e, shown here, was the major production variant featuring an automatic pilot and wide cabin doors to facilitate rapid loading and deployment of paratroopers. Subsequent versions had the wheel fairngs removed, as they were found to clog with sand and mud. 'Auntie', as the Ju 52 was affectionately known to German troops, formed the backbone of the Luftwaffe transport fleet throughout World War II, and served in every theatre with German forces. Pictured here is a Ju 52/3mg7e of 2.Staffel, KGrzbV 1, based at Milos in Greece, in May 1941 prior to the invasion of Crete. The operation, codenamed 'Mercury' involved para-dropping a sizable force from a fleet of 493 Ju 52s, but confusion over the drop zone and delays in providing support for the initial assault. Out of every four men who dropped on Crete one was killed, and by the end of the operation more than 170 Ju 52/3ms had been lost.

Country of origin:	Germany
Type:	(Ju 52/3mg7e) three-seat transport with accommodation for 18 troops, or 12 litters, or freight
Powerplant:	three 730hp (544kW) BMW 132T-2 nine-cylinder radial engines
Performance:	maximum speed 286km/h (178mph); climb to 3000m (9845ft) in 17 minutes 30 seconds; service ceiling 5900m (19,360ft); range 1305km (811 miles)
Weights:	empty 6500kg (14,328lb); maximum take-off 11,030kg (24,317lb)
Dimensions:	span 29.20m (95ft 10in); length 18.90m (62ft); height 4.52m (14ft 10in)
Armament:	one 13mm or 7.92mm trainable rearward-firing machine gun in rear dorsal position, provision for one 7.92mm trainable machine gun in forward dorsal position, and one 7.92mm trainable lateral-firing machine gun in each of the two beam positions

Junkers Ju 86

The Junkers Ju 86 was planned as a medium bomber. The first two production variants were the Ju 86D and Ju 86E that entered service in spring 1936 and differed in their powerplants, the latter type having 810hp (655kW) BMW 132 radial engines. Operational service revealed that performance was poor, so the type was then developed as the Ju 86B, Ju 86F and Ju 86Z civil transports, the Ju 86G bomber trainer, and Ju 86K bomber for export . The final versions were the Ju 86P and Ju 86R for the high-altitude role with a pressurised cabin: the Ju 86P bomber had 950hp (708kW) Jumo 207A-1 engines and a span of 84ft 0in (25.60m), while the Ju 86R reconnaissance type had 1000hp (746kW) Jumo 207B-3 engines and a span of 104 ft 11.75in (32.00m) for a ceiling of 47,245ft (14,400m). Production totalled 470 aircraft. Pictured is a Ju-86D-1 medium bomber of 5/Kampfgeschwader 254, based at Eschwege in September 1939.

Country of origin:	Germany
Type:	(Ju 86D-1) four-seat medium bomber
Powerplant:	two 600hp (447kW) Junkers Jumo 205C-4 vertically opposed Diesel engines
Performance:	maximum speed 325km/h (202mph); service ceiling 5900m (19,360ft); range 1140km (708 miles) with maximum bomb load
Weights:	empty 5800kg (12,786lb); maximum take-off 8200kg (18,078lb)
Dimensions:	span 22.50m (73ft 9.75in); length 17.57m (58ft 7.13in); height 5.06m (16ft 7.25 in)
Armament:	one 7.92mm trainable forward-firing machine gun in the nose position, one 7.92mm trainable rearward-firing machine gun in the dorsal position, and one 7.92mm trainable rearward-firing machine gun in the retractable ventral 'dustbin', plus an internal bomb load of 1000kg (2205lb)

Junkers Ju 87B-1

With its inverted-gull wing, massive landing gear and screaming dive trumpets, the Ju 87 remains synonymous with German success at the beginning of World War II. The Ju 87 was planned as a *Stuka* (short for *Sturzkampfluzeug*), or dive-bomber) a name that became synonymous with the type, to provide 'flying artillery' to support the armoured forces that would spearhead Germany's Blitzkrieg (lightning war) tactics. The Ju 87 first flew in 1935 with twin vertical tail surfaces and a British engine, but was then developed into the Ju 87A initial production model (200 aircraft) with a single vertical surface and the 680hp (507kW) Junkers Jumo 210 inverted-Vee engine. The Ju 87A entered service in the spring of 1937 and was soon supplanted by the Ju 87B-1 that was the first major model with a considerably uprated powerplant to provide improved performance as well as allow a doubling of the bomb load.

Country of origin:	Germany
Type:	two-seat dive-bomber and close support warplane
Powerplant:	one 1200hp (895kW) Junkers Jumo 211Da 12-cylinder inverted-Vee engine
Performance:	maximum speed 383km/h (238mph); climb to 2000m (6560ft) in 4 minutes 18 seconds; service ceiling 8000m (26,245ft); range 790km (491 miles)
Weights:	empty 2710kg (5974lb); maximum take-off 4340kg (9568lb)
Dimensions:	span 13.80m (45ft 3.33in); length 11.10m (36ft 5in); height 4.01m (13ft 2in)
Armament:	two 7.92mm fixed forward-firing machine guns in the leading edges of the wing and one 7.92mm trainable rearward-firing machine gun in the rear of the cockpit, plus an external bomb load of 500kg (1102lb)

Junkers Ju 87B-2

By the end of 1939 the Ju 87B-1 had been replaced in production by the Ju 87B-2 that introduced individual ejector exhaust stubs for a measure of thrust augmentation, hydraulically rather than manually operated radiator cooling gills, an improved propeller with broader-chord blades, and a bomb load of 2205lb (1000kg) when flown as a single-seater. Subvariants produced by the incorporation of factory conversion sets included the Ju 87B-2/U2 with improved radio, Ju 87B-2/U3 with extra armour protection for the close-support role, and Ju 87B-2/U4 with ski landing gear. There was also a Ju 87B-2/Trop version for service in North Africa with sand filters and a pack of desert survival equipment, and both this model and the Ju 87B-2 were delivered to Italy (which named them *Picchiatello*), while the Ju 87B-2 was delivered to Bulgaria, Hungary and Romania. At the beginnig of World War II Germany had 336 Ju-87B aircraft on strength.

Country of origin:	Germany
Type:	two-seat dive-bomber and close support warplane
Powerplant:	one 1200hp (895kW) Junkers Jumo 211Da 12-cylinder inverted-Vee engine
Performance:	maximum speed 383km/h (238mph); climb to 2000m (6560ft) in 4 minutes 18 seconds; service ceiling 8000m (26,245ft); range 790km (491 miles)
Weights:	empty 2710kg (5974lb); maximum take-off 4340kg (9568lb)
Dimensions:	span 13.80m (45ft 3.33in); length 11.10m (36ft 5in); height 4.01m (13ft 2in)
Armament:	two 7.92mm fixed forward-firing machine guns in the leading edges of the wing and one 7.92mm trainable rearward-firing machine gun in the rear of the cockpit, plus an external bomb load of 1000kg (2205lb)

Junkers Ju 87D

By the spring of 1940, the new Jumo 211J-1 inverted-Vee piston engine was ready for service, and the Junkers design team set about evolving a development of the Ju 87B to exploit this engine, which offered not only greater power but also the possibility of a considerably cleaner installation. Other changes in the new variant were a complete redesign of the cockpit enclosure to reduce drag, a reduction in the size and complexity of the main landing gear fairings, an increase in the internal fuel capacity, improvement of crew protection through the introduction of more and thicker armour, the doubling of the defensive firepower, and the strengthening of the lower fuselage and attached crutch for the ability to carry one 3968lb (1800kg) bomb. There were seven subvariants of the Ju 87D between the Ju 87D-1 and Ju 87D-8 for a variety of roles ranging form glider-towing (Ju 87D-2) to night ground attack (Ju 87D-7).

Country of origin:	Germany
Type:	(Ju 87D-1) two-seat dive-bomber and close support warplane
Powerplant:	one 1400hp (1044kW) Junkers Jumo 211J-1 12-cylinder inverted-Vee engine
Performance:	maximum speed 410km/h (255mph); climb to 5000m (16,405ft) in 19 minutes 48 seconds; service ceiling 7300m (23,950ft); range 1535km (954 miles)
Weights:	empty 3900kg (8598lb); maximum take-off 6600kg (14,550lb)
Dimensions:	span 13.80m (45ft 3.33in); length 11.50m (37ft 8.75in); height 3.88m (12ft 9.25in)
Armament:	two 7.92mm fixed forward-firing machine guns in the leading edges of the wing and one 7.92mm trainable two-barrel rearward-firing machine gun in the rear of the cockpit, plus an external bomb load of 1800kg (3968lb)

Junkers Ju 87G

As the increasing ineffectiveness of standard bombs against steadily more heavily armoured tanks became clear to the Luftwaffe in 1942, serious consideration was belatedly given to the adoption of more capable anti-tank armament for the Ju 87, which was now the service's primary anti-tank weapon. The obvious solution was a high-velocity cannon firing a moderately large projectile: the 37mm Flak 18 light anti-aircraft gun was selected, and the revised weapon became the BK 3,7 which, with its magazine and long ejector chute for spent cases, was installed in a pod that could be installed under the wing of the Ju 87 outboard of the main landing gear legs on hardpoints that could otherwise carry bombs. Validated on a Ju 87D-3 conversion, the new armament was introduced on the Ju 87G-1 that entered service in the autumn of 1942. This was the final operational version of the Stuka, with production of all versions totalling 5700.

Country of origin:	Germany
Type:	two-seat anti-tank and close support warplane
Powerplant:	one 1400hp (1044kW) Junkers Jumo 211J-1 12-cylinder inverted-Vee engine
Performance:	maximum speed 410km/h (255mph); climb to 5000m (16,405ft) in 19 minutes 48 seconds; service ceiling 7300m (23,950ft); range 1535km (954 miles)
Weights:	empty 3900kg (8598lb)
Dimensions:	span 13.80m (45ft 3.33in); length 11.50m (37ft 8.75in); height 3.88m (12ft 9.25in)
Armament:	two 7.92mm fixed forward-firing machine guns in the leading edges of the wing, one 7.92mm trainable two-barrel machine gun in the rear of the cockpit, and two 37mm fixed cannon under the wings, plus provision for an external bomb load as an alternative to the cannon

Junkers Ju 87R

Produced in parallel with the Ju 87B, the Ju 87R (Reichweite, or range) was a long-range version of the Ju 87B for anti-ship and other long-endurance missions. The primary changes in the Ju 87R were a structural revision of the outer wing panels to incorporate two 150-litre (33imp gal) tanks that supplemented the standard pair of 240-litre (53imp gal) tanks in the inboard wing panels, and the introduction of 'plumbed' hardpoints under the outer wings, which thus carried two 300-litre (66imp gal) drop tanks in place of the quartet of 50kg (110lb) bombs, so the bomb load was just one 250kg (551lb) weapon. The Ju 87R entered limited service in the spring of 1940, and was produced in four subvariants as the Ju 87R-1 to Ju 87R-4 – equivalent to the Ju 87B-1 to Ju 87B-4. During the Battle of Britain and in the latter stages of the war on the eastern front the Stuka proved itself vulnerable, particularly if no fighter cover was provided.

Country of origin:	Germany
Type:	two-seat dive-bomber
Powerplant:	one 1200hp (895kW) Junkers Jumo 211Da 12-cylinder inverted-Vee engine
Performance:	maximum speed 383km/h (238mph); climb to 2000m (6560ft) in 4 minutes 18 seconds; service ceiling 8000m (26,245ft)
Weights:	empty 3187kg (7026lb)
Dimensions:	span 13.80m (45ft 3.33in); length 11.10m (36ft 5in); height 4.01m (13ft 1.8in)
Armament:	two 7.92mm fixed forward-firing machine guns in the leading edges of the wing, and one 7.92mm trainable rearward-firing machine gun in the rear cockpit, plus an external bomb load of 500kg (1102lb)

Junkers Ju 88A, D, H, S and T

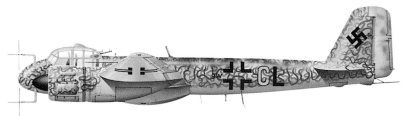

Rivalling the Mosquito as the most versatile warplane of World War II, and of vital importance to Germany right through this war, the Ju 88 was schemed as a high-speed level and dive bomber and first flew in December 1936 for entry into service during 1939. The most important early model was the Ju 88A, of which some 7000 or more were delivered in variants up to the Ju 88A-17 with steadily uprated engines, enhanced defensive armament and improved offensive capability. The Ju 88D was a long-range reconnaissance development of which some 1450 were delivered. The Ju 88H was another reconnaissance model of which small numbers were completed with 1700hp (1267.5kW) BMW 801 radial engines, and the Ju 88S was a high-speed bomber of which modest numbers were produced with radial or Vee engines. The Ju 88T was a reconnaissance derivative of the Ju 88S. The final total of 15,000 Ju 88s of all models gives an idea of the significance of this aircraft.

Country of origin:	Germany
Type:	(Ju 88A-4) four-seat high-speed, level and dive bomber
Powerplant:	two 1340hp (999kW) Junkers Jumo 211J-1/2 12-cylinder engines
Performance:	Maximum speed 470km/h (292mph); climb to 5400m (17,715ft) in 23 minutes; service ceiling 26,900ft (8200m); range 2730km (1696 miles)
Weights:	empty 9860kg (21,737lb); maximum take-off 14,000kg (30,865lb)
Dimensions:	Span 20.00m (65ft 7.5in); length 14.40m (47ft 2.75in); height 4.85m (15ft 11in)
Armament:	one 7.92mm fixed or trainable forward-firing machine gun in windscreen, one 13mm or two 7.92mm forward-firing machine guns in nose position, two 7.92mm machine guns in rear of cockpit, and one 13mm or two 7.92mm trainable rearward-firing machine guns in rear of undernose gondola, plus a bomb load of 2500kg (5511lb)

Junkers Ju 88G

After its introduction in 1942 the Ju 88C-6 proved effective in its role as the first night-fighter derivative of the Ju 88C heavy fighter development program. However, it was appreciated from an early date that the addition of extra equipment would lead to an inevitable increase in both weight and drag, and result in a degradation of performance. This led to the development and appearance (in spring 1943) of the Ju 88 V58 (Ju 88G V1) prototype of a considerably improved night-fighter model. This prototype was a conversion from Ju 88R standard with the more angular tail unit of the Ju 188. There followed some 2800 or more production aircraft in the Ju 88G-1, G-4, G-6 and G-7 variants, each of the last two in three subvariants with different radar and armament, for service from the summer of 1944. Pictured here is a Ju-88G-7a of IV/NJG 6 during the winter of 1944-45, with the tail painted to represent a Ju 88C for deception purposes.

Country of origin:	Germany
Type:	(Ju 88G-7b) four-seat night-fighter
Powerplant:	two 1725hp (1286kW) Junkers Jumo 213E 12-cylinder inverted-Vee engines
Performance:	maximum speed 626km/h (389mph); climb to 9200m (30,185ft) in 26 minutes 24 seconds; service ceiling 10,000m (32,810ft); range 2250km (1398 miles)
Weights:	normal take-off 13,110kg (28,902lb); maximum take-off 13,825kg (30,478lb) or 32,352lb (14,765kg) overload
Dimensions:	span 20.08m (65ft 10.5in); length 15.55m (51ft 0.25in) or, with tail-warning radar, 16.36m (53ft 8in); height 4.85m (15ft 11in)
Armament:	four 20mm fixed forward-firing cannon in the ventral tray, two 20mm fixed obliquely forward/upward-firing cannon in the rear fuselage, and one 13mm machine gun in the rear of the cockpit

Junkers Ju 188

On the outbreak of World War II the design of the Ju 288 as the Ju 88's successor was already well advanced, but by 1941 delays to the Ju 288 programme meant that an interim successor was required. The aircraft selected was the Ju 188, which had emerged from the Ju 88B prototype that had flown in 1940. The Ju 188 entered service in 1942, and production of about 1100 aircraft included the Ju 188A bomber with two 1776hp (1324kW) Junkers Jumo 213A engines, Ju 188D reconnaissance version of the Ju 188A, Ju 188E bomber with radial rather than Vee engines, Ju 188 reconnaissance version of the Ju 188E, Ju 188S high-altitude intruder, and Ju 188T high-altitude reconnaissance aeroplane. Many other variants were trialled or projected for roles that included night-fighting and adverse-weather interception. Pictured here is one of the Ju 188D-2 aircraft on the strength of 1.(F)/124 based at Kirkenes in northern Finland during 1944.

Country of origin:	Germany
Type:	(Ju 188E-1) four-seat medium bomber
Powerplant:	two 1677hp (1250kW) BMW 801D-2 14-cylinder two-row radial engines
Performance:	maximum speed 544km/h (338mph); climb to 6000m (19,685ft) in 17 minutes 24 seconds; service ceiling 10,100m (33,135ft); range 2480km (1541 miles) with a 1500kg (3307lb) bomb load
Weights:	empty 9410kg (20,745lb); maximum take-off 14,570kg (32,121lb)
Dimensions:	span 22.00m (72ft 2in); length 15.06m (49ft 4.9in); height 4.46m (14ft 7.3in)
Armament:	one 20mm trainable forward-firing cannon in nose position, one 13mm machine gun in dorsal turret, one 13mm rearward-firing machine gun in rear of cockpit, and one 7.92mm two-barrel machine gun in undernose gondola, plus a bomb load of 3000kg (6614lb)

Kawanishi N1K-J Shiden 'George'

The Shiden (Violet Lightning) resulted from the realisation of the Kawanishi design team in December 1941 that its N1K1 Kyofu floatplane fighter, which had yet to fly, possessed so much potential that a landplane derivative was clearly a possibility. There followed nine prototypes, the first of them flying in December 1942 at the start of a protracted test programme, before the delivery of 1098 N1K1-J production aircraft in three subvariants differentiated by their armaments. These entered service early in 1944, and were later complemented by 415 examples of the two subvariants of the N1K2-J with a redesigned fuselage and tail unit as well as the wing lowered from the mid- to low-set position allowing the use of shorter main landing gear units. The N1K proved an effective fighter although it was troubled by a temperamental engine. Shown here is late-production N1K2-J KAI of the 343rd Kokutai, Imperial Japanese Navy Air Force during 1945.

Country of origin:	Japan
Type:	(N1K1-J) single-seat fighter and fighter-bomber
Powerplant:	one 1990hp (1557kW) Nakajima NK9H Homare 21 18-cylinder two-row radial engine
Performance:	maximum speed 581km/h (361mph); climb to 6000m (19,685ft) in 7 minutes 50 seconds; service ceiling 12,500m (41,010ft); range 2544km (1581 miles)
Weights:	empty 2897kg (6387lb); maximum take-off 4321kg (9526lb)
Dimensions:	span 12.00m (39ft 4.5in); length 8.88m (29ft 1.88in); height 4.06m (13ft 3.85in)
Armament:	two 20mm fixed forward-firing cannon in the leading edges of the wing, two 20mm fixed forward-firing cannon in underwing gondolas, and two 7.7mm fixed forward-firing machine guns in the forward fuselage, plus an external bomb load of 120kg (265lb)

Kawanishi H6K 'Mavis'

The H6K flying boat resulted from a 1933 requirement and was one of the best warplanes of the Imperial Japanese navy at the start of World War II's Pacific campaign. The type remained in useful service throughout the war as it was supplemented although never really replaced by the superb Kawanishi H8K 'Emily'. The first of four prototypes flew in July 1936, and successful trials led to the H6K2 production model, of which 10 were completed for service from January 1938 with four 1000hp (746kW) Mitsubishi Kinsei 43 radial engines. Further production comprised 127 examples of the H6K4 with revised armament and, in some aircraft, an uprated powerplant, and 36 examples of the H6K5 with greater power. Lesser variants (with numbers) were the H6K2-L transport (16), H6K3 VIP transport (two) and H6K4-L transport (20), many of which remained in service until the end of the war. Pictured is an H6K5 of the Imperial Japanese Navy Air Force.

Country of origin:	Japan
Type:	(H6K5) nine-seat maritime reconnaissance flying boat
Powerplant:	four 1300hp (969kW) Mitsubishi Kinsei 51/53 14-cylinder two-row radial engines
Performance:	maximum speed 385km/h (239mph); climb to 5000m(16,405ft) in 13 minutes 23 seconds; service ceiling 9560m (31,365ft); range 6772 km (4208 miles)
Weights:	empty 12,380kg (27,117lb); maximum take-off 23,000kg (50,706lb)
Dimensions:	span 40.00m (131ft 2.75in); length 25.63m (84ft 0.75in); height 6.27m (20ft 6.75in)
Armament:	one 20mm trainable rearward-firing cannon in tail turret, one 7.7mm machine gun in bow turret, one 7.7mm rearward-firing machine gun in dorsal position, and two 7.7mm trainable lateral-firing machine gun in blister positions, plus a torpedo and bomb load of 3527lb (1600kg)

Kawasaki Ki-61 Hien 'Tony'

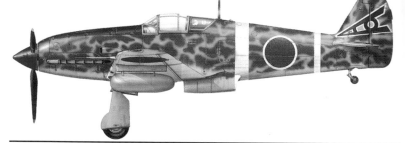

The Hien (Swallow) was unique among Japanese first-line warplanes of World War II in being powered by an inverted-Vee piston engine. This was a Kawasaki Ha-40 unit, a licence-built version of the German Daimler-Benz DB 601A. The first of 12 prototype and pre-production aircraft flew in December 1941, and revealed excellent performance and good handling. The Ki-61-I entered service in February 1943, and was delivered to the extent of 1380 aircraft in two subvariants differentiated by their armament, before the advent of 1274 Ki-61 Kai fighters with a lengthened fuselage and different armament fits. Further development resulted in the Ki-61-II Kai optimised for high-altitude operations with the Kawasaki Ha-140 engine, and deliveries amounted to 374 aircraft in two subvariants again distinguishable by their different armament fit. Like other Japanese fighters, it was soon eclipsed by its American counterparts.

Country of origin:	Japan
Type:	(Ki-61-Ib) single-seat fighter
Powerplant:	one 1175hp (876kW) Kawasaki Ha-40 (Army Type 2) 12-cylinder inverted-Vee engine
Performance:	maximum speed 592km/h (368mph); climb to 5000m (16,405ft) in 5 minutes 31 seconds; service ceiling 11,600m (37,730ft); range 1100km (684 miles)
Weights:	empty 2210kg (4872lb); normal take-off 2950kg (6504lb); maximum take-off 3250kg (7165lb)
Dimensions:	Span 12.00m (39ft 4.25in); length 8.75m (28ft 8.5in); height 3.70m (12ft 1.75in)
Armament:	two 12.7mm fixed forward-firing machine guns in the upper part of the forward fuselage and two 12.7mm fixed forward-firing machine guns in the leading edges of the wing

Kawasaki Ki-45 Toryu 'Nick'

Designed to a 1937 requirement, the Toryu (Dragon Killer) was a twin-engined heavy fighter that became one of the Imperial Japanese Army Air Force's most important warplanes. The first of six prototype and 12 pre-production aircraft flew in January 1939, but considerable development had to be undertaken before the type entered service in autumn 1942 with 1050hp (783kW) Nakajima Ha-25 radial engines as the Ki-45 Kai-a fighter and Ki-45 Kai-b ground-attack/anti-shipping fighter. The Ki-45 Kai-c was a night-fighter development and introduced Mitsubishi engines, while the Ki-45 Kai-d was a ground-attack/anti-shipping model with revised armament including provision to carry 500kg (1102lb) of bombs. Production of the Ki-45 Kai-c reached 477 aircraft, and that of the other three variants 1198 machines. Pictured here is a Ki-45 KAI-c of the 53rd Sentai, Imperial Japanese Army Air Force based at Matsudo in Chiba Prefecture for the defence of the mainland in early 1945.

Country of origin:	Japan
Type:	(Ki-45 Kai-c) two-seat night-fighter
Powerplant:	two 1080hp (805kW) Mitsubishi Ha-102 (Army Type 1) 14-cylinder two-row radial engines
Performance:	maximum speed 540km/h (336mph); climb to 5000m (16,405ft) in 7 minutes; service ceiling 10,000m (32,810ft); range 2000km (1243 miles)
Weights:	empty 4000kg (8818lb); maximum take-off 5500kg (12,125lb)
Dimensions:	span 15.02m (49ft 3.25in); length 11.00m (36ft 1in); height 3.70m (12ft 1.75in)
Armament:	One 37mm fixed forward-firing cannon in underside of forward fuselage, two 20mm fixed obliquely forward/upward-firing cannon in central fuselage, and one 7.92mm trainable rearward-firing machine gun in rear cockpit, plus a bomb load of 500kg (1102lb)

Kawasaki Ki-100

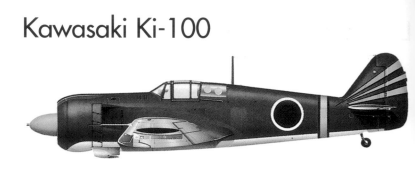

The Ki-61-II Kai was potentially an excellent high-altitude fighter, but was plagued by the unreliability of the Kawasaki Ha-140 Vee engine and a low production rate. By autumn 1944, therefore, Kawasaki were forced to store a number of airframes for lack of the appropriate engines, and in an inspired piece of improvisation combined the Ki-61-II Kai airframe with the Mitsubishi Ha-112-II radial engine. This was wider than the Ha-140, but a remarkably neat installation was devised to combine the radial engine with a narrow fuselage, and the first of three prototype conversions made its maiden flight in February 1945. There followed 272 and 118 new-build aircraft that entered service in two subvariants, including the Ki-100-Ib with an all-round vision canopy, for service from March 1945. The Ki-100 was soon established as the Imperial Japanese Army Air Force's best fighter.

Country of origin:	Japan
Type:	(Ki-100-Ia) single-seat fighter and fighter-bomber
Powerplant:	one 1500hp (1118kW) Mitsubishi Ha-112-II (Army Type 4) 14-cylinder two-row radial engine
Performance:	maximum speed 580km/h (360mph); climb to 5000m (16,405ft) in 6 minutes; service ceiling 11,000m (36,090ft); range 1367 miles (2000km)
Weights:	empty 2525kg (5567lb); maximum take-off 3495kg (7705lb)
Dimensions:	span 12.00m (39ft 4.5in); length 8.82m (28ft 11.25in); height 3.75 m (12ft 3.63in)
Armament:	two 20mm fixed forward-firing cannon in upper part of the forward fuselage, and two 12.7mm fixed forward-firing machine guns in the leading edges of the wing, plus an external bomb load of 500kg (1102lb)

Latécoére Laté 298

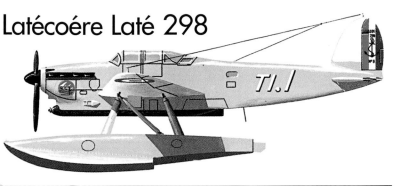

Designed to meet a 1933 requirement, the Laté 298.01 prototype first flew in May 1936. Successful trials led to the Laté 298 production model that entered service in the later part of 1938 with the French naval air arm, which received 24 and 12 (eventually 27) examples of the Laté 298A and Laté 298B with fixed and folding wings respectively. First ordered to the extent of five aircraft in April 1938, the Laté 298D was a Laté 298B development with a fixed wing, and in April and November totals of 25 and 65 more aircraft were ordered. In the event, total deliveries amounted to only about 60 machines. In 1942 the Germans allowed a resumption of Laté 298 production against a Vichy French requirement for 30 aircraft, but it is uncertain how many of these Laté 298F machines (Laté 298D aircraft with simplified controls) were completed. Pictured here is a 298 of Escadrille T1, Aéronavale, based at Berre, near Marseilles, in late 1939.

Country of origin:	France
Type:	(Laté 298D) three-seat coastal reconnaissance and torpedo bomber floatplane
Powerplant:	one 880hp (656kW) Hispano-Suiza 12Ycrs-1 12-cylinder Vee engine
Performance:	maximum speed 290km/h (180mph); climb to 1500m (4,920ft) in 5 minutes 39 seconds; service ceiling 6500m (21,325ft); range 2200 km (1367 miles)
Weights:	empty 3062kg (6750lb); maximum take-off 4800kg (10,582lb) in the reconnaissance role
Dimensions:	Span 15.50m (50ft 10.25in); length 12.56m (41ft 2.5in); height 5.23m (17ft 1.25in)
Armament:	Two 7.5mm fixed forward-firing machine guns in the leading edges of the wing, and one 7.5mm trainable machine gun in the rear of the cockpit, plus an external torpedo and bomb load of 670kg (1477lb)

Lavochkin LaGG-1 and LaGG-3

The LaGG-1 was one of several new monoplane fighters whose development was ordered by the Soviet authorities in 1939 in an effort to modernise the Soviet air forces at a time of deepening European crisis. Based on a wooden airframe to capitalise on the USSR's abundance of the material, the LaGG-1 was a 'modern' monoplane fighter in its low-wing layout with an enclosed cockpit and retractable main landing gear units. The prototype first flew in March 1940, and trials revealed good speed but poor acceleration, climb rate, range, service ceiling and, most notably, handling. Even so, the type was rushed into production; no fewer than 100 interim LaGG-1 and 6427 slightly improved LaGG-3 fighters being completed by autumn 1941. Suffering enormous losses, the aircraft helped the USSR to survive the German invasion of 1941. The aircraft pictured was operated by a Soviet Air Force unit over the Ukrainian front during 1942.

Country of origin:	USSR
Type:	(LaGG-3) single-seat fighter and fighter-bomber
Powerplant:	one 1260hp (939.5kW) Klimov VK-105PF-1 12-cylinder Vee engine
Performance:	maximum speed 575km/h (357mph); climb to 5000m (16,405ft) in 5 minutes 48 seconds; service ceiling 9700m (31,825ft); range 1000km (621 miles)
Weights:	empty 2620kg (5776lb); maximum take-off 3190kg (7032lb)
Dimensions:	span 9.80m (32ft 1.75in); length 8.81m (28ft 11in); height 2.54m (8ft 4in)
Armament:	one 20mm fixed forward-firing cannon in an engine installation and two 7.62mm fixed forward-firing machine guns in the upper part of the forward fuselage, plus an external bomb and rocket load of 200kg (441lb)

Lavochkin La-5

The LaGG-3 mentioned previously was an indifferent fighter of wooden construction that was accepted largely because it was easy to build and provided just about adequate capability. The La-5 was a superb fighter, however, which offered truly excellent capabilities through the replacement of the LaGG-3's Klimov M-105 Vee engine by the more potent Shvetsov M-82 radial engine. The change was ordered in August 1941, and the first of several prototypes flew in March 1942. Intensive development led to an early start to the production run, which lasted until late 1994 and amounted to 9920 aircraft in variants such as the La-5 with the 1480hp (1103.5kW) M-82A engine, La-5F with the 1540hp (1148kW) M-82F (later ASh-82F) engine, definitive La-5FN, La-5FN Type 41 with a metal rather than wooden wing, and La-5UTI two-seat conversion trainer of which only a few were completed. Pictured is a Czech La-5FN, based at Malacky during 1945-46.

Country of origin:	USSR
Type:	(La-5FN) single-seat fighter and fighter-bomber
Powerplant:	one 1630hp (1215kW) Shvetsov ASh-82FN 14-cylinder two-row radial engine
Performance:	maximum speed 648km/h (403mph); climb to 5000m (16,405ft) in 5 minutes; service ceiling 11,000m (36,090ft); range 765km (475 miles)
Weights:	empty 2605kg (5743lb); normal take-off 3265kg (7198lb); maximum take-off 3402kg (7500lb)
Dimensions:	span 9.80m (32ft 1.75in); length 8.67m (28ft 5.33in); height 2.54m (8ft 4in)
Armament:	two 20mm fixed forward-firing cannon in the upper part of the forward fuselage, plus an external bomb and rocket load of 500kg (1102lb)

Letov S 328

Entering service in 1934 with the Czechoslovak Air Force, the S 328 was a development from the original S 28 reconnaissance biplane of 1929 via the S 128 and S 228 with steadily more powerful engines, and was designed to a Finnish requirement that in the event yielded no order. The S 328F prototype was followed by 445 examples of the S 328 production model, 13 examples of the S 328N night-fighter model with four fixed and two trainable machine guns, and four examples of the S 328V twin-float seaplane for the target-towing role. The surviving aircraft were seized by Germany after its occupation of Czechoslovakia in March 1939. Most were retained as trainers, but some were passed to allies such as Bulgaria and Slovakia. Slovak insurgents operated a few aircraft against the Germans in autumn 1944. The aircraft pictured was operated by the Slovak Insurgent Air Force from Tri Duby airfield in September 1944.

Country of origin:	Czechoslovakia
Type:	(S 326) two-seat reconnaissance bomber with secondary ground-attack capability
Powerplant:	one 635hp (474kW) Walter-built Bristol Pegasus IIM2 nine-cylinder single-row radial engine
Performance:	maximum speed 280km/h (174mph); climb to 5000m (16,405ft) in 17 minutes; service ceiling 7200m (23,620ft); range 795 miles (1280km)
Weights:	empty 1680kg (3704lb); maximum take-off 2640kg (5820lb)
Dimensions:	span 13.71m (44ft 11.75in); length 10.36m (33ft 11.75in); height 3.40m (11ft 2in)
Armament:	two or four 7.92mm fixed forward-firing machine guns in the leading edges of the upper and lower wings, and one or two 7.92mm machine guns in the rear cockpit, plus a bomb load of 300kg (661lb)

Lioré-et-Olivier LeO 451

The finest bomber developed by the French aero industry in the period leading up to World War II, the LeO 451 was an aesthetic masterpiece that helped to confirm in a very striking manner that French designers had finally abandoned the angular, slab-sided machines that had trundled about in the skies of France throughout most of the 1930s. Resulting from a November 1934 requirement for an advanced four-seat day bomber, the first of two LeO 45.01 prototypes made its maiden flight in January 1937. These were followed by the LeO 451B.4 production model, which entered service in the autumn of 1939. Production was then rapid, and deliveries totalled about 580 aircraft. The survivors continued in service after the fall of France, some being converted as 12-passenger civil and 17-passenger military transports, with a few remaining in service into the mid-1950s. The example shown here was on the strength of GB1/11 at Oran-La-Sénia (Morocco).

Country of origin:	France
Type:	(LeO 451B.4) four-seat medium bomber
Powerplant:	two 1140hp (850kW) Gnome-Rhòne 14N-48/49 14-cylinder two-row radial engines
Performance:	maximum speed 495km/h (307mph); climb to 5000m (16,405ft) in 14 minutes; service ceiling 9000m (29,530ft); range 2300km (1429 miles) with a 500kg (1102lb) bomb load
Weights:	empty 7815kg (17,229lb); normal take-off 11,400kg (25,133lb)
Dimensions:	span 22.52m (73ft 10.5in); length 17.17m (56ft 4in); height 5.24m (17ft 2.25in)
Armament:	one 7.5mm fixed forward-firing machine gun in the forward fuselage, one 20mm rearward-firing cannon in the dorsal turret, and one 7.5mm machine gun in the ventral turret, plus an external bomb load of 2000kg (4409lb)

LN (Loire-Nieuport) .40

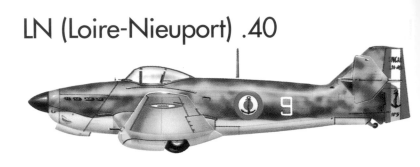

First flown in LN.40.01 prototype form in June 1938, the LN.40 was schemed as a carrierborne dive-bomber for the French naval air arm. The first of 23 or more LN.401BP.1 production aircraft (out of an order for 42 machines) were delivered from mid-1939 for service with two shore-based units. The only other model to enter service was the LN.411BP.1, of which 40 were ordered by the French Air Force. The LN.411 was in essence a version of the LN.401 adapted for the solely land-based role by the removal of carrierborne features such as the arrester hook, wing-folding mechanism and flotation bags. Only a very small number was completed before the fall of France. Some 24 more LN.401 and LN.411 aircraft were completed in 1942 for the Vichy French air force through the assembly of existing components. The aircraft pictured here is an LN,401 that formed part of Escadrille AB.2 of the Aéronavale, based at Berck in France in May 1940.

Country of origin:	France
Type:	(LN.401BP.1) single-seat carrierborne and land-based dive-bomber
Powerplant:	one 690hp (514kW) Hispano-Suiza 12Xcrs 12-cylinder Vee engine
Performance:	maximum speed 380km/h (236mph); initial climb rate not available; service ceiling 9500m (31,170ft); range 1200km (746 miles)
Weights:	empty 2135kg (4707lb); maximum take-off 2823kg (6224lb)
Dimensions:	span 14.00m (45ft 11.25in); length 9.75m (31ft 11.75in); height 3.50m (11ft 5.75in)
Armament:	one 20mm fixed forward-firing cannon in an engine installation, and two 7.5mm fixed forward-firing machine guns in the leading edges of the wing, plus an external bomb load of 225kg (496lb)

Lockheed Hudson

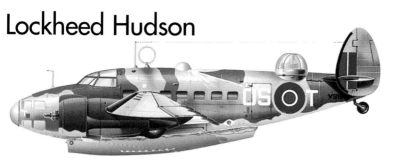

The Hudson was a development of the Model 14 Super Electra transport to meet a British and commonwealth coastal reconnaissance bomber requirement, and first flew in December 1938. The first of 351 Hudson Mk I aircraft reached the UK by sea in February 1939, and further deliveries of this important type included the Hudson Mk II (20 aircraft) with the same Wright R-1820-G102A engines but different propellers, Hudson Mks III and IIIA (about 428 and 601 aircraft) improved version of the Mk I with 1200hp (895kW) GR-1820-G205A engines, Hudson Mks IV and IVA (130 and 52 aircraft) with 1050hp (918.5kW) Pratt & Whitney R-1830-SC3G Twin Wasp engines, Hudson Mk V (409 aircraft) with 1200hp (895kW) R-1830-S3C4G engines, and Hudson Mk VI (450 A-28A aircraft) delivered under Lend-Lease. The aircraft pictured is a Mk III of No 279 Squadron, RAF, based at Sturgate in 1942, and is carrying an underfuselage load of an airborne lifeboat.

Country of origin:	USA
Type:	(Hudson Mk I) six-seat coastal reconnaissance bomber
Powerplant:	two 1100hp (820kW) Wright GR-1820-G102A Cyclone nine-cylinder single-row radial engines
Performance:	maximum speed 357km/h (222mph); climb to 3050m (10,000ft) in 10 minutes; service ceiling 6400m (21,000ft); range 3154km (1960 miles)
Weights:	empty 5484kg (12,091lb); maximum take-off 8845kg (19,500lb)
Dimensions:	span 19.96m (65ft 6in); length 13.50m (44ft 3.75in); height 3.32m (10ft 10.5in)
Armament:	two 0.303in fixed forward-firing machine guns in upper part of forward fuselage, two 0.303in trainable machine guns in dorsal turret, two 0.303in machine guns in beam positions, and one 0.303in machine gun in ventral position; internal bomb load of 612kg (1350lb)

Lockheed A-28 and A-29

These designations were applied to versions of the Hudson built with US funding largely for deliveries under the Lend-Lease scheme to America's allies. The A-28 (52 with 1050hp/783kW Pratt & Whitney R-1830-45 engines) was delivered to Australia as the Hudson Mk IVA, while the A-28A (450 with a convertible trooping interior) was delivered to the UK as the Hudson Mk VI. The A-29 series had Wright R-1820 engines, and comprised the A-29 (416 with 1200hp/895kW R-1820-87 engines) that was delivered to the UK as 243 Hudson Mk IIIA aircraft with the others retained by the USA, the A-29A convertible version of the A-29 (384) delivered to the UK as the Hudson Mk IIIA, and the A-29B (24 conversions of the A-29 and A-29A for the photo-reconnaissance role) retained by the USA. There were also 217 and 83 AT-18 armed and AT-18A unarmed trainers. Pictured here is an A-29 of the US Army Air Corps, in pre-war markings and camouflage.

Country of origin:	USA
Type:	(A-29) four-seat coastal reconnaissance bomber
Powerplant:	two 1200hp (895kW) Wright R-1820-97 nine-cylinder single-row radial engines
Performance:	maximum speed 407km/h (253mph); climb to 3050m (10,000ft) in 6 minutes 18 seconds; service ceiling 8075m (26,500ft); range 2494km (1550 miles)
Weights:	empty 5817kg (12,825lb); maximum take-off 9299kg (20,500lb)
Dimensions:	span 19.96m (65ft 6in); length 13.51m (44ft 4in); height 3.63m (11ft 11in)
Armament:	two 0.3in fixed forward-firing machine guns in upper part of forward fuselage, two 0.3in trainable machine guns in optional dorsal turret, and one 0.3in trainable rearward-firing machine gun in ventral position, plus an internal bomb load of 726kg (1600lb)

Lockheed P-38 Lightning

The P-38A heavy fighter had its empennage carried by two booms supporting the main units of the tricycle landing gear as well as the two engines' turbochargers. The pilot sat in the central nacelle behind heavy nose armament and nosewheel unit. The XP-38 prototype first flew in January 1939, and considerable development paved the way for the P-38D initial operational variant (36 aircraft) that entered service in August 1941. Total production was 9393 aircraft including conversions to F-4 and F-5 reconnaissance standards. The most important fighter variants, featuring steadily more power, were the P-38E (210), P-38F (527), P-38G (1082), P-38H (601), P-38J (2970) and P-38L (3923). There were also night-fighter, trainer and bomber leader conversions, and the type served successfully in every US theatre. The aircraft pictured is a P-38J-5, the most numerous of all the models, with many detail changes during the production run.

Country of origin:	USA
Type:	(P-38L) single-seat long-range fighter and fighter-bomber
Powerplant:	two 1600hp (1193kW) Allison V-1710-111/113 (F30) 12-cylinder Vee engines
Performance:	maximum speed 666km/h (414mph); climb to 6095m (20,000ft) in 7 minutes; service ceiling 13,410m (44,000ft); range 4184km (2600 miles)
Weights:	empty 5806kg (12,800lb); maximum take-off 9798kg (21,600lb)
Dimensions:	span 15.85m (52ft 0in); length 11.53m (37ft 10in); height 3.91m (12ft 10in)
Armament:	one 20mm fixed forward-firing cannon and four 0.5in fixed forward-firing machine guns in the nose, plus an external bomb and rocket load of 1814kg (4000lb)

Lockheed F-4 and F-5

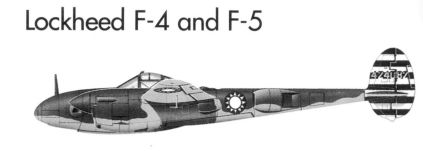

The Lockheed P-38 has often been unfairly overshadowed by its single-engined compatriots, the P-47 and P-51, yet the aircraft proved to be a highly effective long-range fighter in all of the many theatres in which it served. One of these often overshadowed roles was that of photo-reconnaissance (which required speed and agility), no less vital a part of the war effort than the fighter squadrons. The first PR version of the P-38 was the F-4, basically an unarmed P-38E with four cameras. Ninety-nine were built in total. These were followed by the F-5 series. Of the 1082 P-38Gs built, 181 were coverted to F-5A reconnaissance aircraft and 200 to F-5Bs. These aircraft eventually equipped 33 squadrons, with some remaining in service after the war. Pictured here is one of the F-5B-1 aircraft supplied to the Chinese Nationalist Air Force (note the distinctive insignia on the side) while it still held a foothold on the mainland of China.

Country of origin:	USA
Type:	(F-5) single-seat photo-reconnaissance aircraft
Powerplant:	two 1600hp (1193kW) Allison V-1710-111/113 (F30) 12-cylinder Vee engines
Performance:	maximum speed 666km/h (414mph); climb to 6095m (20,000ft) in 7 minutes; service ceiling 13,410m (44,000ft); range 4184km (2600 miles)
Weights:	empty 5806kg (12,800lb); maximum take-off 9798kg (21,600lb)
Dimensions:	span 15.85m (52ft 0in); length 11.53m (37ft 10in); height 3.91m (12ft 10in)
Armament:	none

Lockheed Ventura

By mid-1939 Lockheed had the Hudson maritime reconnaissance bomber derivative of its Model 14 Super Electra civil transport in production for the UK. The company then started to consider further evolution along the same basic line, using the Model 18 Lodestar with its longer fuselage. Lockheed prepared a preliminary design and it was offered to the British in coastal reconnaissance and light bomber forms as successor to the Hudson and Bristol Blenheim respectively. The British approved of the light bomber idea, but the resulting Ventura Mk I (188 aircraft) that entered service in October 1942 was unsuccessful in the daylight bomber role and therefore retasked to the maritime role. Other orders included 487 Ventura Mk II (235 of them repossessed by the USA), 200 Ventura Mk IIA, and 387 Ventura GR.Mk V machines. The Ventura served with all the Commonwealth nations, the Free French air force and also with the Brazilian Air Force.

Country of origin:	USA
Type:	(Ventura GR.Mk V) five-seat coastal reconnaissance bomber
Powerplant:	two 2000hp (1491kW) Pratt & Whitney R-2800-31 Double Wasp 18-cylinder two-row radial engines
Performance:	maximum speed 518km/h (322mph); initial climb rate 680m (2230ft) per minute; service ceiling 8015m (26,300ft); range 2671km (1660 miles)
Weights:	empty 9161kg (20,197lb); maximum take-off 15,422kg (34,000lb)
Dimensions:	span 19.96m (65ft 6in); length 15.77m (51ft 9in); height 3.63m (11ft 11in)
Armament:	two 0.5in machine guns in forward fuselage; (late aircraft without bombardier's window had three 0.5in machine guns in an undernose gun pack), two 0.5in machine guns in dorsal turret, and two 0.303in machine guns in ventral position, plus a bomb load of 2268kg (5000lb)

Lockheed B-34 Lexington, B-37 and PV Ventura

B-34 was the US Army Air Force designation for the 200 Ventura Mk IIA aircraft built with US funding for Lend-Lease delivery. The B-34A and B-34B were 101 and 13 aircraft repossessed from the production lines for service as 57 B-34A-2 bomber trainer, 28 B-34A-3 gunnery trainer, 16 B-34A-4 target tug, and 13 navigator trainer aircraft. The B-37 (18 aircraft only built from an initial order for 550) was an armed reconnaissance derivative with two 2000hp (1491kW) R-2600-13 engines. The US Navy also operated a derivative of the Model 18 transport as the PV Ventura for the patrol bomber role. The core model was the PV-1, of which 1,800 were built and 387 transferred to the UK as Ventura GR.Mk V machines. The US Marine Corps converted a few to use as nightfighters with British radar equipment, and some PV-1 machines were converted as PV-1P photo-reconnaissance aircraft. The designation PV-3 was applied to 27 repossessed Ventura Mk II machines.

Country of origin:	USA
Type:	(PV-1 Ventura) five-seat patrol bomber
Powerplant:	two 2000hp (1491kW) Pratt & Whitney R-2800-31 Double Wasp 18-cylinder two-row radial engines
Performance:	maximum speed 518km/h (322mph); initial climb rate 680m (2230ft) per minute; service ceiling 8015m (26,300ft); range 2671km (1660 miles)
Weights:	empty 9161kg (20,197lb); maximum take-off 15,422kg (34,000lb)
Dimensions:	span 19.96m (65ft 6in); length 15.77m (51ft 9in); height 3.63m (11ft 11in)
Armament:	two 0.5in machine guns in upper part of forward fuselage; (late aircraft without bombardier's window had three 0.5in machine guns in an undernose gun pack), two 0.5in machine guns in dorsal turret, and two 0.303in guns in ventral position; bomb load of 2268kg (5000lb)

Macchi MC.200 Saetta

The Saetta (Lightning) was one of the first generation of Italian low-wing monoplane fighters with advanced features such as retractable main landing gear units, but like many of it's contemporaries was limited in capability by a low-powered engine. Designed from 1936 and first flown in prototype form during December 1937, the MC.200 won the fighter contest held in 1938 and entered service in October 1939. The original type of enclosed cockpit was initially altered to an open and finally a semi-enclosed type ostensibly because Italian pilots preferred this layout! Production totalled 1,150 aircraft, later aircraft having the outer wings of the MC.202 with two 7.7mm machine guns. With the advent of the more capable MC.202, the MC.200 was generally relegated to the escort fighter and fighter-bomber roles (MC.200CB), and the MC.20AS was a tropicalised type for North African service.

Country of origin:	Italy
Type:	(MC.200CB) single-seat fighter and fighter-bomber
Powerplant:	one 870hp (649kW) Fiat A.74 RC.38 14-cylinder two-row radial engine
Performance:	maximum speed 503km/h (312mph); climb to 5000m (16,405ft) in 5 minutes 51 seconds; service ceiling 8900m (29,200ft); range 870km (541 miles)
Weights:	empty 2019kg (4451lb); normal take-off 2339kg (5597lb)
Dimensions:	span 10.58m (34ft 8.5in); length 8.19m (26ft 10.4in); height 3.51m (11ft 5.75in)
Armament:	two 12.7mm fixed forward-firing machine guns in the upper part of the forward fuselage, plus an external bomb load of 320kg (705lb)

Macchi MC.205V Veltro

After producing the excellent MC.202 Folgore development of the MC.200 with a licence-built version of the Daimler-Benz DB 601A engine, Macchi created the MC.205 as a still further improved version of the same basic concept with a licence-built version of the DB 605 engine. The MC.205 prototype was an MC.202 conversion that first flew in April 1942 with the new engine as well as larger outer wing panels. The new fighter entered production and was built to the extent of 262 MC.205V Veltro (greyhound) aircraft that were committed to combat from July 1943. Later machines had 20mm cannon rather than 7.7mm machine guns in the wings, and most of the aircraft served with Aeronautica Nazionale Repubblicana (the air force of the revised Fascist state) after Italy's September 1943 armistice with the Allies. A high-altitude version completed only in prototype form was the MC.205N Orione.

Country of origin:	Italy
Type:	(MC.205V) single-seat fighter and fighter-bomber
Powerplant:	one 1475hp (1100kW) Fiat RA.1050 RC.58 Tifone 12-cylinder inverted-Vee engine
Performance:	maximum speed 642km/h (399mph); climb to 5000m (16,405ft) in 4 minutes 47 seconds; service ceiling 11,000m (36,090ft); range 1040km (646 miles)
Weights:	empty 2581kg (5691lb); normal take-off 3224kg (7108lb); maximum take-off 3408kg (7514lb)
Dimensions:	span 10.58m (34ft 8.5in); length 8.85m (29ft 0.5in); height 3.04m (9ft 11.5in)
Armament:	two 12.7mm fixed forward-firing machine guns in the upper part of the forward fuselage, and two 20mm forward-firing cannon in the leading edges of the wing, plus bomb load of 320kg (705lb)

Martin B-10 and B-12

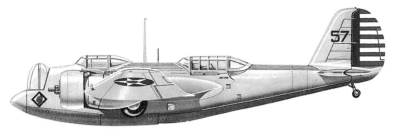

The first American-designed bomber to be flown in combat (albeit by an overseas air force), the B-10 bomber series was obsolete by the beginning of World War II but in its time was a pioneering type. It was the first American bomber of all-metal construction to enter large-scale production, the first American warplane to be fitted with turreted armament, and the US Army Air Corps' first cantilever low-wing monoplane. The USAAC received 151 examples of the B-10 and B-12 bombers, all retired before World War II, but some export aircraft saw combat service. The basic Model 139 was exported to Argentina, China, Thailand and Turkey (35, 9, 26 and 20 machines). The Japanese fought against the Chinese machines as well as the 120 Model 139W and Model 166 aircraft of the Netherlands East Indies in the late 1930s and early 1940s. Shown here is a Martin B-10B of the 28th Bombardment Squadron, US Army Air Corps, based at Luzon in the Phillipines from 1937 to 1941.

Country of origin:	USA
Type:	(Model 139W) four-seat medium bomber
Powerplant:	two 775hp (578kW) Wright R-1820 G-102 Cyclone 9-cylinder single-row radial engines
Performance:	maximum speed 322km/h (200mph); initial climb rate 567m (1860ft) per minute; service ceiling 7680m (25,200ft); range 950km (590 miles) with maximum bomb load
Weights:	empty 4682kg (10,322lb); maximum take-off 7210kg (15,894lb)
Dimensions:	span 21.60 m (70ft 10.5in); length 13.46m (44ft 2in); height 3.53m (11ft 7in)
Armament:	one 0.3in trainable forward-firing machine gun in nose turret, one 0.3in trainable rearward-firing machine gun in dorsal position, and one 0.3in trainable rearward-firing machine gun in the ventral position, plus an internal and external bomb load of 1025kg (2260lb)

Martin B-26 Marauder

The B-26 Marauder was one of the most important tactical warplanes operated by the USA and its allies in World War II. The type was difficult for an inexperienced pilot to handle as a result of its high wing loading and high landing speed, but once mastered was an excellent warplane that achieved good results at a low loss rate. Entering service in summer 1941, the Marauder was built in a number of variants; the most important were the B-26 (201 machines), B-26A (139 machines with provision for a torpedo), B-26B and identical B-26C (1883 and 1235 machines with uprated engines and, in later aircraft, increased wing span), and B-26F and essentially similar B-26G (300 and 893 machines with increased wing incidence). The British designations for the B-26A, B, C and F/G were Marauder Mk I, IA, II and III respectively. The aircraft pictured is a B-26G-1 of the 456th Bomb Squadron, 323rd Bomb Group, US 9th Air Force, based at Laon-Athies in late 1944.

Country of origin:	USA
Type:	(Marauder Mk I) seven-seat medium attack bomber
Powerplant:	two 1850hp (1379kW) Pratt & Whitney R-2800-5 18-cylinder two-row radial engines
Performance:	maximum speed 507km/h (315mph) at 4570 m (15,000ft); climb to 4570m (15,000ft) in 12 minutes 30 seconds; service ceiling 7620m (25,000ft); range 1609km (1000 miles)
Weights:	empty 9696kg (21,375lb); maximum take-off 14,515kg (32,000lb)
Dimensions:	span 18.81m (65ft); length 17.07m (56ft); height 6.05m (19ft 10in)
Armament:	one 0.5in trainable forward-firing machine gun in the nose position, two 0.5in trainable machine guns in the dorsal turret, and one 0.5in trainable rearward-firing machine gun in the tail position, plus an internal and external bomb load of 4800lb (2177kg)

Messerschmitt Bf 109B, Bf 109C and Bf 109D

The Bf 109 is by any standard a classic fighter and, with more than 30,500 examples built before and during World War II, was of vital importance to the German war effort throughout that conflict. The type resulted from the German Air Force's requirement for its first 'modern' monoplane fighter, and the first of 13 prototypes flew in September 1935. The Bf 109B (two variants) entered service in April 1937 with the armament of three 7.92mm machine guns, and was followed by the Bf 109C (two variants) with an armament of four or five machine guns. Both the Bf 109B and Bf 109C saw service in the Spanish Civil War. They were followed by the Bf 109D, which was built to the extent of about 175 aircraft with the 986hp (735kW) Daimler-Benz DB 600Aa engine and an armament of one 20mm cannon and two 7.92mm machine guns. Although some were transferred to night-fighter units most had been relegated to training use by 1939.

Country of origin:	Germany
Type:	(Bf 109C-1) single-seat fighter
Powerplant:	one 700hp (522kW) Junkers Jumo 210Ga 12-cylinder inverted-Vee engine
Performance:	maximum speed 470km/h (292mph); climb 5000m (16,405ft) in 8 minutes 45 seconds; service ceiling 8400m (27,560ft); range 652km (405 miles)
Weights:	empty 1597kg (3522lb), maximum take-off 2296kg (5062lb)
Dimensions:	span 9.87m (32ft 4.5in); length 8.55m (28ft 0.67in); height 2.40m (7ft 3.75in)
Armament:	two 7.92mm fixed forward-firing machine guns in the upper part of the forward fuselage, and two 7.92mm fixed forward-firing machine guns in the leading edges of the wing

Messerschmitt Bf 109E-1 to E-4

Germany's standard single-seat fighter at the beginning of World War II, the Bf 109E was instrumental in the Luftwaffe's success over the Polish, Scandinavian and North-West European battlefields between September 1939 and June 1940. It was only when the type was committed at longer range against British fighters in the Battle of Britain that its limitations were first realised. Entering service at the end of 1938 and built to the extent of more than 4000 aircraft, the Bf 109E 'Emil' was in essence the Bf 109D revised with the more powerful DB 601 engine and cannon armament. The main early variants were the Bf 109E-1 with the 1075hp (801.5kW) DB 601A-1 engine, Bf 109E-3 with an uprated engine, improved armour and provision for an engine-mounted 20mm cannon, and Bf 109E-4 with no engine cannon. The *Emil* was regarded by pilots as one of the finest of the Me 109 models, and was at least equal to early Spitfire models.

Country of origin:	Germany
Type:	(Bf 109E-4) single-seat fighter
Powerplant:	one 1175hp (876kW) Daimler-Benz DB 601Aa 12-cylinder inverted-Vee engine
Performance:	maximum speed 560km/h (348mph); climb to 6000m (19,685ft) in 7 minutes 45 seconds; service ceiling 10,500m (34,450ft); range 660km (410 miles)
Weights:	empty 2125kg (4685lb); normal take-off 2510kg (5534lb); maximum take-off 2665kg (5875lb)
Dimensions:	span 9.87m (32ft 4.5in); length 8.64m (28ft 4.5in); height 2.50m (8ft 2.33in)
Armament:	two 20mm fixed forward-firing cannon in the leading edges of the wing, and two 7.92mm fixed forward-firing machine guns in the upper part of the forward fuselage

Messerschmitt Bf 109E-5 to E-9

Ｆrom 1940 the Bf 109E was used primarily in the fighter-bomber role with one 250kg (551lb) bomb (variants suffixed /B), while the Bf 109E-5 and E-6 were reconnaissance fighters with no cannon armament and, in the case of the E-6, the 1200hp (895kW) DB 601N engine. The Bf 109E-7 was developed from the E-4/N with provision for a drop tank in place of the bomb, and important subvariants were the tropicalised Bf 109E-7/Trop, the Bf 109E-7/U2 with better protection for the ground-attack role, and the Bf 109E-7/Z with a nitrous oxide power boost system. The Bf 109E-8 was an 109E-7 development with the 1350hp (1006.5kW) DB 601E engine, and the Bf 109E-9 was the reconnaissance fighter derivative of the E-8 with no wing cannon and a camera installation. Bf 109E production ended early in 1942. Nearly all E versions were fitted with two or three 20mm cannon, which had a greater range and striking power than a battery of machine guns.

Country of origin:	Germany
Type:	(Bf 109E-7) single-seat fighter
Powerplant:	one 1200hp (895kW) Daimler-Benz DB 601N 12-cylinder inverted-Vee engine
Performance:	(estimated) maximum speed 560km/h (348mph); climb to 6000m (19,685ft) in 7 minutes 45 seconds; service ceiling 34,450ft (10,500m); range 660km (410 miles)
Weights:	(estimated) empty 2125kg (4685lb); maximum take-off 2915kg (6426lb)
Dimensions:	span 9.87m (32ft 4.5in); length 8.64m (28ft 4.5in); height 2.50m (8ft 2.33in)
Armament:	two 20mm fixed forward-firing cannon in the leading edges of the wing, and two 7.92mm forward-firing machine guns in the upper part of the forward fuselage, plus an external bomb load of 250kg (551lb)

Messerschmitt Bf 109F

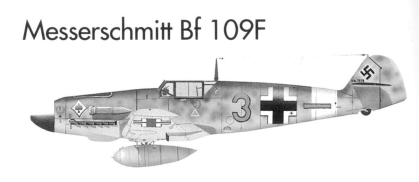

Entering service in spring 1941, the Bf 109F marked the apogee of the Bf 109's development in terms of aerodynamic refinement (improved cowling, rounded wing tips and cantilever tailplane) and handling, although these were achieved only at the expense of armament, which was generally considered too light. It was for this reason that production of the Bf 109F was terminated after the delivery of some 2200 aircraft. The Bf 109F-1 featured two 7.92mm machine guns and a slow-firing 20mm cannon in the engine, the F-2 had a faster-firing 15mm cannon, the F-3 was powered by the 1350hp (1006.5kW) DB 601E engine, the F-4 introduced a fast-firing 20mm cannon and improved protection, the F-5 was a reconnaissance fighter without the cannon, and the F-6 was an unarmed reconnaissance model. The aircraft pictured has the centreline drop tank fitted, a secondary measure to try and wring greater range from the aircraft.

Country of origin:	Germany
Type:	(Bf 109F-2) single-seat fighter
Powerplant:	one 1200hp (895kW) Daimler-Benz DB 601N 12-cylinder inverted-Vee engine
Performance:	maximum speed 600km/h (373mph); climb to 5000m (16,405ft) in 5 minutes 12 seconds; service ceiling 11,000m (36,090ft); range 880km (547 miles)
Weights:	empty 2353kg (5188lb); maximum take-off 3066kg (6760lb)
Dimensions:	span 9.92m (32ft 6.5in); length 8.94m (29ft 3.88in); height 2.60m (8ft 6.33in)
Armament:	one 15mm fixed forward-firing cannon in an engine installation and two 7.92mm fixed forward-firing machine guns in the upper part of the forward fuselage

Messerschmitt Bf 109G

Still in production (23,500 aircraft) at the end of World War II, the Bf 109G was numerically the most important Bf 109 variant. Few of the pilots who flew it would dispute that improvements in the type's speed and firepower – gained by the introduction of the more powerful DB 605 engine – resulted in poorer overall handling qualities. The Bf 109G was delivered in pressurised (even-numbered) and unpressurised (odd-numbered) subvariants for service from summer 1942. Principal among these were the G-1 and G-2 with the DB 605A engine, one 20mm and two 7.92mm weapons, G-3 and G-4 with different radio, G-5 and G-6 with heavier gun armament and later a wooden tail unit, G-8 reconnaissance fighter, G-10 with the 1850hp (1379.5kW) DB 605D, G-12 tandem seat trainer, G-14 improved G-6, and G-16 improved G-14. Pressurisation was deleted from the 109G-6 and subsequent subvariants onward.

Country of origin:	Germany
Type:	(Bf 109G-6) single-seat fighter and fighter-bomber
Powerplant:	one 1474hp (1100kW) Daimler-Benz DB 605AM 12-cylinder inverted-Vee engine
Performance:	maximum speed 386mph (621km/h); climb to 5700m (18,700ft) in 6 minutes; service ceiling 11,550m (37,890ft); range 1000km (621 miles)
Weights:	empty 2673kg (5893lb); maximum take-off 3400kg (7496lb)
Dimensions:	span 9.92m (32ft 6.5in); length 8.85m (29ft 0.5in); height 2.50m (8ft 2.5in)
Armament:	one 20mm or 30mm fixed forward-firing cannon in an engine installation, and two 13mm fixed forward-firing machine guns in the upper part of the forward fuselage, plus an external bomb load of 250kg (551lb)

Messerschmitt Bf 110C/D

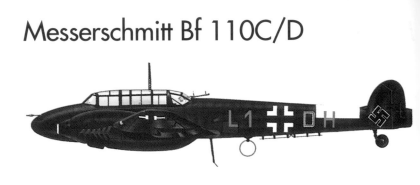

A heavy fighter that first flew in May 1936 and remained in production through
World War II for a total of about 6000 aircraft, the Bf 110 entered service as the
Bf 110B with two 700hp (522kW) Junkers Jumo 210 engines. Only 45 of Bf 110Bs
aircraft were completed before the advent of the Bf 110C with two Daimler-Benz DB
601 engines. About 1300 of the Bf 110C-1 to C-3 fighter variants were built before
production switched to the Bf 110C-4 to C-7 models with better protection and
provision for the fighter-bomber and reconnaissance roles. The Bf 110D, built in D-1
to D-3 variants, had greater fuel capacity (internal and external) for the long-range
fighter, fighter-bomber and shipping escort roles, although some were later adapted
as interim night-fighters, the type serving until a time early in 1943 when they were
superceded by the purpose-built E series. The Bf 110 proved highly vulnerable
during the Battle of Britain against smaller, lighter fighter aircraft.

Country of origin:	Germany
Type:	(Bf 110C-4) two/three-seat heavy fighter
Powerplant:	two 1100hp (820kW) Daimler-Benz DB 601A-1 12-cylinder inverted-Vee engines
Performance:	maximum speed 560km/h (248mph); climb to 6000m (19,685ft) in 10 minutes 12 seconds; service ceiling 10,000m (32,810ft); range 1095km (680 miles)
Weights:	empty 5150kg (11,354lb); maximum take-off 6750kg (14,881lb)
Dimensions:	span 16.20m (53ft 1.8in); length 12.10m (39ft 8.33in); height 4.13m (13ft 6.5in) with the tail up
Armament:	two 20mm fixed forward-firing cannon and four 7.92mm fixed forward-firing machine guns in the nose, and one 7.92mm trainable rearward-firing machine gun in the rear cockpit

Messerschmitt Bf 110E and Bf 110F

From autumn 1940 production of the indifferent Bf 110C/D was scaled down, but in the spring of 1941 two new variants appeared as the Bf 110E and Bf 110F. The Bf 110E was a relatively simple development of the Bf 110D with updated equipment, improved crew protection, a measure of structural strengthening, and racks under the outer wing panels for four 50kg (110lb) bombs as well as the standard pair of 1102lb (500kg) bombs under the fuselage. Bf 110E production stretched through the E-1 to E-3 variants. Appearing slightly later than the Bf 110E and then built in parallel with it, the Bf 110F was introduced to take advantage of the greater power offered by the new DB 601F engine, and there were F-1 to F-3 fighter and fighter-bomber variants before the advent of the F-4 night-fighter with early *Lichtenstein* radar equipment. A total of about 6050 Bf 110 aircraft of all models were built before production ended in March 1945.

Country of origin:	Germany
Type:	(Bf 110F-2) two-seat heavy fighter
Powerplant:	two 1350hp (1007kW) Daimler-Benz DB 601F 12-cylinder inverted-Vee engines
Performance:	maximum speed 565km/h (351mph); climb to 6000m (19,685ft) in 9 minutes 12 seconds; service ceiling 10,900 m (35,760ft); range 1200km (746 miles)
Weights:	empty 5600kg (12,346lb); maximum take-off 7200kg (15,873lb)
Dimensions:	span 16.20m (53ft 1.8in); length 12.10m (39ft 8.33in); height 4.13m (13ft 6.5in) with the tail up
Armament:	two 20mm forward-firing cannon and four 7.92mm fixed forward-firing machine guns in the nose, and one 7.92mm trainable rearward-firing machine gun in the rear cockpit

Messerschmitt Bf 110G and Bf 110H

The Bf 110G was created to fill the operational gap left by the failure of the Messerschmitt Me 210, and appeared in 1942 as a development of the Bf 110F with the more powerful DB 605 engine. The type was used mainly for the defence of Germany in G-1 to G-3 day fighter and G-4 night-fighter variants, the last with radar and all of them in increasingly heavily armed subvariants. The Bf 110 came into its own as a night-fighter, a task in which its size, weight and relative lack of agility were not important .The Bf 110H-1 to H-4 were basically similar to the Bf 110G with DB 605E engines, a strengthened fuselage and retractable tailwheel. In 1944 the Luftwaffe night fighter units were at the peak of their capability and could call on about 320 Bf 110 aircraft for this role, representing somne 60 percent of the total night fighters available. A year later more modern aircraft such as the Heinkel He 219 Uhu began to enter service, and the Bf 110 was slowly withdrawn.

Country of origin:	Germany
Type:	(Bf 110G-4c/R3) two/three-seat night-fighter
Powerplant:	two 1475hp (1100kW) Daimler-Benz DB 605B-1 12-cylinder inverted-Vee engines
Performance:	maximum speed 550km/h (342mph); initial climb rate 661m (2170ft) per minute; service ceiling 8000m (26,245ft); range 1300km (808 miles)
Weights:	empty 5094kg (11,230lb); maximum take-off 9888kg (21,799lb)
Dimensions:	span 16.25m (53ft 3.25in); length 13.05m (42ft 9.75in) including antennae; height 4.18 m (13ft 8.5in) with the tail up
Armament:	two 30mm fixed forward-firing cannon in the nose, two 20mm fixed forward-firing cannon in the ventral tray, and one 7.92mm two-barrel machine gun in the dorsal position or, in the alternative *shräge Musik* installation, two 20mm cannon in the rear fuselage

Messerschmitt Me 163 Komet

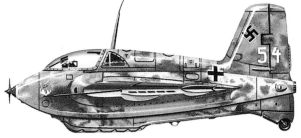

This was truly one of the most remarkable aircraft of World War II, and also revealed the German flair for bringing toward practical use an apparently far-fetched concept. Germany was one of the few countries that during the 1930s believed it was worth pursuing the concept of a rocket-powered aeroplane for manned use and began development of the Me 163 interceptor in response to Allied bomber raids. The first of 76 prototype and development aircraft made its maiden flight in August 1941 as a swept-wing tailless aeroplane that took off from a detachable trolley and landed on an extending skid. It was only after protracted and difficult development that the Me 163B entered limited service in May 1944. Production totalled some 300 Me 163B-1 aircraft whose successes were limited by the fighter's very limited powered endurance and the tendency of its liquid-fuelled rocket engine to explode in the course of a heavy landing.

Country of origin:	Germany
Type:	(Me 163B-1a) single-seat point interceptor
Powerplant:	one 3748lb st (16.67kN) Walter HWK 109-509A-1/2 liquid-propellant rocket motor
Performance:	maximum speed 955km/h (593mph); climb to 9145m (30,000ft) in 2 minutes 36 seconds; service ceiling 12,000m (39,370ft); radius of action 35.5km (22 miles)
Weights:	empty 1908kg (4206lb); maximum take-off 4310kg (9502lb)
Dimensions:	span 9.33m (30ft 7.33in); length 5.85m (19ft 2.33in); height 2.76m (9ft 0.7in) on take-off dolly
Armament:	two 30mm or 20mm fixed forward-firing cannon in the wing roots

Messerschmitt Me 262A-1

The Me 262 was undoubtedly the most far-sighted warplane to enter production during World War II. For the time the concept of a turbojet-powered fighter was extremely advanced. Devlopment of the aircraft was extremely protracted, due to problems with the engines producing insufficient power. The Me 262A-7 was the immediate precursor to the production model, the Me 262A-1a. Although first flown in definitive form in July 1942, precious time was wasted before Hitler authorised production in November 1943, and then only as a high-speed bomber. Some brave subterfuge among the development team ensured the Me 262 was produced as a fighter as well as a bomber, and the type entered service in the summer of 1944 with Luftwaffe fighter units. The first combat mission was flown in October 1944. Pictured is one of the aircraft on the strength of the 9.Staffel Jagdgeschwader Nr 7, based at Parchim in early 1945.

Country of origin:	Germany
Type:	(Me 262A-1a) single-seat interceptor
Powerplant:	two 1984 lb st (8.825kN) Junkers Jumo 004B-1/2/3 turbojet engines
Performance:	maximum speed 870km/h (540mph); climb to 6000m (19,685ft) in 6 minutes 48 seconds; service ceiling 11,450m (37,565ft); range 1050km (652 miles)
Weights:	empty 4420kg (9742lb); maximum take-off 7130kg (15,720lb)
Dimensions:	span 12.51m (41ft 0.5in); length 10.60m (34ft 9.5in); height 3.83m (11ft 6.75in)
Armament:	four 30mm fixed forward-firing cannon in the nose

Messershmitt Me 262A-2

It was realised in mid-1944 that Allied air power during the North African and Italian landings had effectively kept the Luftwaffe and German Navy at bay, forcing a reappraisal of the role of the Me-262 that had not yet entered service. Senior German officers and Hitler himself considered that the new jet should be adapted to the role of fighter-bomber, and the decision was taken to fit aircraft with Schloss 503A-1 bomb racks under the wings. The Me 262A-2a entered service thus configured in July 1944 with *Erprobugskommando Schenk*. Total production of the Me 262 was in the order of 1100 aircraft, but of these perhaps only 200 Me 262A single- and Me 262B two-seat machines entered first-line service, soon acquiring an almost legendary reputation among their opponents but a somewhat dire reputation among their pilots for their axial-flow engines' lack of reliability. Introduced earlier the aircraft could have had a major impact on the air war.

Country of origin:	Germany
Type:	(Me 262A-1a) single-seat fighter-bomber
Powerplant:	two 1984 lb st (8.825kN) Junkers Jumo 004B-1/2/3 turbojet engines
Performance:	maximum speed 870km/h (540mph); climb to 6000m (19,685ft) in 6 minutes 48 seconds; service ceiling 11,450m (37,565ft); range 1050km (652 miles)
Weights:	empty 4420kg (9742lb); maximum take-off 7130kg (15,720lb)
Dimensions:	span 12.51m (41ft 0.5in); length 10.60m (34ft 9.5in); height 3.83m (11ft 6.75in)
Armament:	four 30mm fixed forward-firing cannon in the nose, plus an external bomb load of 500kg (1102lb)

Messerschmitt Me 410 Hornisse

This multi-role warplane was evolved as successor to the unsuccessful Messerschmitt Me 210 heavy fighter and was an altogether more capable as well as more successful warplane. The failings of the Me 210 had in fact been solved just before the type's cancellation, and it was from this ultimately excellent type that the Me 410 was evolved with basically the same revised aerodynamic and structural features in combination with modified outer wing panels and the different powerplant of two Daimler-Benz DB 603A inverted-Vee piston engines. The Me 410 first flew in prototype form during autumn 1942, and there were 1137 production aircraft in variants such as the Me 410A (three major variants) and the Me 410B. Five major variants of the 410B were produced with the DB 603G engines. The B-5 anti-shipping torpedo bomber, the B-7 day reconnaissance and B-8 night reconnaissance aircraft were still in experimental stage at the war's end

Country of origin:	Germany
Type:	(Me 410A-1/U2) two-seat heavy fighter
Powerplant:	two 1750hp (1305kW) Daimler-Benz DB 603A 12-cylinder inverted-Vee engines
Performance:	maximum speed 624km/h (388mph); climb to 6700m (21,980ft) in 10 minutes 42 seconds; service ceiling 10,000m (32,810ft); range 1670km (1050 miles)
Weights:	empty 7518kg (16,574lb); normal take-off 9651kg (21,276lb)
Dimensions:	span 16.35m (53ft 7.75in); length 12.48m (40ft 11.5in); height 4.28m (14ft 0.5in)
Armament:	two 20mm fixed forward-firing cannon in the nose, two 20mm fixed forward-firing cannon in a ventral tray, two 7.92mm fixed forward-firing machine guns in the nose, and one 13mm machine gun in each of the two barbettes on the sides of the fuselage

Messerschmitt Me 410 Hornisse

Five major variants of the 410B were produced with the DB 603G engines. The B-5 anti-shipping torpedo bomber, the B-7 day reconnaissance and B-8 night reconnaissance aircraft were still in experimental stage at the war's end. A number of variants were produced exclusively for the task of shooting down Allied bombers. The /U2/R2 versions had the bomb bay fitted with two 30mm MK103 or MK 108 guns; the UR/R5 installed four MG 151s in the bomb bay, giving six forward-firng 20mm cannon; the U2/R4 added two further MG 151s in the bomb bay. The most heavily armed was the remarkable Me 410A-2/U4, which carried a 5cm BK5 cannon in the nose, and on new-build models also twin MG 151s and twin MG 17s . Field conversion kits were also supplied to fit the BK5 gun plus two 30mm MK 103 cannon. These aircraft were designated B-2/U4. Pictured is an Me 410A-2/U4 of 6./ZG26, operating from Hildesheim in spring 1944.

Country of origin:	Germany
Type:	(Me 410A-2/U4) two-seat heavy fighter
Powerplant:	two 1750hp (1305kW) Daimler-Benz DB 603A 12-cylinder inverted-Vee engines
Performance:	maximum speed 624km/h (388mph); climb to 6700m (21,980ft) in 10 minutes 42 seconds; service ceiling 10,000m (32,810ft); range 1670km (1050 miles)
Weights:	empty 7518kg (16,574lb); normal take-off 9651kg (21,276lb)
Dimensions:	span 16.35m (53ft 7.75in); length 12.48m (40ft 11.5in); height 4.28m (14ft 0.5in)
Armament:	one 5cm BK5 gun in nose, two 20mm fixed forward-firing cannon in the nose, plus one , and one 13mm trainable lateral/rearward-firing machine gun in each of the two remotely controlled barbettes on the sides of the fuselage

Mikoyan-Gurevich MiG-1 and MiG-3

The MiG-1 and MiG-3 series of aircraft were placed in large-scale production largely because they possessed very high performance and despite the fact that they were extremely difficult to fly, not least because of a very short fuselage that resulted in a distinct lack of longitudinal stability. The MiG-1 was developed for an urgent Soviet air force requirement, issued early in 1938, for a high-altitude fighter, and first flew in prototype form in April 1940. Production totalled 100 aircraft, with the armament of one 12.7mm and two 7.62mm machine guns and either open or enclosed accommodation. These were followed by the improved MiG-3 of which 3322 were delivered up to spring 1942 with improved protective features, a rearward-sliding rather than side-hinged canopy, and increased dihedral. Pictured is a MiG-3 of an unidentified Soviet fighter unit operating on the Eatern Front in the summer of 1942.

Country of origin:	USSR
Type:	(MiG-3) single-seat fighter and fighter-bomber
Powerplant:	one 1350hp (1007kW) Mikulin AM-35A 12-cylinder Vee engine
Performance:	maximum speed 640km/h (398mph); climb to 5000m (16,405ft) in 5 minutes 42 seconds; service ceiling 12,000m (39,370ft); range 1195km (742 miles)
Weights:	empty 2595kg (5721lb); maximum take-off 3350kg (7385lb)
Dimensions:	span 10.20m (33ft 5.5in); length 8.25m (27ft 0.8in); height 2.65m (8ft 8.33in)
Armament:	one 12.7mm and two 7.62mm fixed forward-firing machine guns in the upper part of the forward fuselage, plus an external bomb and rocket load of 200kg (441lb)

Mitsubishi A6M Reisen 'Zeke' and 'Zero'

The A6M was generally known in the West as the Zero, a name derived from its Japanese name Reisen (meaning zero fighter) that resulted from its adoption in the Japanese year 2600 (1940). The A6M rightly remains the most famous of all Japanese warplanes of World War II and in its heyday was a superb naval fighter. It is also important as the first carrierborne fighter anywhere in the world to achieve full parity with the best of its land-based contemporaries, but for lack of an adequate successor was maintained in development and production (11,280 aircraft) past its effective limits. The type reached its apogee as a dogfighting warplane in the A6M2, while the A6M3 had greater power but shorter range, the A6M5 heavier firepower, and the A6M6 better protection and greater fighter-bomber capability. When fitted with a drop tank the Zero had phenomenal range, afforded by a sophisticated engine/propeller management techniques.

Country of origin:	Japan
Type:	(A6M2 Model 21) single-seat carrierborne and land-based fighter and fighter-bomber
Powerplant:	one 950hp (708kW) Nakajima NK1C Sakae 12 14-cylinder two-row radial engine
Performance:	maximum speed 534km/h (332mph); climb to 6000m (19,685ft) in 7 minutes 27 seconds; service ceiling 10,000m (32,810ft); range 3104km (1929 miles)
Weights:	empty 1680kg (3704lb); maximum take-off 2796kg (6164lb)
Dimentions:	span 12.00m (39ft 4.5in); length 9.06m (29ft 8.75in); height 3.05m (10ft)
Armament:	two 20mm fixed forward-firing cannon in the leading edges of the wing, and two 7.7mm fixed forward-firing machine guns in the forward fuselage, plus an external bomb load of 120kg (265lb)

Mitsubishi A5M 'Claude'

It is impossible to overstate the importance of the A5M carrierborne fighter in the development of Japanese industry and Japanese military capabilities in the mid-1930s. With this type Japan moved from dependence on Western imports and thinking to a completely indigenous product that was Japan's first carrierborne monoplane fighter and also in every way comparable in terms of performance and capabilities with the best of its Western equivalents. The first of six prototypes made the type's maiden flight in February 1935, and the A5M1 entered service in spring 1937. Production of the series, which departed first-line service in 1943, totalled 980 aircraft in the A5M1 to A5M4 series, the last with open rather than enclosed cockpits There were also 103 examples of the A5M4-K two-seat trainer development. In total it is estimated that nearly 1000 A5Ms were built, the aircraft proving very popular with naval pilots.

Country of origin:	Japan
Type:	(A5M4) single-seat carrierborne and land-based fighter
Powerplant:	one 785hp (585kW) Nakajima Kotobuki 41 or Kotobuki 41 Kai nine-cylinder single-row radial engine
Performance:	maximum speed 435km/h (270mph); climb to 3000m (9845ft) in 3 minutes 35 seconds; service ceiling 9800m (32,150ft); range 1400km (870 miles)
Weights:	empty 1263kg (2874lb); maximum take-off 1822kg (4017lb)
Dimensions:	span 11.00m (36ft 1.13in); length 7.57m2 (4ft 9.88in); height 3.27m (10ft 8.75in)
Armament:	two 7.7mm fixed forward-firing machine guns in the upper part of the forward fuselage, plus an external bomb load of 60kg (132lb)

Mitsubishi G3M 'Nell'

Although it was already obsolescent when Japan entered World War II in 1941, the G3M belied this technical limitation by scoring a number of stunning successes in the opening phases of Japan's offensive onslaught. The lack of an adequate replacement meant that the 'Nell' was forced to soldier on into total obsolescence and suffered devastatingly heavy losses. First flown in July 1935, the G3M was designed to provide the Imperial Japanese Navy Air Force with the means to project its air power deep into the Pacific. The variant that entered service in 1937 was the G3M1, but these 34 aircraft were soon supplanted by an eventual 993 examples of the G3M2 (uprated engines and greater fuel capacity) and G3M3 (further uprated engines and increased fuel capacity). Some aircraft were also converted as L3Y armed transport aircraft. Pictured here is a G3M3 of the Takao Kokutai, 21st Koku Sentai, operating from Hanoi during March 1941.

Country of origin:	Japan
Type:	(G3M2) seven-seat medium attack bomber
Powerplant:	two 1075hp (801.5kW) Mitsubishi Kinsei 41,42 or 45 14-cylinder two-row radial engines
Performance:	maximum speed 373km/h (232mph); climb to 3000m (9845ft) in 8 minutes 19 seconds; service ceiling 9130m (29,950ft); range 4380km (2722 miles)
Weights:	empty 4965kg (10,936lb); maximum take-off 8000kg (17,637lb)
Dimentions:	span 25m (82ft 0.25in); length 16.45m (53ft 11.63in); height 3.69m (12ft 1in)
Armament:	one 20mm trainable rearward-firing cannon in dorsal turret, one 7.7mm trainable machine gun in retractable dorsal turret, one 7.7mm machine gun in each beam position, and provision for one 7.7mm machine gun in cockpit, plus a bomb load of 800kg (1764lb)

Mitsubishi G4M1 'Betty'

The G4M was the ultimate expression of the Imperial Japanese Navy Air Force's desire to project land-based air power from its island garrisons deep into the Pacific Ocean for the destruction of enemy warships and the support of its own forces' amphibious operations. The G4M certainly possessed remarkable range but, as combat was to prove, this capability was purchased only at the expense of features that were just as important: crew protection, self-sealing fuel tanks and a sturdy structure able to absorb battle damage. Resulting from a 1937 requirement, the first of two G4M1 prototypes flew in October 1939, and the type entered service early in 1941. Production totalled 1200 G4M1 aircraft in variants such as the Convoy Fighter escort (five 20mm trainable cannon), Model 11 attack bomber and Model 12 attack bomber, the last with MK4E engines. Trainer and transport variants were then created as conversions. Pictured is a G4M1 of the 708th Kokutai.

Country of origin:	Japan
Type:	(G4M1 Model 11) seven-seat medium attack bomber
Powerplant:	two 1530hp (1141kW) Mitsubishi MK4A Kasei 11 14-cylinder two-row radial engines
Performance:	maximum speed 428km/h (266mph); climb to 7000m (22,965ft) in 18 minutes; range 6033km (3749 miles)
Weights:	empty 6800kg (14,991lb); maximum take-off 9500kg (20,944lb)
Dimensions	span 25.00m (82ft 0.25in); length 20.00m (65ft 7.25in); height 6.00m (19ft 8.25in)
Armament:	one 20mm trainable rearward-firing cannon in the tail position, one 7.7mm trainable rearward-firing machine gun in the dorsal blister position, and one 7.7mm trainable lateral-firing machine gun in each of the two beam positions, plus an external bomb and torpedo load of 800kg (1764lb)

Mitsubishi G4M2 'Betty'

Following the G4M1, the G4M2 was built to the extent of 1154 aircraft for service from mid-1943 with an uprated powerplant, a laminar-flow wing, a larger tailplane, additional fuel capacity and heavier defensive armament for better overall capability but only at the cost of reduced agility. There were three attack bomber Model 22 subvariants (about 350 aircraft) with different armaments, and four attack bomber Model 24 subvariants (about 790 aircraft) with 1850hp (1379kW) MK4T engines and different armaments. A small number of aircraft were converted as engine test beds, and some machines were adapted as Model 24J carriers for the Yokosuka MXY7 Okha rocket-powered kamikaze warplane. The G4M2 remained in service right to the end of World War II. The delegation bringing the final declaration of surrender from the Japanese high command was brought to Ie-Shima in two 'Bettys'.

Country of origin:	Japan
Type:	(G4M2 Model 22) seven-seat medium attack bomber
Powerplant:	two 1800hp (1342kW) Mitsubishi MK4P Kasei 21 14-cylinder two-row radial engines
Performance:	maximum speed 438km/h (272mph); climb to 8000m (26,245ft) in 30 minutes 24 seconds; range 6059km (3765 miles)
Weights:	empty 8160kg (17,990lb); maximum take-off 12,500kg (27,557lb)
Dimensions:	span 25.00m (82ft 0.25in); length 20.00m (65ft 7.25in); height 6.00m (19ft 8.25in)
Armament:	two 7.7mm trainable forward-firing machine guns in nose position, one 20mm trainable cannon in dorsal turret, one 20mm trainable lateral-firing cannon in each beam position, and one 20mm trainable rearward-firing cannon in tail position, plus a bomb and torpedo load of 800kg (1764lb)

Mitsubishi G4M3 'Betty'

By the second half of 1942 the Imperial Japanese Navy Air Force had belatedly realised that the G4M had a major problem of survivability as a result of its lack of armour protection and self-sealing fuel tanks. Many crew members and aircraft were lost as a result after they had been hit and caught fire. In November 1942, therefore, Mitsubishi began work on the G4M3 with armour for the crew areas and the wing revised with self-sealing tanks. At the same time the opportunity was taken to improve the tail gunner's position along the lines of American aircraft, the consequent shortening of the fuselage and forward movement of the centre of gravity requiring the introduction of dihedral on the tailplane to restore stability. The G4M3 entered too late to be of any real use, however, and only 60 of these Attack Bomber Model 34 aircraft had been completed before Japan's surrender in August 1945.

Country of origin:	Japan
Type:	(G4M3) seven-seat medium attack bomber
Powerplant:	two 1825hp (1361kW) Mitsubishi MK4T Kasei 25 14-cylinder two-row radial engines
Performance:	maximum speed 470km/h (292mph); climb to 7000m (22,965ft) in 20 minutes 10 seconds; service ceiling 9200m (30,185ft); range 4335km (2694 miles)
Weights:	empty 8350kg (18,409lb); maximum take-off 12,500kg (27,558lb)
Dimensions:	span 25.00m (82ft 0.25in); length 19.50m (63ft 11.75in); height 6.00m (19ft 8.25in)
Armament:	two 7.7mm trainable forward-firing machine guns in nose, one 20mm trainable cannon in dorsal turret, one 20mm trainable cannon in each beam position, and one 20mm trainable rearward-firing cannon in tail position, plus a bomb load of 800kg (1764lb)

Mitsubishi J2M Raiden 'Jack'

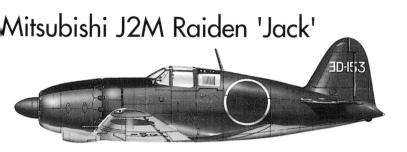

The Raiden (thunderbolt) was designed as land-based successor to the legendary A6M Reisen, but failed to live up to its initial promise, was very slow in development, and finally entered service with performance little better than that of its predecessor despite the use of a more potent engine. On the other side of the coin, however, the Allies assessed the Raiden as the best point interceptor available to the Japanese in the second half of World War II for its excellent blend of performance, stability, handling and field performance. First flown in March 1942, the J2M entered service only in the second half of 1943, and production totalled a mere 475 or so aircraft in variants such as the initial J2M2, the J2M3 – with heavier armament – and J2M4 – optimised for the high-altitude role. The aircraft pictured was on the strength of the 302nd Kokutai, Imperial Japanese Navy Air Force, based in Japan for the defence of the homeland in 1945.

Country of origin:	Japan
Type:	(J2M3) single-seat interceptor fighter
Powerplant:	one 1870hp (1394kW) Mitsubishi MK4R-A Kasei 23a 14-cylinder two-row radial engine
Performance:	maximum speed 587km/h (365mph); climb to 6000m (19,685ft) in 6 minutes 14 seconds; service ceiling 11,700m (38,385ft); range 1899km (1180 miles)
Weights:	empty 2460kg (5423lb); normal take-off 3435kg (7573lb); maximum take-off 3945kg (8697lb)
Dimesions:	span 10.80m (35ft 5.25in); length 9.95m (31ft 9.75in); height 3.95m (12ft 11.25in)
Armament:	four 20mm fixed forward-firing cannon in the leading edges of the wing, plus an external bomb load of 120kg (265lb)

Mitsubishi Ki-15 and C5M 'Babs'

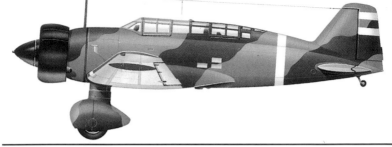

Designed for the high-speed reconnaissance and communications roles, the Ki-15 first flew in May 1936 and entered Imperial Japanese Army Air Force service in the late 1930s as the Ki-15-I with the 640hp (477kW) Nakajima Ha-8 (Army Type 94) radial engine. Production of the Ki-15 series totalled 435 aircraft, the later aircraft completed to Ki-15-II standard with an uprated engine. The same basic type appealed to the Imperial Japanese Navy Air Force, which acquired a development of the Ki-15-II with the designation C5M, of which 50 were delivered in the form of 20 C5M1 machines with the 875hp (652kW) Mitsubishi Zuisei 12 radial engine and 30 C5M2 aircraft with the 940hp (701kW) Nakajima Sakae 12 radial engine. Both army and navy models were relegated to second-line tasks from 1943, but were used for *kamikaze* attacks later in the war. Pictured is a Ki-15-I, operated by the 1sr Chuitai, 15th Hikosentai, of the Imperial Japanese Army air service.

Country of origin:	Japan
Type:	(Ki-15-II) two-seat reconnaissance aeroplane
Powerplant:	one 900hp (671kW) Mitsubishi Ha 26-I (Army Type 99 Model 1) 14-cylinder two-row radial engine
Performance:	maximum speed 510km/h (317mph); climb to 5000m (16,405ft) in 6 minutes 49 seconds; service ceiling not available; range not available
Weights:	empty 1592kg (3510lb); normal take-off 2189kg (4826lb); maximum take-off 2481kg (5470lb)
Dimensions:	span 12.00m (39ft 4.5in); length 3.34m (28ft 6.5in); height 3.34m (10ft 11.5in)
Armament:	one 7.7mm trainable rearward-firing machine gun in the rear cockpit

Mitsubishi Ki-21 'Sally' and 'Gwen'

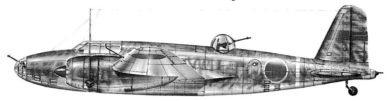

The best bomber that was available in significant numbers to the Imperial Japanese Army Air Force in World War II, the Ki-21 was yet another example of Japan's short-sighted policy of insisting on high speed and long range achieved only by sacrificing protection, defensive firepower and offensive warload. The type resulted from a February 1936 requirement for a modern bomber, and the first of eight prototypes made its maiden flight in December 1936. The Ki-21 entered service in mid-1938; production totalled 774 examples of the Ki-21-I with 850hp (634kW) Nakajima Ha-5 radial engines in three subvariants differentiated by their defensive armaments and fuel capacities, and 1278 examples of the Ki-21-II with a different and uprated powerplant in two subvariants. Some Ki-21-Is were converted as MC-21 unarmed civil transports. Pictured here is a Ki-21-IIb of the Imperial Japanese Army air service in 1944.

Country of origin:	Japan
Type:	(Ki-21-IIb) five/seven-seat 'heavy' (actually medium) bomber
Powerplant:	two 1500hp (1118kW) Mitsubishi Ha-101 (Army Type 100) 14-cylinder two-row radial engines
Country	maximum speed 486km/h (302mph); climb to 6000m (19,685ft) in 13 minutes 13 seconds; service ceiling 10,000m (32,810ft); range 2700km (1678 miles)
Weights:	empty 6070kg (13,382lb); maximum take-off 10,610kg (23,391lb)
Dimensions:	span 22.50m (73ft 9.75in); length 16.00m (52ft 6in); height 4.85m (15ft 11in)
Armament:	one 12.7mm trainable machine gun in dorsal turret, one 7.7mm machine gun in nose position, one 7.7mm machine gun in ventral position, one 7.7mm machine gun in tail position, and one 7.7mm machine gun in each beam position; bomb load of 1000kg (2205lb)

Mitsubishi Ki-30 'Ann'

This aeroplane was the Imperial Japanese Army Air Force's first operational warplane with a double-row radial piston engine, variable-pitch propeller, internal weapons bay and split flaps. Despite these modern features, however, the Ki-30 was a basically undistinguished type that saw most of its service in the Chinese theatre, where lack of effective fighter opposition allowed it to operate generally without molestation. The origins of the type can be traced to the mid-1930s, when the Imperial Japanese Army Air Force launched an ambitious programme of expansion based on aircraft of Japanese design and manufacture. The first of 18 prototype and service trials aircraft flew in February 1937. There followed 686 production aircraft, of which the survivors were relegated to the crew training role from 1942. The aircraft shown here is a Ki-30 of the 2nd Chutai, 10th Hikosentai, Imperial Japanese Army air service in 1942.

Country of origin:	Japan
Type:	two-seat light attack bomber
Powerplant:	one 950hp (708kW) Nakajima Ha-5 Kai (Army Type 97) 14-cylinder two-row radial engine
Performance:	maximum speed 432km/h (263mph); climb to 5000m (16,405ft) in 10 minutes 36 seconds; service ceiling 8570m (28,120ft); range 1700km (1056 miles)
Weights:	empty 2230kg (4916lb); maximum take-off 3322kg (7324lb)
Dimensions:	span 14.55m (47ft 8.75in); length 10.34m (33ft 11in); height 3.645m (11ft 11.5in)
Armament:	one 7.7mm fixed forward-firing machine gun in leading edge of the port wing, and one 7.7mm trainable rearward-firing machine gun in the rear cockpit, pus an internal bomb load of 400kg (882lb)

Mitsubishi Ki-46-I and Ki-46-II 'Dinah'

One of the finest machines of its type to see service in World War II and also one of the most elegant aircraft of all time, the Ki-46 was designed specifically as a high-altitude reconnaissance aeroplane to meet a 1937 requirement, and the prototype made its maiden flight in November 1939. Trials indicated excellent performance and handling, and there followed 34 Ki-46-I initial production aircraft with 900hp (671kW) Mitsubishi Ha-26-I radial engine before production switched to the first fully operational model, the Ki-46-II. Some 1093 examples of the Ki-46-II were delivered with an uprated powerplant and they proved virtually impossible to intercept. A number of these aircraft were later adapted to Ki-46-II Kai standard as radio and navigation trainers with an additional stepped cockpit above and behind the standard unit. The aircraft were an important asset in the early Pacific campaign, but as the capability of Allied fighters improved Ki-46-II losses mounted.

Country of origin:	Japan
Type:	(Ki-46-II) two-seat high-altitude reconnaissance aeroplane
Powerplant:	two 1055hp (787kW) Mitsubishi Ha-102 (Army Type 1) 14-cylinder two-row radial engines
Performance:	maximum speed 604km/h (375mph); climb to 8000m (26,245ft) in 17 minutes 58 seconds; service ceiling 10,720m (35,170ft); range 2474km (1537 miles)
Weights:	empty 3263kg (7194lb); normal take-off 5050kg (11,133lb); maximum take-off 5800kg (12,787lb)
Dimensions:	span 14.70m (48ft 2.75in); length 11.00m (36ft 1in); height 3.88m (12ft 8.75in)
Armament:	one 7.7mm trainable rearward-firing machine gun in the rear cockpit

Mitsubishi Ki-46-III 'Dinah'

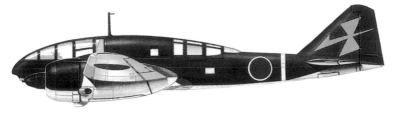

Anticipating that Allied fighters capable of intercepting the Ki-46-II would appear in the later part of 1942, the Imperial Japanese Army Air Force had ordered an improved version as the Ki-46-III. The first of two such prototypes made its maiden flight in December 1942 with an uprated powerplant, fuel capacity increased for another hour of endurance, and an unstepped and therefore lower-drag cockpit enclosure. Production of the Ki-46-III (609 aircraft) was undertaken between 1942 and 1945, proceeding in parallel with the later production stages of the Ki-46-II that was built between 1940 and 1944. The Ki-46-III was without doubt the best strategic reconnaissance aeroplane used in significant numbers in World War II, offering long range as well as high speed and a good service ceiling, making it virtually impossible to intercept for Allied aircraft. Production of all versions of the Ki-46 totalled 1742.

Country of origin:	Japan
Type:	(Ki-46-III) two-seat high-altitude reconnaissance aeroplane
Powerplant:	two 1500hp (1118kW) Mitsubishi Ha-112-II (Army Type 4) 14-cylinder two-row radial engines
Performance:	maximum speed 630km/h (391mph); climb to 8000m (26,245ft) in 20 minutes 15 seconds; service ceiling 10,500m (34,450ft); range 4000km (2486 miles)
Weights:	empty 3831kg (8446lb); maximum take-off 6500kg (14,330lb)
Dimensions:	span 14.70m (48ft 2.75in); length 11.00m (36ft 1in); height 3.88m (12ft 8.75in)
Armament:	one 7.7mm trainable rearward-firing machine gun in the rear cockpit

Mitsubishi Ki-46-III Kai 'Dinah'

The good performance of the Ki-46-III suggested that the type could be adapted for the bomber interceptor role pending the arrival of purpose-designed interceptors. The resulting Ki-46-III Kai was produced as an unknown number of conversions from Ki-46-III standard with the reconnaissance equipment removed, the nose revised for the accommodation of two 20mm cannon, and the upper centre fuel tank removed to provide volume for a 37mm fixed obliquely forward/upward-firing cannon. The type entered service in November 1944, but proved disappointing because of its poor climbing performance. The only other type to be produced as a conversion, and then only in small numbers, was the Ki-46-IIIb intended for the attack role with the fixed armament reduced to just two 20mm nose cannon. Ki-46-IV prototypes, with high-performance turbo-charged engines producing 1500hp (1119kW), were under test when the war ended.

Country of origin:	Japan
Type:	(Ki-46-III Kai) two-seat high-altitude interceptor fighter
Powerplant:	two 1500hp (1118kW) Mitsubishi Ha-112-II (Army Type 4) 14-cylinder two-row radial engines
Performance:	maximum speed 630km/h (391mph); climb to 8000m (26,245ft) in 19 minutes; service ceiling 10,500m (34,450ft); range not available
Weights:	empty 3831kg (8446lb); normal take-off 5722kg (12,619lb); maximum take-off 6230kg (13,735lb)
Dimensions:	span 14.70m (48ft 2.75in); length 11.00m (36ft 1in); height 3.88m (12ft 8.75in)
Armament:	two 20mm fixed forward-firing cannon in the nose, and one 37mm obliquely forward/upward-firing cannon in the upper part of the central fuselage

Mitsubishi Ki-67 Hiryu 'Peggy'

The Ki-67 Hiryu (flying dragon) was without doubt the finest bomber to see service with the Imperial Japanese Army or Imperial Japanese Navy Air Forces in World War II, for it combined high performance with good defensive firepower, adequate offensive weapon load, and a structure that was sturdy and provided good protection for the crew and fuel supply. Mitsubishi submitted the winning design to a 1940 requirement and the flight of the first of 19 prototypes took place in in December 1942. Service entry of the Ki-67-I began in the summer of 1944 after a development programme that had been much protracted by the army's desire to develop the Hiryu in several variants exploiting its excellent performance and handling. Production totalled 698 aircraft, of which some were converted as explosives-laden *kamikaze* aircraft. Pictured is a Ki-67 of the Imperial Japanese Army Air Force.

Country of origin:	Japan
Type:	(Ki-67-I) six/eight-seat 'heavy' (actually medium) bomber
Powerplant:	two 1900hp (1417kW) Mitsubishi Ha-104 (Army Type 4) 18-cylinder two-row radial engines
Performance:	maximum speed 537km/h (334mph); climb to 6000m (19,685ft) in 14 minutes 30 seconds; service ceiling 9470m (31,070ft); range 3800km (2361 miles)
Weights:	empty 8649kg (19,068lb); maximum take-off 13,765kg (30,347lb)
Dimensions:	span 22.50m (73ft 9.75in); length 18.70m (61ft 4.25in); height 7.70m (25ft 3in)
Armament:	one 20mm trainable cannon in dorsal turret, two 12.7mm trainable rearward-firing machine guns in tail position, one 12.7mm trainable machine gun in nose position, and one 12.7mm machine gun in each beam position, plus a bomb or torpedo load of 1070kg (2359lb)

Morane-Saulnier MS.406

The MS.406 was France's first 'modern' monoplane fighter with a cantilever low-set wing, enclosed cockpit and tailwheel landing gear that included inward-retracting main units, but was obsolescent by World War II and suffered heavy losses in combat against the superior fighters fielded by the Luftwaffe. The type resulted from a 1934 requirement and was first conceived as the MS.405 that flew in prototype form during August 1935 and led to 15 MS.405C.1 pre-production fighters. There followed the MS.406C.1 production model of which an initial 1,000 examples were ordered in March 1938. The MS.406 was built on two production lines, and construction of 1077 aircraft was completed between June 1938 and June 1940. Exports were made to Switzerland and Turkey, and captured aircraft were passed to Croatia and Finland. Shown here is an MS.405C-1of the Escadron d'Entrainement, Vichy French Air Force, based at Toulouse in 1941.

Country of origin:	France
Type:	(MS.406C.1) single-seat fighter
Powerplant:	one 860 hp (641kW) Hispano-Suiza 12Y-31 12-cylinder Vee engine
Performance:	maximum speed 490km/h (304mph); climb to 5000m (16,405ft) in 6 minutes 30 seconds; service ceiling 9400m (30,850ft); range 1500km (932 miles)
Weights:	empty 1872kg (4127lb); maximum take-off 2722kg (6000lb)
Dimensions:	span 10.62m (34ft 9.63in); length 8.17m (26ft 9.33in); height 3.25m (10ft 8in) with the tail up
Armament:	one 20mm fixed forward-firing cannon or 7.5mm fixed forward-firing machine gun in an engine installation, and two 7.5mm fixed forward-firing machine guns in the leading edges of the wing

Naval Aircraft Factory N3N

The XN3N-1 prototype made its maiden flight in August 1935, and 179 N3N-1 production aircraft were delivered from June 1936 with provision for wheeled landing gear or float alighting gear. The first 159 had the 220hp (164kW) Wright R-790-8 radial engine, but later aircraft switched to the uprated R-760-8 engine. This unit was also used in the 816 examples of the N3N-3 delivered from 1938 with a vertical tail surface of revised shape, a modified main landing gear arrangement with a single strut on each side, and an uncowled engine installation that was retrospectively adopted for the N3N-1 in 1941 and 1942. The N3N series served with great utility throughout the period of World War II, but most of the surviving aircraft were sold to civil operators soon after the end of this conflict. A typically brightly coloured aircraft is pictured here, this example being a N3N-1 based at Pensacola in 1939.

Country of origin:	USA
Type:	(N3N-3) two-seat primary flying trainer
Powerplant:	one 235hp (175kW) Wright R-760-2 Whirlwind seven-cylinder single-row radial engine
Performance:	maximum speed 203 km/h (126mph); initial climb rate 244m (800ft) per minute; service ceiling 4635m (15,200ft); range 756km (470 miles)
Weights:	empty 948kg (2090lb); maximum take-off 1266kg (2792lb)
Dimensions:	span 10.36m (34ft); length 7.77m (25ft 6in); height 3.30m (10ft 10in)
Armament:	none

Nakajima B5N 'Kate'

The B5N was the torpedo and level bomber counterpart of the Aichi D3A dive-bomber, and as such was a major weapon in the first part of the Japanese campaign in the Pacific theatre from December 1941. The type resulted from a 1934 requirement, and the first of two prototypes flew in January 1937. Successful development paved the way for the B5N1 initial production model with the powerplant of one 840hp (626kW) Nakajima Hikari 3 radial engine. Production of the B5N1 bomber was complemented by that of its B5N1-K advanced trainer derivative, and by 1941 the type had been replaced in first-line service by the improved B5N2 with a more potent engine. B5N production totalled 1147, and the B5N2 remained in first-line service up to mid-1944, thereafter being retasked to less demanding roles such as maritime reconnaissance. Shown here is a B5N2 of the Imperial Japanese Navy Air Force, based on the fated carrier *Akagi* in 1941-42.

Country of origin:	Japan
Type:	(B5N2) three-seat carrierborne and land-based torpedo and level bomber
Powerplant:	one 1000hp (746kW) Nakajima NK1B Sakae 11 nine-cylinder single-row radial engine
Performance:	maximum speed 378km/h (235mph); climb to 3000m (9845ft) in 7 minutes 40 seconds; service ceiling 8260m (27,100ft); range 1991km (1237 miles)
Weights:	empty 2279kg (5024lb); maximum take-off 4100kg (9039lb)
Dimensions:	span 15.52 m (50ft 11in); length 10.30m (33ft 9.5in); height 3.70m (12ft 1.75in)
Armament:	one 7.7mm trainable rearward-firing machine gun in the rear cockpit, plus an external torpedo and bomb load of 800kg (1764lb)

Nakajima B6N Tenzan 'Jill'

Designed to a 1939 requirement for a B5N successor, the B6N Tenzan (heavenly mountain) may be regarded as a extension of the design philosophy that inspired the B5N with considerably more power for significantly improved performance. The first of two prototypes flew in the spring of 1941, but the time needed to eradicate the problems that were encountered meant that the first of 133 B6N1 production aircraft entered service only late in 1943 with the 1870hp (1394kW) Nakajima NK7A Mamoru 11 radial engine. Further development of this engine was then cancelled, forcing Nakajima to develop the B6N2 with a different powerplant. Production of the B6N2 totalled 1133 aircraft in two subvariants, but little effective use could be made of these aircraft for lack of capable aircrew. The B6N3 was a purely land-based development that did not enter production. The aircraft pictured is a B6N2 of the Imperial Japanese Navy Air Force duirng 1944.

Country of origin:	Japan
Type:	(B6N2) three-seat carrierborne and land-based torpedo bomber
Powerplant:	one 1850hp (1379kW) Mitsubishi MK4T Kasei 25 14-cylinder two-row radial engine
Performance:	maximum speed 481km/h (299mph); climb to 5000m (16,405ft) in 10 minutes 24 seconds; service ceiling 9040m (29,660ft); range 3045km (1892 miles)
Weights:	empty 3010kg (6636lb); maximum take-off 5650kg (12,456lb)
Dimensions:	span 14.89m (48ft 10.6in); length 10.87m (35ft 7.8in); height 3.80m (12ft 5.6in)
Armament:	one 7.7mm trainable rearward-firing machine gun in the rear of the cockpit, and one 7.7mm trainable rearward-firing machine gun in the ventral tunnel position, plus an external torpedo and bomb load of 800kg (1764lb)

Nakajima Ki-27 'Nate'

The Imperial Japanese Army Air Force's counterpart to the naval A5M, the Ki-27 was a cantilever low-wing fighter with fixed landing gear but advanced features such as an enclosed cockpit, and offered very creditable performance and a very high level of agility. The type first flew in October 1936 and was the army's standard fighter between 1937 and mid-1942. Production totalled some 3495 aircraft; the main variants were the Ki-27 pre-production type with a clear-view canopy, the Ki-27a production type with an uprated engine and a metal-faired canopy, and the Ki-27b definitive type with a clear-view canopy as well as provision for underwing bombs. After 1942 the Ki-27 was used mainly as a trainer, but numbers were expended as kamikaze attack warplanes in the closing stages of World War II. This particular aircraft was the personal mount of Lieutenant Colonel Toshio Katoh, commander of the 1st Sentai, based at Kagamigahara in June 1939.

Country of origin:	Japan
Type:	(Ki-97b) single-seat fighter and fighter-bomber
Powerplant:	one 780hp (581.5kW) Nakajima Ha-1b (Army Type 97) nine-cylinder single-row radial engine
Performance:	maximum speed 470km/h (292mph); climb to 5000m (16,405ft) in 5 minutes 22 seconds; service ceiling 12,250m (40,190ft); range 1710km (1063 miles)
Weights:	empty 1110kg (2447lb); maximum take-off 1790kg (3946lb)
Dimensions:	span 11.31m (37ft 1.25in); length 7.53m (24ft 8.5in); height 3.25m (10ft 8in)
Armament:	two 7.7mm fixed forward-firing machine guns in the upper part of the forward fuselage, plus an external bomb load of 100kg (220lb)

Nakajima Ki-43 Hayabusa 'Oscar'

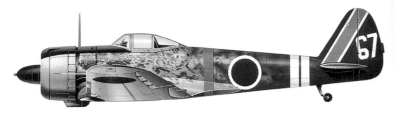

The Ki-43 Hayabusa (Peregrine Falcon) was the most advanced fighter available to the Imperial Japanese Army Air Force in the opening phases of World War II, and as such the type came as a very considerable shock to the Allied air forces. The type was also the most important of all the Imperial Japanese Army Air Force's fighters in numerical terms, with production totalling more than 5900 aircraft right up to the end of the war, by which time the Ki-43 was decidedly obsolete in terms of firepower and protection. The main variants were the Ki-43-I (three subvariants) with the 980hp (731kW) Ha-25 engine driving a two-blade propeller, Ki-43-II (three subvariants) with an uprated engine driving a three-blade propeller, and the Ki-43-III (one subvariant) with the 1230hp (917kW) Ha-115-II engine. Shown here is a Ki-43IIb of the 3rd Chutai, 25th Sentai, Imperial Japanese Army air force, based at Hankow in China in January 1944.

Country of origin:	Japan
Type:	(Ki-43-IIb) single-seat fighter and fighter-bomber
Powerplant:	one 1150hp (857kW) Nakajima Ha-115 (Army Type 1) 14-cylinder two-row radial engine
Performance:	maximum speed 530km/h (329mph); climb to 5000m (16,405ft) in 5 minutes 49 seconds; service ceiling 11,200m (36,750ft); range 3200km (1988 miles)
Weights:	empty 1910kg (4211lb); normal take-off 2590kg (5710lb); maximum take-off 2925kg (6450lb)
Dimensions:	span 10.84m (35ft 6.75in); length 8.92m (29ft 3.25in); height 3.27m (10ft 8.75in)
Armament:	two 12.7mm fixed forward-firing machine guns in the upper part of the forward fuselage, plus an external bomb load of 500kg (1102lb)

Nakajima Ki-44 Shoki 'Tojo'

The Shoki (Demon) was designed as a small and highly loaded fighter specifically for the interception role. The type was the only interceptor to serve with the Imperial Japanese Army Air Force, and after the start of strategic attacks on the Japanese home islands by American bombers the Shoki proved its worth as the fastest-climbing Japanese fighter. The Ki-44 entered service in the second half of 1942 as a type that was initially unpopular among pilots accustomed to more lightly loaded and agile fighters. Production of 1222 aircraft included the Ki-44-I (three subvariants) with the 1250hp (932kW) Ha-41 engine and machine gun armament, the Ki-44-II (three subvariants) with a m ore powerful engine and heavier armament. The Ki-44-III (two subvariants) had the 2000hp (1491kW) Ha-145 engine and armament of either four 20mm cannon (Ki-44-IIIa) or two 20mm and two 37mm cannon (Ki-44-IIIB). Shown here is a Ki-44-IIb.

Country of origin:	Japan
Type:	(Ki-44-II) single-seat fighter
Powerplant:	one 1520hp (1133kW) Nakajima Ha-109 (Army Type 2) 14-cylinder two-row radial engine
Performance:	maximum speed 605km/h (376mph); climb to 5000 m (16,405ft) in 4 minutes 17 seconds; service ceiling 11,200m (36,745ft); range 1700km (1056 miles)
Weights:	empty 2106kg (4643lb); normal take-off 2764kg (6094lb); maximum take-off 2993kg (6598lb)
Dimensions:	span 9.45m (31ft); length 8.79m (28ft 9.9in); height 3.25m (10ft 8in)
Armament:	two 12.7mm machine guns in the upper part of the forward fuselage, and two 12.7mm fixed forward-firing machine guns in the leading edges of the wing, plus a bomb load of 200kg (441lb)

Nakajima Ki-49 Donryu 'Helen'

The Donryu (Storm Dragon) was planned from 1938 as replacement for the Mitsubishi Ki-21 but proved so indifferent that it supplemented rather than replaced the older type. The first of three prototypes made its maiden flight in August 1939, and the evaluation of seven pre-production aircraft paved the way for the introduction from August 1941 of the Ki-49-I initial production variant, of which 129 were delivered with a powerplant of two 1250hp (932kW) Nakajima Ha-41 radial engines. There followed 667 examples of the Ki-49-II in two subvariants with an uprated and different powerplant, improved protection and heavier defensive firepower. There were also three prototypes of the Ki-58 escort derivative with no bombs but a trainable armament of five 20mm cannon and three 12.7mm machine guns. The inability of the Ki-49 to fulfill its intended role meant that the aircraft was increasingly relegated to secondary duties in the later stages of the war.

Country of origin:	Japan
Type:	(Ki-49-IIa) eight-seat 'heavy' (actually medium) bomber
Powerplant:	two 1500hp (1118kW) Nakajima Ha-109 (Army Type 2) 14-cylinder two-row radial engines
Performance:	maximum speed 492km/h (306mph); climb to 5000m (16,405ft) in 13 minutes 39 seconds; service ceiling 9300m (30,510ft); range 2950km (1833 miles)
Weights:	empty 6530kg (14,396lb); maximum take-off 11,400kg (25,133lb)
Dimensions:	span 20.42m (67ft); length 16.50m (54ft 1.6in); height 4.25m (13ft 1.2in)
Armament:	one 20mm trainable cannon in dorsal turret, one 12.7mm machine gun in nose position, one 12.7mm machine gun in tail position, one 12.7mm machine gun in ventral position, and one 7.7mm machine gun in each beam position; bomb load of 1000kg (2205lb)

Nakajima Ki-84 Hayate 'Frank'

Designed as successor to the Ki-43, the Hayate (Gale) was one of the best fighters available to the Imperial Japanese Army Air Force in the closing stages of World War II. Its high level of basic capability was boosted by the fact that, unlike several other high-performance Japanese fighters, it was available in useful numbers and without the teething problems that affected many of these other types. Entering service in the first half of 1944, the Ki-84 was built to the extent of 3512 aircraft in two primary variants, namely the Ki-84-I (four subvariants distinguished by their steadily more capable armament) and the Ki-84-II (two subvariants) derivative of the Ki-84-I with a wooden rear fuselage and fittings in an effort to reduce the drain on Japan's dwindling reserves of strategic light alloys. The final variant was the Ki-116, a conversion by Mansyu from a standard Ki-84-1a with a lighter powerplant. Pictured is a Ki-84-1a of the 58th Shimbu-tai in August 1944.

Country of origin:	Japan
Type:	(Ki-84-la) single-seat fighter and fighter-bomber
Powerplant:	one 1900hp (1417kW) Nakajima Ha-45 (Army Type 4) Model 23 18-cylinder two-row radial engine
Performance:	maximum speed 631km/h (392mph); climb to 5000m (16,405ft) in 5 minutes 54 seconds; service ceiling 10,500m (34,450ft); range 2168km (1347 miles)
Weights:	empty 2660kg (5864lb); normal take-off 3613kg (7955lb); maximum take-off 4170kg (9193lb)
Dimensions:	span 11.24m (36ft 10.5in); length 9.92m (32ft 6.5in); height 3.39m (11ft 1.25in)
Armament:	two 20mm fixed forward-firing cannon in the leading edges of the wing, and two 12.7mm fixed forward-firing machine guns in the forward fuselage, plus an external bomb load of 500kg (1102lb)

North American B-25A/B Mitchell

O ne of the most important US tactical warplanes of World War II and built to the extent of 9816 aircraft, the Mitchell was a classic medium bomber that was also developed into a potent anti-ship warplane. The origins of the type can be found in 1938, when North American gambled that the US Army Air Corps would need a new attack bomber. In response work commenced on the NA-40 that first flew in January 1939 before conversion into the NA-40B to meet the definitive USAAC requirement issued in January 1939. The concept was then refined as the NA-62, subsequently ordered as 24 B-25 initial production aircraft which were delivered from February 1941. Later deliveries comprised 40 and 120 B-25A and B-25B aircraft, the former with self-sealing fuel tanks and the latter with dorsal and ventral turrets but no tail gun position. the B-25B was used in the 'Doolittle raid' of April 1942, when 16 aircraft lifted off from an aircraft carrier to bomb Tokyo.

Country of origin:	USA
Type:	(B-25B) five-seat medium bomber
Powerplant:	two 1700hp (1267kW) Wright R-2600-9 14-cylinder two-row radial engines
Performance:	maximum speed 483km/h (300mph); service ceiling of 7175m (23,500ft); range 2172km (1350 miles) with a 1361kg (3000lb) bomb load
Weights:	empty 9072kg (20,000lb); maximum take-off 12,909kg (28,460lb)
Dimensions:	span 30.66m (67ft 7in); length 16.13 m (52ft 11in), height 4.80m (15ft 9in)
Armament:	one 0.3in trainable forward-firing machine gun in the nose position, two 0.5in trainable machine guns in the dorsal turret, and two 0.5in trainable machine guns in the ventral turret, plus an internal bomb load of 1361kg (3000lb)

North American B-25C/D Mitchell

The B-25 series entered combat service in 1942. Some early concerns were expressed by pilots regarding the type's often tricky handling qualities, but these were soon dispelled and the aircraft began to make a notable impact on the air war. The B-25B was followed into service by the virtually identical B-25C and B-25D. These were actually the first variants to enter large-scale production in the form of 1619 Inglewood-built B-25C and 2290 Kansas City-built B-25D machines with an uprated powerplant, an autopilot, external hardpoints for one 907kg (2000lb) torpedo or eight 113kg (250lb) bombs, provision for forward-firing machine guns in packs scabbed onto the sides of the forward fuselage and, in later aircraft, increased fuel capacity. The two models were used in most American theatres, and 533 B-25C/D aircraft were delivered to the UK as Mitchell Mk II aircraft to supplement 23 Mitchell Mk I (B-25B) machines.

Country of origin:	USA
Type:	(B-25C) five-seat medium bomber
Powerplant:	two 1700hp (1267.5kW) Wright R-2600-13 18-cylinder two-row radial engines
Performance:	maximum speed 457km/h (284mph); climb to 4570m (15,000ft) in 16 minutes 30 seconds; service ceiling 6460m (21,200ft); range 2454km (1525 miles) with a 1452kg (3200lb) bomb load
Weights:	empty 9208kg (20,300lb); maximum take-off 18,960kg (41,800lb)
Dimensions:	span 20.60m (67 ft 7in); length 16.12m (52ft 11in); height 4.82m (15ft 10in)
Armament:	two 0.5in trainable forward-firing machine guns in the nose position, two 0.5in trainable machine guns in the dorsal turret, and two 0.5in trainable machine guns in the ventral turret, plus an internal and external bomb and torpedo load of 1361kg (3000lb)

North American B-25G/H/J Mitchell

Delivered to the extent of 405 aircraft including five B-25C conversions, the B-25G was a dedicated anti-ship model evolved for use in the Pacific theatre with a four-man crew and a 75mm M4 gun in the nose, together with two 0.5in (12.7mm) Browning fixed forward-firing machine guns and four 'package' guns. The 1000 examples of the B-25H had a lighter 75mm gun, eight 0.5in fixed forward-firing machine guns, six 0.5in trainable machine guns (two each in the dorsal and new tail positions and one in each of the two new beam positions), and provision for eight 5in rockets under the wings. The 4318 examples of the B-25J had no 75mm gun and either a glazed B-25D nose or, in later aircraft, a 'solid' nose with eight 0.5in guns. Some 313 B-25Js were delivered to the UK as Mitchell Mk III aircraft. The aircraft was exported widely and continued in service well after the war. The USAF retired its last B-25 staff transport in May 1960.

Country of origin:	USA
Type:	(B-25H) five-seat medium bomber
Powerplant:	two 1700hp (1267.5kW) Wright R-2600-13 18-cylinder two-row radial engines
Performance:	maximum speed 442km/h (275mph); climb to 4570m (15,000ft) in 19 minutes; service ceiling 7255m (23,800ft); range 4345km (2700 miles)
Weights:	empty 9061kg (19,975lb); maximum take-off 16,351kg (36,047lb)
Dimensions:	span 20.6m (67ft 7in); length 15.7m (51ft 3.8in); height 4.8m (15ft 9in)
Armament:	one 75mm forward-firing gun in port lower side of nose, four 0.5in machine guns in forward fuselage, two 0.5in machine guns in dorsal turret, two 0.5in trainable machine guns in tail position, and one 0.5in machine gun in each beam position; internal load of 2449kg (5400lb)

North American P-51A /C Mustang

The Mustang was the finest all-round fighter of World War II, for it was a truly superb warplane that combined phenomenal performance, good acceleration, very good manoeuvrability, an extremely sturdy airframe and other operationally significant attributes in an aesthetically attractive package whose totality somehow seemed to be greater than the sum of its parts. The Mustang resulted from a British requirement and first flew in October 1940 with the Allison V-1710 engine, which was also used in the 1045 examples of the P-51 and P-51A (Mustang Mks I and II) that served from April 1942 in the low-level fighter and reconnaissance fighter roles. The P-51B and P-51C (1988 and 1750 aircraft respectively) then switched to the Packard V-1650 American-made version of a classic British engine, the Rolls-Royce Merlin. This transformed the Mustang from a mediocre aircraft into one of the most important fighters of World War II.

Country of origin:	USA
Type:	(P-51B) single-seat fighter and fighter-bomber
Powerplant:	one 1400hp (1044kW) Packard V-1650-3 12-cylinder Vee engine
Performance:	maximum speed 708km/h (440mph); climb to 3050m (10,000ft) in 1 minute 48 seconds; service ceiling 12,800m (42,000ft); range 3540km (2,200 miles)
Weights:	empty 3103kg (6840lb); maximum take-off 5080kg (11,200lb)
Dimensions:	span 11.89m (37ft 0.25in); length 9.83m (32ft 3in); height 2.64m (8ft 8in)
Armament:	six 0.5in fixed forward-firing machine guns in the leading edges of the wing, plus an external bomb load of 907kg (2000lb)

North American P-51D to P-51K Mustang

The combination of the Mustang airframe and Merlin engine had proved ideal in the P-51B/C and paved the way for most later developments. The first of these was the definitive P-51D of which 7966 were completed with a cut-down rear fuselage and clear-view 'bubble' canopy, and later with increased fuel capacity and underwing provision for rocket projectiles as alternatives to bombs for the increasingly important ground-attack role. The P-51D was one of the decisive weapons of World War II, and was complemented by the P-51H lightweight model (555 aircraft) and the P-51K version of the P-51D with a different propeller (1337 aircraft). Variants of the P-51 series for other roles included the a-36A Apache dive-bomber and ground-attack model, and the F-6 series of photo-reconnaissance aircraft. Orders for 1700 P-51L aircraft and 1628 P-51M fighters were cancelled at VJ Day, but not before Mustang production had totalled 15,386.

Country of origin:	USA
Type:	(P-51D) single-seat fighter and fighter-bomber
Powerplant:	one 1695hp (1264kW) Packard V-1650-7 12-cylinder Vee engine
Performance:	maximum speed 703km/h (437mph); climb to 6095m (20,000ft) in 7 minutes 18 seconds; service ceiling 12,770m (41,900ft); range 3703km (2301 miles)
Weights:	empty 3103kg (6840lb);maximum take-off 5493kg (12,100lb)
Dimensions:	span 11.28m (37ft 0.25in); length 9.84m (32ft 3.25in); height 4.16m (13ft 8in) with the tail down
Armament:	six 0.5in fixed forward-firing machine guns in the leading edges of the wing, plus an external bomb and rocket load of 907kg (2000lb)

Northrop A-17

The A-17 was a development of the Gamma 2 transport for the attack role, and the first of 110 A-17 aircraft was delivered in July 1935. There followed 129 examples of the A-17A with an uprated engine and retractable landing gear, and two examples of the A-17AS three-seat command transport. All the American aircraft had been relegated to second-line tasks before the USA's entry into World War II, but a number of aircraft (built as DB-8s after Douglas's take-over of Northrop) were exported and some of these played a more active role. The exports included 102 (including licence-built) aircraft for Sweden as well as 17, 20, 36 and 10 for Iraq, the Netherlands, Norway and Peru respectively. Peru also ordered 34 other aircraft that were impressed for US service as A-33s. These aircraft were armed with six 7.62mm machine guns and had a potential bomb load of 816kg (1800lb). France and the UK received 32 and 61 aircraft respectively.

Country of origin:	USA
Type:	(A-17A) two-seat attack warplane
Powerplant:	one 825hp (615kW) Pratt & Whitney R-1535-13 14-cylinder two-row radial engine
Performance:	maximum speed 354km/h (220mph); climb to 1525m (5000ft) in 3 minutes 54 seconds; service ceiling 5915m (19,400ft); range 1923km (1195 miles)
Weights:	empty 2316kg (5106lb); maximum take-off 3425kg (7550lb)
Dimensions:	span 14.55m (47ft 9in); length 9.65m (31ft 8in); height 3.66m (12ft)
Armament:	four 0.3in fixed forward-firing machine guns in leading edges of the wing, and one 0.3in trainable rearward-firing machine in the rear of the cockpit with provision for its use in the ventral hatch position, plus an internal and external bomb load of 544kg (1200lb)

Northrop N-3PB

The N-3PB clearly owed much to the cantilever low-wing monoplanes that 'Jack' Northrop had designed while part of the Douglas Aircraft Company. In 1940 a Norwegian purchasing commission placed an order for 24 of the floatplanes, but shortly after this the Germans invaded the country and soon overran it. The Norwegian government-in-exile maintained its order for the N-3PB, and the first example flew in January 1941. By April 1941 all the aircraft had been delivered to 'Little Norway', the Norwegian base area in Canada. One squadron operated the type, flying 18 of the floatplanes from three bases in Iceland on convoy escort patrols under the auspices of an RAF unit. By the summer of 1942 it was clear that the N-3PB was unsuitable for the task and the aircraft were relegated to the training role. Pictured here is an N3-PB of the Royal Norwegian Naval Air Service, operating as No 330 Squadron RAF Coastal Command during 1941-42.

Country of origin:	USA
Type:	(N-3PB) three-seat coastal reconnaissance and convoy escort floatplane
Powerplant:	one 1100hp (820kW) Wright GR-1820-G205A Cyclone nine-cylinder single-row radial engine
Performance:	maximum speed 414km/h (257mph); climb to 4570m (15,000ft) in 14 minutes 24 seconds; service ceiling 7315m (24,000ft); range 1609 km (1000 miles)
Weights:	empty 2808kg (6190lb); maximum take-off 4808kg (10,600lb)
Dimensions:	span 14.91m (48ft 11in); length 10.97m (36ft); height 3.66m (12ft)
Armament:	four 0.5in fixed forward-firing machine guns in leading edges of wing, one 0.3in machine gun in rear of cockpit, and one 0.3in machine gun in ventral position, plus a load of 907kg (2000lb)

Northrop P-61A Black Widow

Although it did not possess the performance or the firepower of the German Heinkel He 219 Uhu, the Black Widow was still an immensely potent and impressive night-fighter with the additional advantage of being able to undertake the nocturnal intruder role with a very heavy disposable load. The first of two XP-61 prototypes made its maiden flight in May 1942 as very large twin-engined aircraft with a central nacelle for the crew, radar and armament, and the tail unit supported by the twin booms that were rearward extensions of the engine nacelles. There followed 13 YP-61 service test aircraft before the P-61A (200 aircraft) entered service in the summer of 1944. All the aircraft had a primary armament of four 20mm cannon, and the first 37 also featured a power-operated dorsal barbette carrying four 0.5in machine guns that was then omitted for reasons of buffet. P-61As began to enter service in the Pacific theatre in the first half of 1944.

Country of origin:	USA
Type:	(P-61A) two/three-seat night-fighter
Powerplant:	two 2250 hp (1678kW) Pratt & Whitney R-2800-65 18-cylinder two-row radial engines
Performance:	maximum speed 594km/h (369mph); climb to 4570m (15,000ft) in 7 minutes 36 seconds; service ceiling 10,090m (33,100ft); range 3058km (1900 miles)
Weights:	empty 9510kg (20,965lb); maximum take-off 15,513kg (34,200lb)
Dimensions:	span 20.12m (66ft); length 14.91m (48ft 11in); height 4.46m (14ft 8in)
Armament:	four 20mm fixed forward-firing cannon in the underside of the forward fuselage and, in the first 37 aircraft, four 0.5in trainable machine guns in a remotely controlled dorsal barbette

Northrop P-61B/C Black Widow

The P-61 was designed from the outset as a radar-equipped night-fighter and after the award of a USAAC contract in January 1941 was developed from the XP-61 prototypes. Even before the P-61A entered operational service Northrop had started delivery of the P-61B with improvements such as a slightly lengthened nose. Deliveries amounted to 450 aircraft, and improvements introduced during the P-61B's production included four underwing hardpoints each able to carry one bomb or drop tank on the P-61B-10 block onward, the four-gun dorsal barbette from the P-61B-15 block onward, and a new General Electric barbette with a revised fire-control system on the P-61B-20 block onward. Although crews were happy with the firepower, and agility of the P-61A and P-61B, they were critical of these two variants' speed and climb, which led to the development of the P-61C of which 41 were completed with two 2800hp (2088kW) R-2800-73 engines.

Country of origin:	USA
Type:	(P-61B) three-seat night-fighter and intruder
Powerplant:	two 2250hp (1678kW) Pratt & Whitney R-2800-65 18-cylinder two-row radial engines
Performance:	maximum speed 589km/h (366mph); climb to 6095m (20,000ft) in 12 minutes; service ceiling 10,090m (33,100ft); range 4828km (3000 miles)
Weights:	empty 10,637kg (23,450lb); maximum take-off 16,420kg (36,200lb)
Dimensions:	span 20.14m (66ft 0.75in); length 15.11m (49ft 7in); height 4.47m (14ft 8in)
Armament:	four 20mm fixed forward-firing cannon in the underside of the forward fuselage, and four 0.5in trainable machine guns in a remotely controlled dorsal barbette, plus an external bomb load of 2903kg (6400lb)

PZL P.23 Karas

Stemming from the P.13 project for a six-passenger transport, the P.23 Karas (Crucian Carp) was a light bomber and army co-operation warplane. The P.23/I Karas was the first of three prototypes and flew in August 1934. A number of problems had to be overcome before the type was ordered into production as the P.23A trainer with the 590hp (440kW) Pegasus IIM2 engine and P.23B operational model with an uprated engine (40 and 210 aircraft respectively). With their fixed landing gear, indifferent performance, poor armament and cramped accommodation, the aircraft suffered very heavy losses in the German invasion of September 1939 before 31 survivors were flown to Romania. Another 54 aircraft were delivered to Bulgaria in two P.43 variants with Gnome-Rhône radial engines. Pictured is a P.23B operated by No 42 Squadron, Polish Air Force attached to the Pomorze Army in September 1939.

Country of origin:	Poland
Type:	(P.23B Karas) three-seat light reconnaissance bomber
Powerplant:	one 680hp (507kW) PZL (Bristol) Pegasus VIII nine-cylinder single-row radial engine
Performance:	maximum speed 300km/h (186mph); climb to 2000m (6560ft) in 4 minutes 45 seconds; service ceiling 7300m (23,950ft); range 1400km (870 miles)
Weights:	empty 1928kg (4250lb); maximum take-off 3526kg (7773lb)
Dimensions:	span 13.95m (45ft 9.25in); length 9.68m (31ft 9.25in); height 3.30m (10ft 10in)
Armament:	one 7.7mm fixed forward-firing machine gun in the forward fuselage, one 7.7mm trainable rearward-firing machine gun with 600 rounds in the rear cockpit, and one 7.7mm machine gun in the ventral position, plus an external bomb load of 700kg (1543lb)

PZL P.24

Poland's best fighter at the time of Germany's invasion in September 1939, the P.24 was a more powerfully engined development of the P.11, itself an upgraded Bristol Mercury-engined version of the P.7 with the Bristol Jupiter engine. All three types were therefore braced gull-wing monoplanes with fixed landing gear. As first flown in 1933, the P.24 introduced the more powerful Gnome-Rhòne 14K engine, spatted main landing gear wheels, and a strengthened structure. Production totalled about 300 aircraft including export models, and the main variants were the P.24A with cannon and an enclosed cockpit, the P.24B with modified wheel spats, the P.24C development of the P.24A with machine gun armament, the P.24E with an uprated engine, and the P.24F and P.24G improved versions of the P.24A with cannon and machine gun armament respectively. The aircraft shown here is a P.24C of the 4th Regiment, Turkish Air Force, based at Kütaha in 1939.

Country of origin:	Poland
Type:	(P.24F) single-seat fighter
Powerplant:	one 970hp (723kW) Gnome-Rhòne 14N-07 14-cylinder two-row radial engine
Performance:	maximum speed 430km/h (267mph); climb to 5000m (16,405ft) in 5 minutes 40 seconds; service ceiling 10,500m (34,450ft); range 700km (435 miles)
Weights:	empty 1332kg (2937lb); maximum take-off 2000kg (4409lb)
Dimensions:	span 10.68m (35ft 0.75in); length 7.60m (24ft 11.5in); height 2.69m (8ft 10.25in)
Armament:	two 20mm fixed forward-firing cannon and two 7.92mm fixed forward-firing machine guns the leading edges of the wing, plus an external bomb load of 40kg (88lb)

PZL P.37 Los

The Los (Elk) was the most modern Polish warplane at the time of the German invasion, and at a technical level compared favourably with the best medium bombers in service anywhere in the world. The P.37/I was the first of three prototypes and flew June 1936. The relatively swift solution to a number of early problems paved the way for orders for 180 production aircraft as the P.37A with 873hp (651kW) Pegasus XIIB engines, a single vertical tail surface and single-wheel main landing gear units, the P.37Abis with twin vertical surfaces, and the P.37B with an uprated powerplant, a redesigned cockpit, twin vertical surfaces and twin-wheel landing gear units: deliveries amounted to 10, 20 and about 60 aircraft respectively. Export aircraft with Gnome-Rhône engines were ordered by Bulgaria, Romania, Turkey and Yugoslavia, but none was completed. Pictured is a P.37B Los B of the Bomber Brigade, Dispositional Air Force, Polish Air Force, in September 1939.

Country of origin:	Poland
Type:	(P.37B) four-seat medium reconnaissance bomber
Powerplant:	two 918hp (684.5kW) PZL (Bristol) Pegasus XX nine-cylinder single-row radial engines
Performance:	maximum speed 445km/h (277mph); service ceiling 9250m (30,350ft); range 1500km (932 miles) with a 2200kg (4850lb) bomb load
Weights:	empty 4280kg (9436lb); maximum take-off 8900kg (19,621lb)
Dimensions:	span 17.93m (58ft 10in); length 12.92m (42ft 4.7in); height 5.08m (16ft 8in)
Armament:	one 7.7mm trainable forward-firing machine gun in nose position, one 7.7mm trainable rearward-firing machine gun in the dorsal position, and one 7.7mm trainable rearward-firing machine gun in ventral position, plus an internal bomb load of 2580kg (5688lb)

Petlyakov Pe-2

The Pe-2 may be regarded as the Soviet counterpart of the de Havilland Mosquito and Junkers Ju 88, although it differed from its British and German counterparts in being optimised for the purely tactical role in a host of variants that were built to the extent of 11,427 aircraft. The origins of the design can be found in the VI-100 prototype for a high-altitude fighter that flew in 1939/40, but the design was then revised as the PB-100 dive-bomber with three rather than two crew members in unpressurised accommodation, a powerplant optimised for lower-altitude operations, and different armament including a lower-fuselage bomb bay. The PB-100 prototype was a conversion of the second VI-100, and first flew in June 1940. Later in the same month the decision was taken for the PB-100 to be placed in immediate production with a number of minor changes as the Pe-2. This proved to be the outstanding Soviet tactical bomber of World War II.

Country of origin:	USSR
Type:	(Pe-2) three-seat multi-role attack bomber
Powerplant:	two 1100hp (820kW) Klimov VK-105RA 12-cylinder Vee engines
Performance:	maximum speed 540km/h (335mph); climb to 5000m (16,405ft) in 7 minutes; service ceiling 8800m (28,870ft); range 1500km (932 miles) with a 2205lb (1000kg) bomb load
Weights:	empty 5870kg (12,943lb); maximum take-off 8495kg (18,728lb)
Dimensions:	span 17.16m (56ft 3.7in); length 12.66m (41ft 6.5in); height 4.00m (13ft 1.5in)
Armament:	two 7.62mm fixed forward-firing machine guns in the nose, one 7.62mm trainable rearward-firing machine gun in the dorsal position, and one 7.62mm trainable rearward-firing machine gun in the ventral position, plus an internal and external bomb load of 1600kg (3527lb)

Petlyakov Pe-2FT

The original version of the Pe-2 was supplanted from the spring of 1942 by the Pe-2FT that featured improved defensive armament (single 7.62mm machine guns in a dorsal turret and either of two beam positions), removal of the underwing dive brakes, reduction of the nose glazing and, as availability permitted from February 1943, an uprated powerplant. Further development resulted in operational models such as the Pe-2R long-range photo-reconnaissance model with greater fuel capacity, the Pe-2UT dual-control trainer with a revised cockpit, and the Pe-3 multi-purpose fighter with a fixed forward-firing armament of two 20mm cannon and two 12.7mm machine guns, single 12.7mm trainable machine guns in the dorsal and ventral positions, and underwing provision for 132mm rockets. There were also many experimental developments. Pictured is a Pe-2FT of the Soviet Air Force, operating over the Eastern Front in the latter part of World War II.

Country of origin:	USSR
Type:	(Pe-2FT) three-seat multi-role attack bomber
Powerplant:	two 1260hp (939.5kW) Klimov VK-105PF 12-cylinder Vee engines
Performance:	maximum speed 580km/h (360mph); climb to 5000m (16,405ft) in 9 minutes 18 seconds; service ceiling 8800m (28,870ft); range 1315km (817 miles) with a 1000kg (2205lb) bomb load
Weights:	empty 5950kg (13,119lb); maximum take-off 8520kg (18,783lb)
Dimensions:	span 17.11m (56ft 1.7in); length 12.78m (41ft 11in); height 3.42m (11ft 2.67in)
Armament:	two 7.62mm or one 7.62mm and one 12.7mm fixed forward-firing machine guns in nose, one 7.62mm machine gun in dorsal turret, one 7.62mm or 12.7mm trainable machine gun in ventral position, and one 7.62mm or 12.7mm trainable lateral-firing machine gun in window positions, plus a bomb load of 1600kg (3527lb)

Plage & Laskiewicz (Lublin) R-XIII

In the late 1920s the Polish Air Force and naval air arm were starting an expansion and upgrade programme involving the procurement of machines of Polish design and manufacture. One of the new types was the R-XIII liaison and observation aeroplane, a development of the R-XIV, and this was then produced in a complex series of variants with wheeled landing gear and float alighting gear. The prototype first flew in July 1931, and total manufacture of 273 aircraft included major variants such as the initial R-XIIIA and follow-on R-XIIIB with an improved gun mounting, the R-XIIIbis floatplane, the R-XIIIC improved R-XIIIB, the R-XIIID improved R-XIIIC, the R-XIIIter/hydro improved floatplane, and R-XIIIF with the 420hp (313kW) Skoda G.1620A Mors A engine. Although already obsolescent by the outbreak of war in 1939, the type equipped seven observation squadrons and suffered heavy losses, mainly to German ground fire.

Country of origin:	Poland
Type:	(R-XIIID) two-seat observation and liaison aeroplane
Powerplant:	one 220hp (164kW) Skoda-built Wright Whirlwind J-5 seven-cylinder single-row radial engine
Performance:	maximum speed 195km/h (121mph); climb to 3000m (9845ft) in 15 minutes 50 seconds; service ceiling 4450m (14,600ft); range 600km (373 miles)
Weights:	empty 887kg (1956lb); normal take-off 1330kg (2932lb)
Dimensions:	span 13.20m (43ft 4in); length 8.46m (27ft 9.25in); height 2.76m (9ft 0.25in)
Armament:	one or two 7.7mm trainable rearward-firing machine guns in the rear cockpit

Plage & Laskiewicz (Lublin) R-XVI

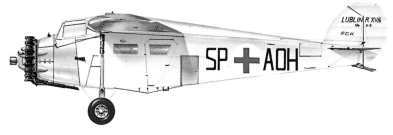

First flown early in 1932, the R-XVI prototype was a high-wing light transport with accommodation for four passengers and a single engine (a licence-built Wright Whirlwind by Skoda) driving a fixed-pitch propeller. This machine proved unsuitable for service with the national carrier LOT and was later taken in hand for modification with a strengthened fuselage revised internally for service as an air ambulance. Successful testing of the prototype at a medical aviation congress held in Spain in 1933 led to an order. There followed five examples of the R-XVIB production model with a variable-pitch propeller, an enclosed cockpit and a further modified fuselage. All six aircraft were still in service with the Polish air force at the time of the German invasion that started World War II in September 1939, and were used only for the casualty evacuation role during this campaign. None of the aircraft survived the war.

Country of origin:	Poland
Type:	(R-XVIB) three-seat air ambulance, light transport and communications aeroplane
Powerplant:	one 220hp (164kW) Skoda-built Wright Whirlwind J-5 seven-cylinder single-row radial engine
Performance:	maximum speed 190km/h (118mph); climb to 1000m (3280ft) in 6 minutes 30 seconds; service ceiling 4460m (14,635ft); range 800km (497 miles)
Weights:	empty 1150kg (2535lb); normal take-off 1630kg (3593lb)
Dimensions:	span 14.93m (49ft); length 10.08m (33ft 1.25in); height 2.96m (9ft 8.75in)
Armament:	none

Polikarpov I-15

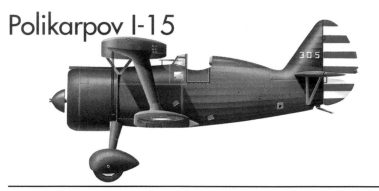

From a time early in 1933 Nikolai Nikolayevich Polikarpov planned the I-15 as successor to his I-5 biplane fighter with a gulled upper wing (intended to improve the pilot's forward fields of vision) and a powerplant of one Wright R-1820-F Cyclone radial piston engine, a US unit being imported in limited numbers pending the start of licensed production as the M-25. The I-15 (404 with the 480hp/358kW M-22 and 270 with the M-25 engine) entered service in 1934. These were complemented and supplanted by the I-15bis (otherwise I-152) that was manufactured to the extent of 2408 aircraft may of which were still in limited service at the time of Germany's June 1941 invasion of the USSR. The I-15bis had the improved M-25V engine in a longer-chord cowling, a conventional upper wing, greater fuel capacity, and doubled gun firepower. Pictured is one of the 186 I-15bis aircraft supplied to support Chinese nationalist forces in Manchuria in 1937-38.

Country of origin:	USSR
Type:	(I-15bis) single-seat fighter
Powerplant:	one 750hp (559kW) M-25B nine-cylinder single-row radial engine
Performance:	maximum speed 370km/h (230mph); climb to 1000m (3280ft) in 1 minute 6 seconds; service ceiling 9000m (29,530ft); range about 530km (329 miles)
Weights:	empty 1310kg (2888lb); maximum take-off 1730kg (3814lb)
Dimensions:	span 10.20m (33ft 5.5in); length 6.33m (20ft 9.25in); height 2.19m (7ft 2.25in)
Armament:	four 7.62mm fixed forward-firing machine guns in the upper part of the forward fuselage, plus an external bomb load of 100kg (220lb)

Polikarpov I-16

Designed at much the same time as the I-15, the I-16 was an altogether more advanced fighter in its basic concept, for it was the USSR's first cantilever low-wing monoplane fighter with retractable main landing gear units (although the landing gear had to be retracted by pumping a handle no less than 100 times!). The type first flew in December 1933, and immediately revealed decidedly tricky handling characteristics, especially in the longitudinal plane as a result of its short fuselage. Even so the type entered large-scale production (7005 aircraft excluding about 1640 two-seat trainers) and saw operational service up to 1942, latterly suffering very heavy losses. The I-16 was produced in 10 main variants between the I-16 Tip 1 with the 480hp (358kW) M-22 radial engine and the definitive I-16 Tip 24 with an altogether more powerful engine as well as considerably heavier and more diverse armament.

Country of origin:	USSR
Type:	(I-16 Tip 24) single-seat fighter and fighter-bomber
Powerplant:	one 1100hp (820kW) Shvetsov M-63 nine-cylinder single-row radial engine
Performance:	maximum speed 489km/h (304mph); climb to 5000m (16,405ft) in 4 minutes; service ceiling 9000m (29,530ft); range 700km (435 miles)
Weights:	empty 1490kg (3285lb); maximum take-off 2095kg (4619lb)
Dimensions:	span 9.00m (29ft 6.33in); length 6.13m (20ft 1.3in); height 2.57m (8ft 5in)
Armament:	two 7.62mm fixed forward-firing machine guns in the upper part of the forward fuselage and two 7.62mm fixed forward-firing machine guns or two 20mm fixed forward-firing cannon in the leading edges of the wing, plus an external bomb and rocket load of 500kg (1102lb)

Polikarpov I-153

Otherwise known as the I-15ter, the I-153 was first flown in 1938 as an attempt to modernise the I-15bis by reducing drag. In this capacity the two most important changes were a reversion to the type of gulled upper wing used on the I-15, and the introduction of manually operated retractable main landing gear units. The type was built to the extent of 3437 aircraft and entered service in time for participation in the border incident with Japan in the summer of 1939. The type was also heavily involved in the Russo-Finnish 'Winter War' of 1939-40, and in the first part of the German invasion of the USSR from June 1941. The surviving I-153 aircraft were relegated to training service from the middle of 1943, although the Finns used captured aircraft as first-line fighters into 1944. The aircraft was flown with some degree of success by experienced pilots, but in the hands of less experienced aviators it could be a handful.

Country of origin:	USSR
Type:	(I-153) single-seat fighter and fighter-bomber
Powerplant:	one 1000hp (746kW) Shvetsov M-62 nine-cylinder single-row radial engine
Performance:	maximum speed 444km/h (276mph); climb to 3000m (9845ft) in 3 minutes; service ceiling 35,105ft (10,700m); range 880km (547 miles)
Weights:	empty 1348kg (2972lb); maximum take-off 2110kg (4652lb)
Dimensions:	span 10.00m (32ft 9.5in); length 6.17m (20ft 2.9in); height 2.80m (9ft 2.25in)
Armament:	four 12.7mm fixed forward-firing machine guns in the forward fuselage, plus an external bomb and rocket load of 200kg (441lb)

Potez 63.11

In 1934 the French air ministry issued a complex requirement for a multi-role warplane to be powered by two examples of the new small-diameter radial engines developed by Gnome-Rhône and Hispano-Suiza, to carry a fixed forward-firing armament that included at least one 20mm cannon, to carry sufficient radio equipment for the type to operate as a controller for single-seat fighters in running engagements with bomber formations, and to possess the capability for operation in three fighter roles. The winning design was the Potez 63 that was then developed in a number of forms including the Potez 63.11 for tactical reconnaissance and army co-operation. First flown in December 1938, the Potez 63.11 entered service in November of the same year, and about 925 Potez 63.11A.3 aircraft had been delivered by June 1940. After this the type was operated by both the Free French and Vichy French forces in North Africa and the Middle East.

Country of origin:	France
Type:	three-seat multi-role warplane
Powerplant:	two 700hp (522kW) Gnome-Rhône 14M-4/5 radial engines
Powerplant:	maximum speed 425km/h (264mph); climb to 3000m (9845ft) in 6 minutes; service ceiling 8500m (27,885ft); range 1500km (932 miles)
Weights:	empty 3135kg (6911lb); maximum take-off 4530kg (9987lb)
Dimensions:	span 16.00m (52ft 6in); length 10.93m (35ft 10.5in); height 3.08m (10ft 1.25in)
Armament:	one 7.5mm machine gun under central fuselage, one 7.5mm machine gun in rear fuselage, and one 7.5mm machine gun in the rear cockpit, or in some aircraft three 7.5mm machine guns in nose and under fuselage, four 7.5mm machine guns in two two-gun underwing packs, three 7.5mm machine guns under fuselage, and two 7.5mm machine guns in cockpit; external bomb load of 300kg (661lb)

Potez 633

Resulting from a 1934 requirement for a multi-role warplane, the Potez 630 paved the way for a number of role-optimised variants. One of the first was a light bomber, which was evaluated from January 1937 as the Potez 632.01 prototype conversion of the Potez 630.02 night-fighter, and in May 1938 an order was placed for 125 examples (only six delivered) of the Potez 633B.2 production version that was basically similar to the Potez 631C.3 fighter except for its accommodation, armament, and the reintroduction of a glazed lower nose to provide a bombardier position. Other sales were made to China, Greece, Romania and Switzerland, and 30 of these aircraft were retained for French service. Another model was the Potez 637A.3 (60 delivered) three-seat attack and reconnaissance model with a ventral gondola and heavier armament. Pictured is one 21 aircraft supplied to Romania, which were used in the German campaign in the Ukraine.

Country of origin:	France
Type:	(Potez 633B.2) two-seat light bomber
Powerplant:	two 700hp (522kW) Gnome-Rhône 14M-6/7 14-cylinder two-row radial engines
Performance:	maximum speed 439km/h (273mph); climb to 4000m (13,125ft) in 8 minutes 30 seconds; service ceiling 8000m (26,250ft); range 1300km (808 miles)
Weights:	empty 2450kg (5401lb); maximum take-off 4500kg (9921lb)
Dimensions:	span 16.00m (52ft 6in); length 11.07m (36ft 4in); height 3.62m (11ft 10.5in)
Armament:	one 7.5mm fixed forward-firing machine gun in the upper starboard side of the forward fuselage, and one 7.5mm trainable rearward-firing machine gun in the rear cockpit, plus an internal bomb load of 400kg (882lb)

Reggiane Re.2000 Falco I

First flown in May 1939, this portly yet capable interceptor was the first fighter designed by Reggiane, a Caproni subsidiary, and bore a striking resemblance to the Seversky (later Sikorsky) fighters designed in the USA. Although it initially failed to win domestic orders the aircraft went into production as the Re.2000 Serie I to meet export orders from Sweden (60 aircraft) and Hungary (70 plus 191 licence-built aircraft with the Gnome-Rhône 14K engine). Of the 27 aircraft retained in Italy, 10 were converted to Re.2000 Serie II shipborne fighter standard with the 1025hp (764kW) P.XIbis engine and the other 17 to the Re.2000 (GA) Serie III long-range fighter-bomber standard with the P.XIbis engine, greater fuel capacity and provision for 2000kg (4409lb) of bombs. The Swedish aircraft remained in service up to 1946. Pictured is an Re.2000 of the 1st Division, Flygflottilj 10, Royal Swedish air force, based at Angelholm early in 1945.

Country of origin:	Italy
Type:	(Re.2000 Serie I) single-seat interceptor fighter
Powerplant:	one 985hp (734.5kW) Piaggio P.XI RC.40 14-cylinder two-row radial engine
Performance:	maximum speed 530km/h (329mph); climb to 6000m (19,685ft) in 6 minutes 10 seconds; service ceiling 10,500m (34,450ft); range 1400km (870 miles)
Weights:	empty 2080kg (4585lb); maximum take-off 2880kg (6349lb)
Dimensions:	span 11.00m (36ft 1in); length 7.99m (26ft 2.5in); height 3.20m (10ft 6in)
Armament:	two 12.7mm fixed forward-firing machine guns in the upper part of the forward fuselage, plus an unspecified internal bomb load

Reggiane Re.2001 Falco II, Re.2002 Ariete and Re.2005 Sagittario

The Re.2000's potential could not initially be realised for lack of adequate power, Italy having ignored the advisability of developing potent Vee engines. The solution was found in the licensed production of German engines, and an early development was the Re.2001 Falco II, first flown in June 1940 as an Re.2000 development with the Alfa Romeo RA.1000 (Daimler-Benz DB 601) engine. Production then totalled 110 Serie I fighters and fighter-bombers, and 124 Serie II, III and IV night-fighters with heavier armament. The Re.2002 Ariete (Ram), of which 227 were completed, was a fighter-bomber development with the 1180hp (880kW) Piaggio P.XIX RC.25 radial engine, and the Re.2005 Sagittario (Archer) was a fighter-bomber of which 37 were completed with the 1475hp (1100kW) Fiat RA.1050 (DB 605) engine. Pictured is an Re.2001 of the 150th Squadriglia, 2nd Gruppo 'Golletto', Regia Aeronautica, based at Pantellaria in August 1942.

Country of origin:	Italy
Type:	(Re.2001 Serie III) single-seat night-fighter
Powerplant:	one 1175hp (876kW) Alfa Romeo RA.1000 RC.41-la Monsonie 12-cylinder inverted-Vee engine
Performance:	maximum speed 545km/h (339mph); climb to 5000m (16,405ft) in 6 minutes 20 seconds; service ceiling 11,000m (36,090ft); range 1100km (684 miles)
Weights:	empty 2460kg (5423lb); maximum take-off 3280kg (7231lb)
Dimensions:	span 11.00m (36ft 1in); length 8.36m (27ft 5in); height 3.15m (10ft 4in)
Armament:	two 12.7mm fixed forward-firing machine guns in the upper part of the forward fuselage and two 7.7mm fixed forward-firing machine guns in the leading edges of the wing

Rogozarski IK-3

Designed as successor to the Ikarus IK-2 gull-wing monoplane fighter, the IK-3 was Yugoslavia's first 'modern' fighter of the cantilever low-wing type with an enclosed cockpit and retractable landing gear. The type first flew in private-venture prototype form in the spring of 1938 and, despite the loss of this aeroplane, the machine was ordered into production. The first 12 aircraft introduced considerable redesign of the cockpit enclosure and main landing gear, as well as a somewhat uprated engine and a strengthened airframe. The aircraft had all been delivered by July 1939, and were flown by the 161 and 162 Eskadrila of the 51 Grupa based at Zemun. After the German invasion of Yugoslavia in April 1941 they proved moderately successful, destroying 11 enemy aircraft before the surviving aircraft were destroyed on the emergency strip at Veliki Radnici to prevent their seizure by the victorious Germans.

Country of origin:	Yugoslavia
Type:	(IK-3) single-seat fighter
Powerplant:	one 980hp (731kW) Avia-built Hispano-Suiza 12Ycrs 12-cylinder Vee engine
Performance:	maximum speed 527km/h (328mph); climb to 5000m (16,405ft) in 7 minutes; service ceiling 9460m (30,800ft); range 785km (488 miles)
Weights:	empty 2068kg (4560lb); maximum take-off 2630kg (5799lb)
Dimensions:	span 10.30m (33ft 9.75in); length 8.00m (26ft 3in); height 3.25m (10ft 8in)
Armament:	one 20mm fixed forward-firing cannon in an engine installation, and two 7.92mm fixed forward-firing machine guns in the upper part of the forward fuselage

Republic P-47M/N Thunderbolt

When the Germans started firing the Fieseler Fi 103 (or V-1) flying bomb at the southern part of the UK in June 1944, the USAAF decided to procure a 'sprint' version of the P-47D as the P-47M (130 built) with the R-2800-57(C) radial engine offering an emergency combat rating of 2800 hp (2088 kW). The last version of the Thunderbolt to be built was the P-47N, largest and heaviest of all Thunderbolt variants. The type was designed for operations in the Pacific theatre with particular emphasis on the maximum range with greater fuel capacity in a wing enlarged to a span of 42ft 7in (12.98m). P-47N production totalled 1816 aircraft with a maximum speed of 460mph (740km/h) and range of more than 2350 miles (3781km) after take-off at a maximum weight of 20,700lb (9390kg). In addition to service with the USAAF during the war the Thunderbolt was used by Brazil, the Free French Air Force, the British Royal Air Force and the Soviet Union.

Country of origin:	USA
Type:	(P-47M) single-seat interceptor fighter
Powerplant:	one 2100hp (1566kW) Pratt & Whitney R-2800-57(C) 18-cylinder two-row radial engine
Performance:	maximum speed 756km/h (470mph); initial climb rate 1067m (3500ft) per minute; service ceiling not available; range 901km (560 miles)
Weights:	empty 4728kg (10,423lb); maximum take-off 7031kg (15,500lb)
Dimensions:	span 12.42m (40ft 9in); length 10.99m (36ft 1in); height 4.44m (14ft 7in)
Armament:	six or eight 0.5in fixed forward-firing machine guns in the leading edges of the wing

Republic P-47B to P-47G

The Thunderbolt is one of the classic warplanes of World War II, and remains an enduring example of the American predilection to 'think big' and produce an item that is visually impressive yet packed with equally impressive capability as a result of the careful combination of high power (a turbocharged engine) and clean design. The XP-47B prototype first flew in May 1941, but depite indications of impressive performance a number of serious design problems had to be resolved before the P-47B could enter combat service in April 1943. The 171 P-47B fighters and 602 generally similar P-47C fighter-bombers were powered by the 2000hp (1491kW) R-2800-21 engine, while the definitive P-47D introduced an uprated powerplant and, in its major subvariant, a clear-view 'bubble' canopy in place of the original framed canopy and 'razorback' rear fuselage. Production of the P-47D and generally similar P-47G 'razorback' model totalled 12,603 and 354 respectively.

Country of origin:	USA
Type:	(P-47D) single-seat fighter and fighter-bomber
Powerplant:	one 2535hp (1890kW) Pratt & Whitney R-2800-59 18-cylinder two-row radial engine
Performance:	maximum speed 700km/h (435mph); climb to 4570m (15,000ft) in 5 minutes 36 seconds; service ceiling 12,800m (42,000ft); range 2776km (1725 miles)
Weights:	empty 4858kg (10,700lb); maximum take-off 7355kg (16,200lb)
Dimensions:	span 12.42m (40ft 9in); length 10.99m (36ft 1in); height 4.44m (14ft 7in)
Armament:	eight 0.5in fixed forward-firing machine guns in the leading edges of the wing, plus an external bomb and rocket load of 1134kg (2500lb)

Saab J21

Sweden wished to ensure its continued neutrality through a policy of armed
strength during World War II but were effectively denied access to foreign
weapons. In response Sweden undertook an indigenous rearmament programme
including an advanced fighter, and for this task the Saab 21 was ultimately designed
round a licence-produced version of the Daimler-Benz DB 605B engine as a low-
wing monoplane with tricycle landing gear, heavy forward-firing armament, a
pilot's ejection seat, and a twin-boom pusher layout that later allowed the type's
revision with a turbojet engine as the J 21R. The first of three J 21 prototypes flew
in July 1943, and 54 J 21A-1 fighters were delivered from December 1945, followed
by 124 and 119 examples respectively of the J 21A-2 with revised armament and the
J 21A-3 fighter-bomber. Pictured is one of the aircraft operated by Flygflottilj 12 of
the Flygvapen.

Country of origin:	Sweden
Type:	(J 21A-1) single-seat interceptor fighter
Powerplant:	one 1475hp (1100kW) SFA DB 605B 12-cylinder Vee engine
Performance:	maximum speed 645km/h (401mph); initial climb rate 850m (2789ft) per minute; service ceiling 11,000m (36,090ft); range 750km (466 miles)
Weights:	empty 3250kg (7165lb); maximum take-off 4413kg (9730lb)
Dimensions:	span 11.60m (38ft 0.75in); length 10.44m (34ft 3.25in); height 3.97m (13ft 3.25in)
Armament:	one 20mm fixed forward-firing cannon and two 13.2mm fixed forward-firing machine guns in the nose, and two 13.2mm fixed forward-firing machine guns in the front of the booms

Savoia-Marchetti SM.79 Sparviero

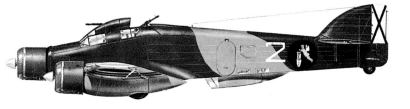

Arguably one of the finest torpedo bombers of World War II, the Sparviero (Sparrowhawk) was notable for its three-engined layout and 'hunchback' fuselage. First flown in 1934 as the SM.79P civil transport prototype with eight-passenger seating, the type was then developed as a medium reconnaissance bomber and entered service as the SM.79-I with the uprated powerplant of three Alfa Romeo 126 radial engines and a large ventral gondola. The following SM.79-II was optimised for the anti-ship role with two 450mm torpedoes and a powerplant of three 1000hp (746kW) Piaggio P.XI RC.40 or 1030hp (768kW) Fiat A.80 RC.41 radial engines. The final Italian model was the SM.79-III improved SM.79-II with heavier defensive armament but no ventral gondola. Deliveries totalled 1230 aircraft. The aircraft continued in service after World War II as a transport with the Aeronautica Militare Italiana.

Country of origin:	Italy
Type:	(SM.79-I) four/five-seat medium reconnaissance bomber
Powerplant:	three 780hp (582kW) Alfa Romeo 126 RC.34 9-cylinder single-row radial engines
Performance:	maximum speed 430km/h (267mph); climb to 5000m (16,405ft) in 19 minutes 45 seconds; service ceiling 6500m (21,325ft); range 1900km (1181 miles) with a 1250kg (2756lb) bomb load
Weights:	empty 6800kg (14,991lb); maximum take-off 10,480kg (23,104lb)
Dimensions:	span 21.20m (69ft 2.7in); length 15.62m (51ft 3.1in); height 4.40m (14ft 5.25in)
Armament:	one 12.7mm fixed forward-firing machine gun above cockpit, one 12.7mm trainable rearward-firing machine gun in dorsal position, one 12.7mm machine gun in ventral position, and one 7.7mm machine gun in two beam positions; bomb load of 2756lb (1250kg)

Savoia-Marchetti SM.79B, JR and K Sparviero

The SM.79 was exported in a number of twin-engined forms. The SM.79B was the SM.79-I version for Brazil (three machines) with 930hp (694kW) Alfa Romeo 128 RC.18 engines, Iraq (four machines) with 1030hp (768kW) Fiat A.80 RC.41 engines and Romania (24 machines) with 1000hp (746kW) Gnome-Rhône 14K Mistral-Major engines, while the SM.79JR was another model for Romania (40 machines), similar to the SM.79B, with 835kW (1,120hp) Junkers Jumo 211Da engines. Sixteen of the latter were built under licence. The last export model was the SM.79K version of the SM.79-I for Yugoslavia (45 machines). Italian variants were the SM.79C VIP transport conversions of 16 SM.79-Is with 1000hp (746kW) Piaggio P.XI RC.40 engines and no dorsal or ventral gun positions, and the SM.79T long-range version of the SM.79C with 780hp (582kW) Alfa Romeo 126 RC.34 engines and significantly increased fuel capacity.

Country of origin:	Italy
Type:	(SM.79JR) four/five-seat medium reconnaissance bomber
Powerplant:	two 1120hp (835kW) Junkers Jumo 211Da 12-cylinder inverted-Vee engines
Performance:	maximum speed 445km/h (276mph); climb to 3000m (9845ft) in 8 minutes 36 seconds; service ceiling 7400m (24,280ft)
Weights:	empty 7185kg (15,840lb); maximum take-off 10,775kg (23,754lb)
Dimensions:	span 21.20m (69ft 2.7in); length 16.10m (52ft 9.9in); height 4.40m (14ft 5.25in)
Armament:	one 13mm fixed forward-firing machine gun above the cockpit, one 13mm trainable rearward-firing machine gun in the dorsal position, one 13mm trainable rearward-firing machine gun in the ventral position, and one 7.92mm machine gun in either of the two beam positions, plus an internal bomb load of 1250kg (2756lb)

Savoia-Marchetti SM.81 Pipistrello

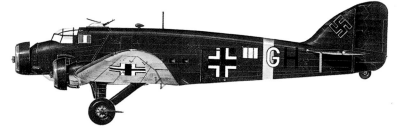

Developed in parallel with the SM.73 transport, with which it shared a basically common airframe, the Pipistrello (Bat) was a dual-role bomber and transport that first flew in 1934 and entered service in 1935. The SM.81 was built to the extent of 535 aircraft in three subvariants that differed only in their powerplants, which could comprise any of three types of radial engine (two Italian and one French, the last from captured stocks). The SM.81 saw extensive service in the Italian conquest of Abyssinia in the mid-1930s and still proved moderately effective in the early part of the Spanish Civil War, but from the time of Italy's June 1940 entry into World War II was used increasingly in the dedicated transport role, although it did undertake night bombing raids in North Africa. The type survived the war in modest numbers and remained in Italian service to 1950. Pictured here is an SM.81 of the Gruppo Transporti 'Terraciano', air force of the Repubblica Sociale Italiana.

Country of origin:	Italy
Type:	(SM.81) five/six-seat bomber and transport
Powerplant:	three 670hp (499.5kW) Piaggio P.X RC.35 nine-cylinder single-row radial engines, or 650hp (485kW) Alfa Romeo 125 RC.35 or 126 RC.34 nine-cylinder single-row radial engines, or 650hp (485kW) Gnome-Rhône 14-K 14-cylinder two-row radial engines
Performance:	maximum speed 340km/h (211mph); climb to 3000m (9845ft) in 12 minutes; service ceiling 7000m (22,965ft); range 2000km (1243 miles)
Weights:	empty 6300kg (13,889lb); maximum take-off 10,055kg (22,167lb)
Dimensions:	span 24.00m (78ft 9in); length 17.80m (58ft 4.75in); height 6.00m (19ft 8.25in)
Armament:	two 7.7mm or one 12.7mm machine guns in dorsal turret, two 7.7mm machine guns in ventral turret, and one 7.7mm machine gun in beam positions, plus an internal bomb load of 4409lb (2000kg)

Seversky P-35

In May 1935 the US Army issued a requirement for a new fighter and the Seversky Aircraft Corporation created the SEV-2XP as its response. This was built with great speed and was developed via the SEV-1XP, SEV-7 and AP-1 stages with a higher-rated engine and a number of significant aerodynamic improvements before it was ordered as the P-35. These 77 aircraft were procured to maintain a production capability as the company (soon Republic) created more advanced types, and were delivered by August 1938. After the delivery of more capable fighters, the surviving P-35 machines became fighter trainers. Sweden ordered 120 of the EP-1 export version, but 60 of these were requisitioned by the USA for service as P-35A fighters, which were mostly lost in the Philippines to air attack in the hours after Japan's entry into the war. Pictured here is a 17th Pursuit Squadron P-35A, based at Nichols Field in the Phillipines during 1941.

Country of origin:	USA
Type:	(P-35) single-seat fighter
Powerplant:	one 950hp (708kW) Pratt & Whitney R-1830-9 14-cylinder two-row radial engine
Performance:	maximum speed 452km/h (281mph); climb to 1525m (5000ft) in 2 minutes 3 seconds; service ceiling 9325m (30,600ft); range 1851km (1150 miles)
Weights:	empty 4315lb (1957kg); maximum take-off 2855kg (6295lb)
Dimensions:	span 10.97m (36ft); length 7.67m (25ft 2in); height 2.77m (9ft 1in)
Armament:	one 0.5in fixed forward-firing machine gun and one 0.3in fixed forward-firing machine gun in the upper part of the forward fuselage, plus an internal bomb load of 159kg (350lb)

Short Singapore

In 1926 Short produced the Singapore Mk I twin-engined flying boat that was built only in prototype form, and in 1931 developed this into the Singapore Mk II with a four-engined powerplant comprising two tandem pairs of tractor/pusher engines. The Singapore Mk II showed considerable promise, and in May 1934 the Air Ministry ordered four development machines, of which the first flew in July of the same year and soon received the designation Singapore Mk III. This paved the way for a further 33 boats, and all 37 machines had been delivered by June 1937 for use by five squadrons. The type was relegated to Far Eastern service in 1940-41, and in December 1941 the last four boats were handed over to the Royal New Zealand Air Force for continued service into 1942. Pictured here is one of the Mk III aircraft on the strength of No 203 Squadron, RAF, based at the British Middle East outpost of Aden in 1940.

Country of origin:	United Kingdom
Type:	(Singapore Mk III) eight-seat maritime reconnaissance flying boat
Powerplant:	four 610hp (455kW) Rolls-Royce Kestrel VIII/XX 12-cylinder Vee engines
Performance:	maximum speed 219km/h (136mph); climb to 1525m (5000ft) in 7 minutes; service ceiling 4510m (14,800ft); range 1987 km (1235 miles)
Weights:	empty 9237kg (20,364lb); maximum take-off 14,692kg (32,390lb)
Dimensions:	span 27.43m (90ft); length 19.56m (64ft 2in); height 7.19m (23ft 7in)
Armament:	one 0.303in trainable forward-firing machine gun in bow position, one 0.303in trainable rearward-firing machine gun in dorsal position, and one 0.303in trainable rearward-firing machine gun in tail position, plus a bomb load of 590kg (1300lb)

Short Stirling Mks I to V

The first four-engined heavy bomber to enter service with Bomber Command of the Royal Air Force during World War II, the Stirling was also the only British four-engined bomber to enter service after having been designed wholly as such, for the Avro Lancaster and Handley Page Halifax were both four-engined developments of two-engined designs. Even so, the Stirling was a workmanlike rather than inspired aeroplane largely as a result of the Air Ministry's demand for a span of less than 30.48m (100ft). The Stirling Mk I entered service in August 1940, and production of 2374 aircraft included 756 Mk I bombers with 1595hp (1189kW) Hercules XI engines, 875 Mk III bombers with a revised dorsal turret, 579 Mk IV paratroop and glider-towing aircraft without nose and dorsal turrets, and 160 Mk V unarmed transports. Pictured here is a Mk V of No 196 Squadron, RAF, based at Sheperd's Grove in the United Kingdom during 1946.

Country of origin:	United Kingdom
Type:	(Stirling Mk III) seven/eight-seat heavy bomber
Powerplant:	four 1650hp (1230kW) Bristol Hercules XVI 14-cylinder two-row radial engines
Performance:	maximum speed 434km/h (270mph); initial climb rate 244m (800ft) per minute; service ceiling 5180m (17,000ft); range 3235km (2010 miles) with a 1588kg (3500lb) bomb load
Weights:	empty 21,274kg (46,900lb); maximum take-off 31,752kg (70,000lb)
Dimensions:	span 30.20m (99ft 1in); length 26.59m (87ft 3in); height 6.93m (22ft 9in)
Armament:	two 0.303in trainable forward-firing machine guns in the nose turret, two 0.303in trainable machine guns in the dorsal turret, and four 0.303in trainable rearward-firing machine guns in the tail turret, plus an internal bomb load of 6350kg (14,000lb)

Short Sunderland Mk I

A 1933 requirement for a modern four-engined monoplane flying boat prompted designs from two companies including Short, which had an ideal starting point for its S.25 in the S.23 'Empire' class of civil flying boats. This proven lineage was a factor that contributed to the Air Ministry's order for 21 production examples of the S.25 in March 1936, some 18 months before the first prototype made its maiden flight in October 1937. The initial production model was the Sunderland Mk I that entered service in the summer of 1938 with an initial two squadrons. By the time World War II started in September 1939, another two British-based squadrons had converted onto the type, and the rising rate of production allowed another three to convert during the first months of the war. Sunderland Mk I production totalled 90 boats, 15 of them by the Blackburn Aircraft Company, all powered by 1010hp (753kW) Bristol Pegasus engines.

Country of origin:	United Kingdom
Type:	(Sunderland Mk I) 10-seat maritime reconnaissance flying boat
Powerplant:	four 1010hp (753kW) Bristol Pegasus XXII nine-cylinder single-row radial engines
Performance:	maximum speed 336km/h (209mph); climb to 1525m (5000ft) in 7 minutes 12 seconds; service ceiling 4570m (15,000ft); range 4023km (2500 miles)
Weights:	empty 13,875kg (30,589lb); maximum take-off 22,226kg (49,000lb)
Dimensions:	span 34.38m (112ft 9.5in); length 26.00m (85ft 3.5in); height 10.52m (34ft 6in)
Armament:	two 0.303in trainable forward-firing machine guns in bow turret, four 0.303in trainable rearward-firing machine guns in tail turret, and one 0.303in machine gun in each beam position, plus an internal bomb, depth charge and mine load of 907kg (2000lb)

Short Sunderland Mks II to V

The Sunderland Mk II first flew in August 1941 as a Mk I development with four 1050hp (783kW) Bristol Pegasus XVIII radial engines and, later in the production run of 58 such boats, the replacement of the single machine guns in the manually operated waist positions by two guns in a dorsal turret and the addition of air-to-surface search radar. first flown in June 1942, the Sunderland Mk III was the first major production model of the family and was in essence a late-production Sunderland Mk II with a revised planing bottom, and production of 407 such boats lasted to late 1943. The last production model was the Sunderland GR.Mk V, of which 143 were completed up to June 1946 with a significantly improved powerplant, better armament and detail modifications. The Mk III was converted for use as a long-range passenger aircraft and operated by BOAC from March 1943 on gradually extending routes.

Country of origin:	United Kingdom
Type:	(Sunderland GR.Mk V) 10-seat maritime reconnaissance flying boat
Powerplant:	four 1200hp (895kW) Pratt & Whitney R-1830-90B Twin Wasp 14-cylinder two-row radial engines
Performance:	maximum speed 343km/h (213mph); climb to 3660m (12,000ft) in 16 minutes; ceiling 5455m (17,900ft); range 2980 miles (4796km)
Weights:	empty 16,738kg (36,900lb); maximum take-off 27,216kg (60,000lb)
Dimensions:	span 34.38m (112ft 9.5in); length 26.00m (85ft 3.5in); height 10.52m (34ft 6in)
Armament:	two 0.303in machine guns in bow turret, provision for four 0.303in machine guns on sides of bow, two 0.303in machine guns in dorsal turret, four 0.303in machine guns in tail turret, and one 0.5in machine gun in each beam positions, plus an internal bomb, depth charge and mine load of 4960lb (2250kg)

Sukhoi Su-2

The Su-2 was designed in competition to the Ilyushin Il-2 as a means of providing the Soviet ground forces with potent close air support. Like the Il-2, therefore, the type's origins can be traced to the Soviet doctrine adopted in the mid-1930s that air power should be seen not as a means of projecting strategic capabilities deep into the enemy's rear areas and homeland but as a tactical adjunct of the ground forces. Pavel Sukhoi had previously worked as head of one of the design brigades in the Tupolev Design Bureau, where his last task had been the development of the ANT-51 tactical reconnaissance and ground-attack monoplane, and on being allowed to establish his own design bureau he set about the evolution of the ANT-51 into the BB-1 prototype, which entered production as the Su-2. Some 2000 aircraft were completed between 1940 and 1942, and this indifferent type was relegated to training use from 1943.

Country of origin:	USSR
Type:	two-seat light attack bomber and reconnaissance warplane
Powerplant:	one 1000hp (746kW) Tumanskii M-88B 14-cylinder two-row radial engine
Performance:	maximum speed 460km/h (286mph); climb to 4000m (13,125ft) in 8 minutes 12 seconds; service ceiling 8800m (28,870ft); range 1200km (746 miles)
Weights:	empty 2970kg (6548lb); maximum take-off 4375kg (9645lb)
Dimensions:	span 14.30m (46ft 11in); length 10.46m (34ft 3.75in)
Armament:	between four and eight 7.62mm fixed forward-firing machine guns in the leading edges of the wings, and one 7.62mm trainable rearward-firing machine gun in the dorsal turret, plus an internal and external bomb and rocket load of 900kg (1984lb)

Supermarine Walrus

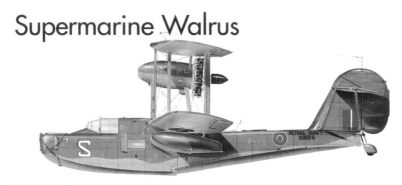

In 1920 Supermarine flew its Channel flying boat, and in 1922 the Seagull Mk I development of this machine. There followed a development programme that led in June 1933 to the Seagull Mk V that introduced a predominantly metal structure. The Australian government ordered 24 of this type, and its success led to a British contract fore 12 catapult-capable 'boats that received the revised designation Walrus Mk I in 1935. Later orders increased the total to 556 boats (the later examples with air-to-surface radar) for service with the Fleet Air Arm and Royal Air Force in the reconnaissance and air/sea rescue roles with the 635hp (473.5kW) Pegasus IIM2 engine. The final model, of which 191 were delivered up to January 1944, was the Walrus Mk II with an uprated engine and a wooden hull. Pictured here is a Walrus Mk I of No 700 Squadron, Fleet Air Arm, based on HMS *Belfast* in the early 1940s.

Country of origin:	United Kingdom
Type:	(Walrus Mk II) four-seat coastal and shipborne air/sea rescue, spotter and anti-submarine amphibian flying boat
Powerplant:	one 775hp (578kW) Bristol Pegasus VI nine-cylinder single-row radial engine
Performance:	maximum speed 217km/h (135mph); climb to 3050m (10,000ft) in 12 minutes 30 seconds; service ceiling 5640m (18,500ft); range 966 km (600 miles)
Weights:	empty 2223kg (4900lb); maximum take-off 3334kg (7350lb)
Dimentions:	span 13.97m (45ft 10in); length 11.58m (38ft); height 5.13m (16ft 10.5in) with the main landing gear units lowered
Armament:	one 0.303in trainable forward-firing machine gun in the bow position, and one or two 0.303in machine guns in the dorsal position, plus a bomb and depth charge load of 272kg (600lb)

Supermarine Spitfire Mks XII and XIV

By the middle years of World War II the best way to wring yet more out of the Spitfire airframe appeared to be the application of considerably more power in the form of the Rolls-Royce Griffon engine. The first such variant was the Spitfire Mk XII, of which 100 were completed with a Griffon III or VI engine. However, the definitive variant was the Spitfire Mk XIV based on the Mk VII airframe but with the Griffon engine in a longer nose, a cut-down rear fuselage and 'clear-view' bubble canopy, a vertical tail surface of greater area, and the E-type wing that added provision for two 0.5in machine guns as alternatives to the four 0.303in weapons. The 527 F.Mk XIV aircraft were complemented by 430 FR.Mk XIV machines optimised for the reconnaissance fighter role with a fuselage-mounted camera. Production of the Spitfire Mk XIV totaled over 900 machines, and which helped to destroyover 300 German flying bombs.

Country of origin:	United Kingdom
Type:	(Spitfire F.Mk XIV) single-seat fighter and fighter-bomber
Powerplant:	one 2050hp (1528.5kW) Rolls-Royce Griffon 65 12-cylinder Vee engine
Performance:	maximum speed 721km/h (448mph); climb to 6095m (20,000ft) in 7 minutes; service ceiling 13,565m (44,500ft); range 1368km (850 miles)
Weights:	empty 2994kg (6600lb); maximum take-off 3856kg (8500lb)
Dimentions:	span 11.23m (36ft 10in); length 9.96m (32ft 8in); height 3.86m (12ft 7.75in)
Armament:	two 20mm forward-firing cannon and either four 0.303 in or two 0.5in fixed forward-firing machine guns in the leading edges of the wing, plus an external bomb or rocket load of 227kg (500lb)

Supermarine Spitfire Mk XVIII

The success of the Spitfire Mk XIV made it sensible to continue this design trend further with the evolution of a longer-range variant with additional fuel tankage in the rear fuselage, even though this demanded some strengthening of the structure and main landing gear units. The wing was also redesigned, and the resulting type entered production as the Spitfire Mk XVIII, of which 300 examples were completed for service from the middle of 1945 as 100 F.Mk XVIII fighters and 200 FR.Mk XVIII reconnaissance fighters. There was also a Spitfire PR.Mk XIX of which 225 were completed as developments of the Mk XIV for the unarmed photo-reconnaissance role, mostly in tropical regions and with a pressurised cabin for operations at high altitude. These PR aircraft were used extensively after the war, making numerous flights over Chinese and Malaysian territory from bases in Hong Kong. In post-war service they were redesignated PR Mk 19

Country of origin:	United Kingdom
Powerplant:	one 2050hp (1528.5kW) Rolls-Royce Griffon 65 12-cylinder Vee engine
Performance:	maximum speed 721km/h (448mph); climb to 6095m (20,000ft) in 7 minutes; service ceiling 13,565m (44,500ft); range more than 1368km (850 miles)
Weights:	empty not available; maximum take-off 4990kg (11,000lb)
Dimensions:	span 11.23m (36ft 10in); length 10.14m (33ft 3.25in); height 3.86m (12ft 7.75in)
Armament:	two 20mm forward-firing cannon and two 0.5in fixed forward-firing machine guns in the leading edges of the wing, plus an external bomb and rocket load of 227kg (500lb)

Spitfire Mks IX and XVI

Entering service in June 1942 as a supposed 'interim' type to tackle the depredations of Focke-Wulf Fw 190 'hit-and-run' raiders over southern England, the Spitfire Mk IX was one of the most successful of all Spitfire variants and was in effect the airframe of the Spitfire Mk VC (Spitfire Mk V with two cannon and two machine guns and provision for carrying bombs) with the uprated Merlin 60 series of engines. Production of the Spitfire Mk IX totalled 5665 aircraft in the low-, medium- and high-altitude subvariants that had been pioneered in the Spitfire Mk V model, and the Spitfire LF.Mk XVI (1054 aircraft) was a development with the 1580hp (1178kW) Packard Merlin 266. There were also the Spitfire PR.Mks IX, X and XI succeeding earlier Spitfire photo-reconnaissance adaptations: the PR.Mk IX was a Mk IX conversion, but the 16 and 471 PR.Mks X and XI were new-build aircraft with Merlin 61, 63 or 70 engines.

Country of origin:	United Kingdom
Type:	(Spitfire F.Mk IX) single-seat fighter and fighter-bomber
Powerplant:	one 1565hp (1167kW) Rolls-Royce Merlin 61 or 1650hp (1230kW) Merlin 63 12-cylinder Vee engine
Performance:	maximum speed 655km/h (408mph); initial climb rate 1204m (3950ft) per minute; service ceiling 12,105m (43,000ft); range 1576km (980 miles)
Weights:	empty 2545kg (5610lb); maximum take-off 4309kg (9500lb)
Dimensions:	span 11.23m (36ft 10in); length 9.46m (31ft); height 3.85m (12ft 7.75in)
Armament:	two 20mm fixed forward-firing cannon and four 0.303in fixed forward-firing machine guns in the leading edges of the wing, plus an external bomb load of 454kg (1000lb)

Supermarine Seafire

Faced with the technical and tactical obsolescence of its two-seat carrierborne fighters, the Royal Navy ordered the Seafire as a navalised version of the Spitfire for service from June 1942. The main variants were the Seafire Mk IB (166 conversions from Spitfire Mk VB standard), Seafire Mk IIC (372 aircraft in low- and medium-altitude fighter as well as reconnaissance fighter forms), and definitive Seafire Mk III (1220 aircraft in the same variants as the Seafire Mk II but with folding wings). There were also 30 Seafire Mk III (Hybrid) aircraft with fixed wings, these later being reclassified as Seafire Mk IIC machines, and the Seafire Mks XV, XVII, 45, 46 and 47 were post-war developments. The Seafire offered good performance, but was hampered for carrierborne operations by its long nose and narrow-track main landing gear units. Nevertheless the aircraft soldiered on after the war, seeing service in Korea with No 800 Sqn until final retirement from RNVR units in 1967.

Country of origin:	United Kingdom
Type:	(Seafire LF.Mk III) single-seat carrierborne fighter and fighter-bomber
Powerplant:	one 1600hp (1193kW) Rolls-Royce Merlin 55M 12-cylinder Vee engine
Performance:	maximum speed 560km/h (348mph); climb to 1525m (5000ft) in 1 minute 54 seconds; service ceiling 7315m (24,000ft); range 890km (553 miles)
Weights:	empty 2814kg (6204lb); maximum take-off 3465kg (7640lb)
Dimentions:	span 11.23m (36ft 10in); length 9.21m (30ft 2.5in); height 3.42m (11ft 2.5in)
Armament:	two 20mm fixed forward-firing cannon and four 0.303in Browning fixed forward-firing machine guns in the leading edges of the wing, plus an external bomb and rocket load of 227kg (500lb)

Supermarine Spitfire Mk I to V

R.J Mitchell began the design of the Spifire in the mid-1930s, with a virtually free reign and unfettered by official specifications. The Type 300 was developed around the Rolls Royce Merlin engine, and the prototype was subsequently ordered into production in June 1936 as the Spitfire Mk 1. Service deliveries of 310 aircraft began in July 1938 to No 19 Squadron at Duxford. These were heavily engaged in the Battle of Britain, proving a better foil to the Bf 109 than the less manoeuvrable Hurricane. The Mk I was followed by 1,566 IBs with twin 20mm cannon, the Mk IIA and IIB with Merlin XII, the one-off experimental Mk III with Merlin XX, the Mk IV (2 Griffon engines prototypes, and 229 photo reconnaissance versions of the Spitfire Mk V, and then by the Mk V with strengthened fuselage for Merlin 45 or Merlin 50, drop tank and bomb provision. Suffix LF designates an aircraft with the low-altitude clipped wing and F the standard wing. A,B, and C are different armament fits.

Country of origin:	United Kingdom
Type:	(Spitfire Mk VA) single-seat fighter and fighter-bomber
Powerplant:	one 1,478hp (1102kW) Rolls-Royce Merlin 45 12-cylinder Vee engine
Performance:	maximum speed 594km/h (394mph); initial climb rate 1204m (3950ft) per minute; service ceiling 11,125m (36,500ft); range 1827km (1,135 miles)
Weights:	empty 2267kg (4998lb); maximum take-off 2911kg (6417lb)
Dimensions:	span 11.23m (36ft 10in); length 9.12m (29ft 11in); height 3.02m (9ft 11in)
Armament:	eight 0.303in fixed forward-firing machine guns in the leading edges of the wing,

Tupolev SB-2

The SB-2 was almost certainly the most capable bomber serving anywhere in the world during the mid-1930s, in purely numerical terms was the most important bomber in the world during the late 1930s, and was also the first 'modern' aeroplane of the stressed-skin type to enter production in the USSR, an event that took place in 1935. The SB-2 was initially delivered with 730hp (544kW) M-100 engines driving fixed-pitch propellers, but then came the 860hp (641kW) M-100A engine in a wider nacelle and driving a variable-pitch propeller. SB-2 series production totalled 6967 aircraft, and the most important variant was the SB-2bis with uprated and different engines and greater fuel capacity. Other variants included 200 SB-RK dive-bombers with 1100hp (820kW) Klimov M-105R engines, and the 111 Czechoslovak licence-built B 71 bombers. Pictured is an SB-2bis of the Red Air Force, captured by the Germans late in 1941.

Country of origin:	USSR
Type:	(SB-2bis) three-seat light bomber
Powerplant:	two 960hp (716kW) Klimov M-103 12-cylinder Vee engines
Performance:	maximum speed 450km/h (280mph); climb to 1000m (3280ft) in 1 minute 48 seconds; service ceiling 9000m (29,530ft); range 2300km (1429 miles)
Weights:	empty 4768kg (10,511lb); maximum take-off 7880kg (17,372lb)
Dimentions:	span 20.33m (66ft 8.5in); length 12.57m (41ft 2.75in); height 3.25m (10ft 8in)
Armament:	two 7.62mm trainable forward-firing machine guns in the nose position, one 7.62mm trainable rearward-firing machine gun in the dorsal turret, and one 7.62mm trainable rearward-firing machine gun in the ventral position, plus an internal bomb load of 600kg (1323lb)

Tupolev Tu-2

First flown in ANT-58 prototype form during January 1941, the Tu-2 was one of the best high-speed bombers to see service in World War II, but was built in larger numbers (2500 or more aircraft) after the end of the war than during the conflict. Developed via the ANT-59 and ANT-60 prototypes then the Tu-2 pre-production model, the Tu-2S initial production model was delivered from the spring of 1944 as a Tu-2 development with uprated engines and heavier offensive and defensive armament. The type proved to possess excellent operational capabilities in terms of its performance, strength and versatility in the attack bomber and ground-attack roles, and the only two other models to see significant combat service during World War II were the Tu-2D long-range model and the Tu-2R photo-reconnaissance model. The aircraft pictured is a Tu-2S of a Soviet bomber regiment operating on the Eastern Front in 1945.

Country of origin:	USSR
Type:	(Tu-2S) four-seat medium attack bomber
Powerplant:	two 1850hp (1379kW) Shvetsov ASh-82FN 14-cylinder two-row radial engines
Performance:	maximum speed 547km/h (340mph); climb to 5000m (16,405ft) in 9 minutes 30 seconds; service ceiling 9500m (31,170ft); range 2100km (1305 miles)
Weights:	empty 7474kg (16,477lb); maximum take-off 11,360kg (25,044lb)
Dimensions:	span 18.86m (61ft 10.5in); length 13.80m (45ft 3.3in); height 4.56m (14ft 11in)
Armament:	two 20mm fixed forward-firing cannon in wing roots, one 12.7mm trainable rearward-firing machine gun in rear of the cockpit, one 12.7mm machine gun in dorsal position, and one 12.7mm machine gun in ventral position, plus an internal bomb load of 4000kg (8818lb)

Vickers Vincent

In the early 1930s the standard army cooperation warplanes operated by the Royal Air Force in overseas theatres were the Fairey IIIF and Westland Wapiti. Both these types were obsolescent, and in its search for a successor type the Air Ministry decided that the new Vildebeest torpedo bomber had the potential to be transformed into an effective general-purpose warplane. In 1932, therefore, a Vildebeest Mk I was converted as prototype of a general-purpose version, and successful evaluation of this conversion resulted in orders for 196 Vincent Mk Is completed between July 1934 and October 1936 as new aircraft or Vildebeest conversions. Some 171 of the aircraft served with the RAF (12 squadrons in India, the Middle East and East Africa), and they continued to serve in Iraq until 1941. Small numbers were transferred to Iraq and New Zealand. Pictured here is a Vincent of the Royal New Zealand Air Force in 1940.

Country of origin:	United Kingdom
Type:	three-seat general-purpose warplane
Powerplant:	one 635hp (473.5kW) Bristol Pegasus IIM3 nine-cylinder single-row radial engine
Performance:	maximum speed 228.5km/h (142mph); initial climb rate 233m (765ft) per minute; service ceiling 5180m (17,000ft); range 2012km (1,250 miles)
Weights:	empty 1918kg (4229lb); maximum take-off 3674kg (8100lb)
Dimensions:	span 14.94m (49ft); length 11.175m (36ft 8 in); height 5.41m (17ft 9in)
Armament:	one 0.303in fixed forward-firing machine gun in the port side of the forward fuselage, and one 0.303in trainable rearward-firing machine gun in the rear cockpit, plus an external bomb load of 499kg (1100lb)

Vickers Wellesley

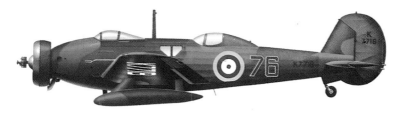

Designed in 1933 as a private venture to meet an official requirement for a general-purpose and torpedo bomber, the Wellesley was based on the novel geodetic structure and emerged for its first flight in June 1935 as a fabric-covered cantilever monoplane with a wing of high aspect ratio. Such were the capabilities of the prototype that the Air Ministry ordered an initial 96 Wellesley Mk I aircraft optimised for the medium bomber role with its bombs carried in two panniers under the wing. The Wellesley Mk I entered service in April 1937, and production up to May 1938 and totalled 176 aircraft, most of the later aircraft being completed (with the unofficial designation Wellesley Mk II) with a continuous 'glasshouse' canopy bridging the front and rear cockpits. The Wellesley saw useful service in East and North Africa during the first part of World War II. Pictured is a Wellesley Mk I of No 76 Squadron, based at Finningley in 1938.

Country of origin:	United Kingdom
Type:	(Wellesley Mk I) two/three-seat general-purpose bomber
Powerplant:	one 835hp (622.5kW) Bristol Pegasus XX nine-cylinder single-row radial engine
Performance:	maximum speed 367km/h (228mph); climb to 6000m (19,685ft) in 17 minutes 30 seconds; service ceiling 7770m (25,500ft); range 4635km (2880 miles) with a 1060lb (481kg) bomb load
Weights:	empty 3066kg (6760lb); maximum take-off 5670kg (12,500lb)
Dimensions:	span 22.73m (74ft 7in); length 11.66m (39ft 3in); height 4.67m (15ft 3.5in)
Armament:	one 0.303in fixed forward-firing machine gun in the leading edge of the port wing, and one 0.303in trainable rearward-firing machine gun in the rear cockpit, plus an internal bomb load of 907kg (2000lb)

Vickers Wellington B.Mks I to X

One of the most important warplanes in the British inventory at the beginning of World War II, the Wellington bore the brunt of the bomber effort until large numbers of four-engined heavy bombers became available in the later stages of 1941. The type then found an important second career in the maritime reconnaissance, transport and training roles until a time well after the end of the war. Total production was 11,461, the last machine not being delivered until October 1945. Entering service in October 1938, the initial model was the Wellington Mk I with 1000hp (746kW) Pegasus XVIII radial engines, and bomber development continued via the Mk III with Rolls-Royce Merlin Vee engines, Mk III with Hercules radial engines, Mk IV with Pratt & Whitney Twin Wasp radial engines, Mk VI with Merlin engines, and Mk X with Hercules engines. Wellingtons formed the major component of the first 1000-bomber raid.

Country of origin:	United Kingdom
Type:	(Wellington Mk X) six-seat medium bomber
Powerplant:	two 1675hp (1249kW) Bristol Hercules XI or XVI 14-cylinder two-row radial engines
Performance:	maximum speed 410km/h (255mph); climb to 4570m (15,000ft) in 27 minutes 42 seconds; service ceiling 6705m (22,000ft); range 3033.5km (1885 miles) with a 680kg (1500lb) bomb load
Weights:	empty 10,194kg (22,474lb); maximum take-off 16,556kg (36,500lb)
Dimensions:	span 26.26m (86ft 2in); length 19.68m (64ft 7in); height 5.31m (17ft 5in)
Armament:	two 0.303in trainable forward-firing machine guns in nose turret, four 0.303in trainable rearward-firing machine guns in tail turret, and one 0.303in trainable lateral-firing machine gun in each beam position, plus an internal bomb load of 2041kg (4500lb)

Vickers Wellington GR.Mks VIII to XIV

As the Wellington became obsolescent in the bomber role for which it had been schemed, its reliability and endurance commended the type's further development as a maritime type for Coastal Command rather than Bomber Command. The first such variant was the Wellington GR.Mk VIII that entered service in the spring of 1942 as a development of the Mk IC bomber with either ASV.Mk II radar or a Leigh Light for anti-ship and anti-submarine operations. These 394 aircraft were followed by 180 GR.Mk XI anti-ship aircraft based on the Mk X bomber with ASV.Mk II or III radar, 58 GR.Mk XII anti-submarine aircraft with ASV.Mk III radar and a Leigh Light, 844 GR.Mk XIII day torpedo bombers with Hercules XVII engines and ASV.Mk II radar, and 841 GR.Mk XIV night aircraft with ASV.Mk III radar and a Leigh Light. Many GR.Mk.IVs were supplied to France in 1944-45 and some were sold to that country in 1946.

Country of origin:	United Kingdom
Type:	(Wellington GR.Mk XIII) six/seven-seat maritime reconnaissance warplane
Powerplant:	two 1735hp (1294kW) Bristol Hercules XVII 14-cylinder two-row radial engines
Performance:	maximum speed 402km/h (250mph); service ceiling 4875m (16,000ft); range 2816km (1750 miles)
Weights:	empty 9974kg (21,988lb); maximum take-off 14,062kg (31,000lb)
Dimensions:	span 26.26m (86ft 2in); length 19.68m (64ft 7in); height 5.38m (17ft 8in)
Armament:	two 0.303in trainable forward-firing machine guns in the nose turret, and four 0.303in trainable rearward-firing machine guns in the tail turret, plus an internal bomb and torpedo load of 2041kg (4500lb)

Vought SB2U Vindicator

Ordered in October 1934, the SB2U was the US Navy's first monoplane scout and dive-bomber, although it is worth noting that lingering doubts about the monoplane's high take-off and landing speed meant that an order was also placed for a single XSB3U-1 biplane prototype. The XSB2U-1 monoplane prototype made its maiden flight in January 1936. In October of the same year the US Navy ordered 54 SB2U-1 production aircraft with the 825hp (615kW) Pratt & Whitney R-1535-96 engine. The SB2U-1 was delivered from December 1937, and there followed 58 and 57 examples of the SB2U-2 with equipment changes and the SB2U-3 with heavier armament and enlarged fuel tankage. The SB2U was phased out of service in 1942. France and the UK bought 39 and 50 generally similar V-156F and Chesapeake Mk I aircraft. Pictured is the SB2U-2 aircraft operated by the 5th section leader of Bombing Squadron VB-2 deployed on the USS *Lexington* in July 1939.

Country of origin:	USA
Type:	(SB2U-3) two-seat carrierborne and land-based scout and dive-bomber
Powerplant:	one 825hp (615kW) Pratt & Whitney R-1535-2 Twin Wasp Junior 14-cylinder two-row radial engine
Performance:	maximum speed 391km/h (243mph); initial climb rate 326m (1070ft) per minute; service ceiling 7195m (23,600ft); range 1802km (1120 miles)
Weights:	empty 2556kg (5634lb); maximum take-off 4273kg (9421lb)
Dimensions:	span 12.77m (41ft 10.9in); length 10.36m (33ft 11.75in); height 4.34m (14ft 3in)
Armament:	one 0.5in fixed forward-firing machine gun in the port upper part of the forward fuselage, and one 0.5in machine gun in the rear cockpit, plus an external bomb load of 454kg (1000lb)

Vought F4U Corsair

Designed with an inverted-gull wing to keep span and main landing gear lengths as short as possible, the F4U Corsair was planned as a carrierborne fighter but matured as a superlative ground-attack and close support fighter that saw service mainly in the Pacific theatre against the Japanese, where it did sterling service in the grim battle of attrition against the Japanese. The type first flew in May 1940 and entered operational service in February 1943 in the land-based role as the type's carrierborne capabilities were initially thought suspect. Armed with bombs and rockets to supplement its fixed guns, the type remained in production until after World War II, but the main war-time variants were the F4U-1 (4399 aircraft in five subvariants), F4U-4 (2651 aircraft in five subvariants), 4006 Goodyear-built FG-1 aircraft in three subvariants, and 735 Brewster-built F3A-1 aircraft in three subvariants.

Country of origin:	USA
Type:	(F4U-4) single-seat carrierborne and land-based fighter and fighter-bomber
Powerplant:	one 2250hp (1678kW) Pratt & Whitney R-2800-18W Double Wasp 18-cylinder two-row radial engine
Performance:	maximum speed 718km/h (446mph); initial climb rate 1180m (3870ft) per minute; service ceiling 12,650m (41,500ft); range 2511km (1560 miles)
Weights:	empty 4175kg (9205lb); maximum take-off 6149kg (13,555lb) as a fighter or 8845kg (19,500lb) as a fighter-bomber
Dimensions:	span 12.49m (40ft 11.75in); length 10.27m (33ft 8.25in); height 4.50m (14ft 9in)
Armament:	six 0.5in fixed forward-firing machine guns in the leading edges of the wing, plus an external bomb and rocket load of 907kg (2000lb)

Vultee A-35 Vengeance

Early in 1940 Vultee received a French order for a dive-bomber, and the contract stipulated the delivery of 300 of these V-72 aircraft by September 1941. France's fall brought a temporary halt to the programme, which was revived by British orders for 700 V-72 warplanes for service with the designations Vengeance Mks I and II. The USA also bought 200 A-31 (Vengeance Mk III) aircraft for Lend-Lease transfer to the UK, and then funded the A-35 with American equipment and greater wing incidence. The A-35 (100 aircraft) had the 1600hp (1193kW) R-2600-11 engine, the A-35A comprised 99 conversions with revised forward-firing armament, and the A-35B (Vengeance Mk IV) comprised 563 further improved aircraft. Only limited operational use was made of the type, which was generally operated as a target tug. Pictured here is an A-35B Vengeance of Groupes de Bombardement 1/32, Free French Air Force, based in North Africa during 1943.

Country of origin:	USA
Type:	(A-35B) two-seat dive-bomber and attack warplane
Powerplant:	one 1700hp (1267.5kW) Wright R-2600-13 14-cylinder two-row radial engine
Performance:	maximum speed 449km/h (279mph); climb to 4570m (15,000ft) in 11 minutes 18 seconds; service ceiling 6795m (22,300ft); range 2253km (1400 miles)
Weights:	empty 4672kg (10,300lb); maximum take-off 7439kg (16,400lb)
Dimensions:	span 14.63m (48ft); length 12.12m (39ft 9in); height 4.67m (15ft 4in)
Armament:	six 0.5in fixed forward-firing machine guns in the leading edges of the wing, and one 0.5in trainable rearward-firing machine gun in the rear cockpit, plus an internal and external bomb load of 907kg (2000lb)

Westland Lysander

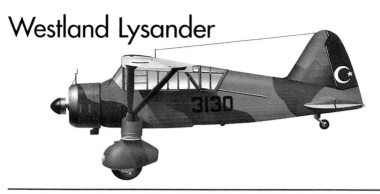

Resulting from a 1934 battlefield reconnaissance and army co-operation requirement, the Lysander was designed to provide its two-man crew with the best possible fields of vision to the front and sides, especially toward the ground, and was therefore planned round a substantial fuselage carrying a large glazed cockpit under the high-set wing. The first of two prototypes flew in June 1936, and production (with totals) comprised the Lysander Mk I (169) for service from June 1938, Lysander Mk II (517) with the 905hp (675hp) Bristol Perseus XII engine, Lysander Mk III (517) with the Mercury XX engine, and Lysander Mk IIIA (347) improved version of the Mk III. From 1941 the type was increased used as a target-tug (100 new TT.Mk IIIA aircraft complementing 70 conversions) and for the delivery of agents into Europe. Pictured is a Lysander Mk II, one of 36 supplied to Turkey. This example was based at Yesilköy in 1940.

Country of origin:	United Kingdom
Type:	(Lysander Mk I) two-seat tactical reconnaissance and army co-operation warplane
Powerplant:	one 890hp (664kW) Bristol Mercury XII nine-cylinder single-row radial engine
Performance:	maximum speed 369km/h (229mph); climb to 3050m (10,000ft) in 6 minutes 48 seconds; service ceiling 7925m (26,000ft); range 966km (600 miles)
Weights:	empty 1844kg (4065lb); maximum take-off 3402kg (7500lb)
Dimensions:	span 15.24m (50ft); length 9.30m (30ft 6in); height 3.35m (11ft)
Armament:	two 0.303in fixed forward-firing machine guns in the wheel fairings, and one 0.303in trainable rearward-firing machine gun in the rear of the cockpit, plus an external bomb load of 227kg (500lb)

Westland Wapiti

In the mid-1920s the Royal Air Force began to appreciate the approaching 'block obsolescence' of its World War I-vintage de Havilland D.H.9A general-purpose biplane and issued a requirement for a replacement offering improved performance, greater load-carrying capability, a durable airframe capable of withstanding the rigours of operations in all the regions in which RAF had to fly and, most taxingly of all, maximum use of D.H.9A components of which the service had abundant stocks. The winning contender was the Westland Wapiti, which used the D.H.9A's wing cellule and tail unit. The Wapiti prototype first flew in March 1927, and after some development the type was built to the extent of 570 aircraft for the UK, Australia, Canada and South Africa in variants up to the Wapiti Mk VI, and for China as the Wapiti Mk VIII. Pictured is a Mk IA of the Royal Australian Air Force, in service as a glider-tug during the 1940s.

Country of origin:	United Kingdom
Type:	(Wapiti Mk III) two-seat general-purpose warplane
Powerplant:	one 490hp (365kW) Armstrong Siddeley Jaguar VI 14-cylinder two-row radial engine
Performance:	maximum speed 225km/h (140mph); climb to 1525m (5000ft) in 4 minutes 18 seconds; service ceiling 6280m (20,600ft); range 1062km (660 miles)
Weights:	empty 1442kg (3180lb); maximum take-off 2449kg (5400lb)
Dimensions:	span 14.15m (46ft 5in); length 9.91m (32ft 6in); height 3.61m (11ft 10in)
Armament:	one 0.303in fixed forward-firing machine gun in the upper part of the forward fuselage, and one 0.303in trainable rearward-firing machine gun in the rear cockpit, plus an external bomb load of 263kg (580lb)

Westland Whirlwind

The Whirlwind was the Royal Air Force's first single-seat twin-engined fighter, a layout conceived so that a fixed forward-firing battery of four 20mm cannon could be grouped in the nose. The powerplant was based on two examples of the Rolls-Royce Peregrine engine that was in essence a modernised version of the classic Kestrel, but this engine's teething problems (at a time when its manufacturer was more concerned with improving its great Merlin engine and maximising its production) meant that the future of the otherwise excellent Whirlwind was curtailed in terms of production and service life. Production totalled only 112 aircraft and they were in service for a short period between between June 1940 and June 1943. The type was flown by only two squadrons, and surviving Whirlwind Mk I fighters were later upgraded to Whirlwind Mk IA fighter-bomber standard. The aircraft also had a high landing speed, limiting its capacity for deployment.

Country of origin:	United Kingdom
Type:	(Whirlwind Mk IA) single-seat long-range fighter-bomber
Powerplant:	two 765hp (570kW) Rolls-Royce Peregrine I 12-cylinder Vee engines
Performance:	maximum speed 579km/h (360mph); initial climb rate 396m (1300ft) per minute with two 227kg (500lb) bombs; service ceiling 30,000ft (9145m); range about 800 miles (1287km)
Weights:	empty 3769kg (8310lb); maximum take-off 5166kg (11,388lb)
Dimensions:	span 13.72m (45ft); length 9.83m (32ft 3in); height 3.20m (10ft 6in)
Armament:	four 20mm fixed forward-firing cannon in the nose, plus an external bomb load of 454kg (1000lb)

Yakovlev Yak-1

First flown during January 1940, the Yak-1 lightweight fighter was one of the most important and successful fighters fielded by the USSR in the course of World War II and, like many of its Soviet contemporaries, was based on an airframe of mixed light alloy and wooden construction. In configuration the Yak-1 was of typical 'modern' fighter design with a cantilever low-set wing, enclosed cockpit and retractable main landing gear units, and entered production late in 1940 in a programme that saw the delivery of 8721 aircraft by the summer of 1943. The main models were the baseline Yak-1, the Yak-1B with a cut-down rear fuselage allowing the incorporation of a clear-view 'bubble' canopy, and the Yak-1M lightened model with a number of significant improvements. Developments were the Yak-3, Yak-7 and Yak-9. This series of fighters were the finest available to the Soviet air forces during the eastern campaign, and undoubtedly helped to turn the tide of the war.

Country of origin:	USSR
Type:	(Yak-1 early production standard) single-seat fighter and fighter-bomber
Powerplant:	one 1100hp (820kW) Klimov M-105P 12-cylinder Vee engine
Performance:	maximum speed 600km/h (373mph); climb to 5000m (16,405ft) in 5 minutes 24 seconds; service ceiling 10,000m (32,810ft); range 700km (435 miles)
Weights:	empty 2347kg (5174lb); maximum take-off 2847kg (6276lb)
Dimensions:	span 10.00m (32ft 9.7in); length 8.48m (27ft 9.9in); height 2.64m (8ft 8in)
Armament:	one 20mm fixed forward-firing cannon in an engine installation, and two 7.62mm fixed forward-firing machine guns in the upper part of the forward fuselage, plus an external bomb and rocket load of 200kg (441lb)

Index

Note: Page numbers in **bold** refer to main entries.